THE
STEVE SPURRIER
STORY

THE
STEVE SPURRIER
STORY

FROM HEISMAN TO
HEAD BALL COACH

Bill Chastain

TAYLOR TRADE PUBLISHING
Lanham • New York • Oxford

Published by Taylor Trade Publishing
A Member of the Rowman & Littlefield Publishing Group
4720 Boston Way
Lanham, Maryland 20706

Distributed by National Book Network

Library of Congress Control Number: 2002111514

ISBN 0-87833-316-9 (cloth: alk. paper)

♾™ The paper used in this publication meets the minimum requirements of
American National Standard for Information Sciences—Permanence of Paper
for Printed Library Materials, ANSI/NISO Z39.48–1992.
Manufactured in the United States of America.

To Mom and Dad

CONTENTS

ACKNOWLEDGMENTS

I wish to give thanks to the following people who helped me write this book: Steve Spurrier, Larry Smith, John Reaves, Norm Carlson, David Alfonso, Ben Bennett, Lee McGriff, Ray Graves, Tom Shannon, Graham McKeel, Kirk Kirkpatrick, Chris Harry, Pepper Rodgers, Tom Butters, Graham Spurrier, Joe Biddle, Jim McVay, Nick Pugliese, Art Chase, Michele Tessier and a special thanks to Tom McEwen—writing this book would not have been possible without his help.

INTRODUCTION

Growing up in Florida in the 1960s, I can remember how all the kids loved Steve Spurrier, glamorous star quarterback for the University of Florida. Nobody stood taller than the Gators' No. 11, who became the epitome of a college football hero: good looking, talented and capable of leading miraculous comebacks.

Looking back, it's funny how the memories of Spurrier's playing career managed to get blurred. While doing the research for this book, I rediscovered the fact that Spurrier truly was the real deal as an athlete, which I believe has been obscured by his coaching success.

Spurrier didn't get by on guile and intelligence as an athlete, though they were part of the package; he did it with athletic ability that he began to develop at an early age. Peeling through the archives of Spurrier's life reaffirmed what he had been as an athlete and became the most enjoyable aspect of writing this biography.

I remembered many of Spurrier's successes from my childhood reading accounts written by Tom McEwen of the *Tampa Tribune*, a man I later worked with while a sportswriter for that same newspaper. Other accounts of Spurrier's wizardry were new to me; Spurrier won the Heisman Trophy, but I had never realized the depth of his success dating back to high school days—when he competed in everything and rarely lost at anything—to the miracle comebacks playing for Florida. Confidence and competitiveness have been his curse and his blessing. Those special qualities complemented his athletic ability on one hand while casting him as an arrogant figure on the other.

Unlike many gifted athletes who excelled playing the games but couldn't coach a lick, Spurrier took coaching football games to another dimension, making him the exception.

There is no gray to Spurrier; the man is as black and white as they come, and he is passionate, which echoes over and over in what his friends and associates say about him. Whether you consider Spurrier an "evil" genius or simply a genius, you can't dispute the fact that he is a football artist, given the creative things he has done as a coach.

Steve Spurrier has led an interesting life, and this is the story of that life.

SOURCE LIST

Jim McVay—Director of college football's Outback Bowl; formerly the marketing director of the Tampa Bay Bandits, the United States Football League team coached by Spurrier.

Graham McKeel—Spurrier's former teammate and roommate at Florida.

Ray Graves—The head coach at Florida when Spurrier was a player.

Tom Shannon—The senior quarterback Spurrier alternated with as a sophomore; Shannon is a successful businessman and remains friends with Spurrier.

Pepper Rodgers—Spurrier's offensive coach at Florida; hired Spurrier as an assistant when he was head coach at Georgia Tech; coached against Spurrier in the USFL; is currently a vice president with the Washington Redskins.

Kirk Kirkpatrick—Played for Spurrier during his first season as head coach of Florida; led the SEC in receiving that season.

Larry Smith—Spurrier's teammate at Florida; played running back, gained All-American honors and played pro football for the Los Angeles Rams and Washington Redskins.

Ben Bennett—Record-setting Duke quarterback who played for Spurrier when he was the Blue Devils' offensive coordinator.

Tom Butters—Duke athletic director who hired Spurrier to be the Blue Devils' head football coach.

Joe Biddle—Sportswriter who grew up with Spurrier in Johnson City, Tennessee, and has since covered him as a coach.

Nick Pugliese—Sportswriter for the *Tampa Tribune*; covered Spurrier when he coached the Bandits.

Chris Harry—Sportswriter for the *Tampa Tribune* and *Orlando Sentinel*; covered Spurrier for 10 years at Florida.

David Alfonso—Sportwriter for the *Tampa Tribune*; covered college football when Spurrier was an assistant at Duke.

Tom McEwen—Longtime sports columnist for the *Tampa Tribune*; covered Spurrier from his playing days through coaching days; won the Red Smith Award for excellence in sportswriting.

Graham Spurrier—Spurrier's older brother.

Lee McGriff—Knew Spurrier when McGriff was a kid and Spurrier was playing pro foot-
    ball; was Spurrier's teammate with the Buccaneers; coached with him at Florida un-
    der head coach Charley Pell; his son played for Spurrier at Florida.
John Reaves—Record-setting quarterback at Florida; played in the NFL and in the
    USFL (for Spurrier, with the Bandits); coached with Spurrier at Florida.
Norm Carlson—Friend and longtime University of Florida athletic director.
Steve Spurrier—Washington Redskins coach and former football coach at the University
    of Florida.

FOREWORD

B ill Chastain's biography on Steve Spurrier is a straightforward and candid account of a man who will be remembered as one of the most influencing college football coaches of all time.

After Spurrier's amazing run at his alma mater, the University of Florida, many of us believe Stephen Orr Spurrier will be just as innovating and dominating in the NFL as the coach of the Washington Redskins.

Those of us who know him well have no doubts about the winning part in the NFL. The questions are how quickly? And for how long he will win.

The book is an easy read, which is a Chastain trademark. Red Smith once declared he preferred to be known as a reporter; so does Chastain. He has chronicled Spurrier's life from his days growing up in Tennessee to the present, gathering information for the project by talking to those who know the "Head Ball Coach" best.

No one coaches quarterbacks better than Spurrier, nor is there another coach out there more daring. He expects a lot from his players. If they do not produce as he expects, they must prepare to take the consequences. Spurrier does not always have the form of others, but he always manages to get the job done.

Spurrier won the Heisman Trophy after taking the Gators to unprecedented heights and later returned to Florida as head coach, raising the level of expectation to where Gator fans expected championships and any other result was a disappointment. Spurrier wouldn't have it any other way.

There is no bigger stage for Spurrier to take on this new challenge than in the nation's capital. And no, he is not bothered one whit that the colors and nickname of his new team are similar to his former in-state rival Florida State Seminoles.

I have known Spurrier and his wife, Jerri, as a friend and day-to-day chronicler of his career since he arrived at Gainesville for his wonderful playing career. In addition, I have known Chastain since he was at Tampa's Plant High School, then for the decade he worked with me at the *Tampa Tribune* after I hired him as a sports writer. So, turn this page and look forward to Chastain's sequel when he tells us all how Spurrier compares with George Halas, Paul Brown, Vince Lombardi, Tom Landry, Don Shula, Bill Walsh, Chuck Noll and all the other great coaches of the NFL.

—Tom McEwen

1

THE HEAD BALL
COACH PULLS
A SHOCKER

Shortly after Steve Spurrier's Florida Gators dominated Maryland in the 2002 Orange Bowl, Spurrier asked Norm Carlson and his wife, Silvia, to dinner at Crescent Beach; Carlson never could have imagined the magnitude of the invitation.

"He said, 'ya'll come up here and we'll go to dinner,'" said Carlson, Spurrier's friend and the longtime University of Florida sports information director. "We actually wanted to return to Gainesville; our dog was in the kennel and there were various other reasons. But Steve kept insisting, so we said we'd better go."

Spurrier called the Carlson's Crescent Beach condominium when they arrived, telling the couple he and his wife, Jerri, would pick them up for dinner.

"Steve and Jerri got there about 5:30 and he said, 'I'm going to tell you something and you need to sit down,'" Carlson said. "Then Jerri told Silvia, 'Silvia, you better sit down and you better have a beer.' Well, my wife doesn't really drink. One beer a month would be pushing it. But Jerri said, 'I'm not kidding, you have to have a beer.' So I got Silvia a beer. As soon as I sat down, Steve said, 'I'm resigning tomorrow.' I told him, 'You're pulling my chain.' He said, 'Here's my statement that I need to make, let's you and I go over it and see how it needs to be changed.' That's how I found out."

And just like that, the most productive coach in Florida Gators football history was out the door and ready to pursue other coaching avenues. A blindsided Gator Nation received the news the following day.

Upon further review, the nature of Spurrier's departure should have been expected; conventional wisdom and Spurrier never have intersected.

"Yeah, I was surprised," Carlson said. "I figured he'd just bought a new house. [The team] had a great year. He had [talented quarterback] Rex Grossman coming back. Blah, blah, blah. But that's always been when Steve will do something you didn't expect. So I shouldn't have been surprised. Actually, I probably would have been more surprised if he had done it any other way."

Spurrier's abrupt resignation hurt some feelings of those close to him, but Carlson said the "Head Ball Coach's" exodus happened in the wisest possible fashion.

"There was no other way to do it," Carlson said. "The timing of it. [Had he told others] it would have started getting out. The players weren't going to be back on campus for another four or five days, so the timing was right for what he needed to do. It's just the way it had to happen."

Gator fans had grown accustomed to Spurrier standing on the sidelines ranting and raving, face balled up like a clinched fist, coaching up his beloved Gators to yet another double-digit victory at Florida Field. The orange and blue montage always roared its collective approval for their Gators, a team synonymous with excellence since Spurrier's arrival in 1990. Most figured Spurrier's trademark visor would surpass Bear Bryant's hounds tooth hat in SEC lore and Gator fans, with their Spurrier-instilled confidence, would continue to swagger well past the day when Spurrier's healthy mop of hair finally turned white. Spur-Dog was born to coach the Gators and, by golly, he'd coach 'em up until he could no longer coach. Alas, one of the traits that makes Spurrier interesting is his unpredictability. Spurrier has always conducted business his way, causing Gators fans to embrace him and others to perceive him as arrogant and cocky.

Spurrier's response to criticism has been consistent.

"If you say the guy's a lousy coach and he's egotistical and he's arrogant, that's OK, that's your opinion," Spurrier said. "That's OK, those are just words. I guess I said something a long time ago. As long as they don't call me a loser, I'll be all right."

Nobody could call Spurrier a loser while he coached the Gators. He won big at a school where expectations ran high despite few successes prior to his arrival.

A former University of Florida vice president, Harry Philpott, qualified the lofty expectations of Gators fans in 1968: "All that [Gator fans] want is a 10-0 season, to beat Notre Dame in the Rose Bowl and then to fire the coach."

Spurrier didn't wait to get fired, dropping the bomb that silenced Gainesville on Friday, January 5, 2002, via a 9:15 phone call telling Florida athletic director Jeremy Foley he was stepping down.

Foley "had no inkling" his highly successful football coach was leaving.

Spurrier issued a 10-paragraph statement the day his resignation was announced, but he did not address the media.

"I'm not burned out, stressed out or mentally fatigued from coaching," Spurrier said. "I just feel my career as a college head coach after 15 years is complete, and if the opportunity and challenge of coaching an NFL team happens, it is something I would like to pursue."

Speculation about Spurrier's next move dominated Florida newspapers. If the NFL's Tampa Bay Buccaneers lost in the first round of the playoffs, would they fire head coach Tony Dungy and hire Spurrier? The Minnesota Vikings had an opening after Dennis Green was fired. Maybe they'd hire Spur-Dog? Perhaps San Diego? Jacksonville? Spurrier loyalists believed if he ever decided to leave the University of Florida, he wouldn't stray from the state of Florida. He liked the beaches and golf way too much to stalk the sidelines anywhere but in the Sunshine State.

Amid the speculation about where Spurrier might go came the speculation about who would replace the coaching legend. Oklahoma coach Bob Stoops was first mentioned; he had been Spurrier's defensive coach when the Gators became the 1996 national champions. When Stoops didn't want the job, Denver Broncos coach Mike Shanahan became the next in line. But he too decided to remain where he was, paving the way for New Orleans Saints assistant Ron Zook to assume control of the Gators.

Only when Zook became the new Gators coach did Florida fans start lamenting what they would be missing without Spurrier, who had taken the program to lofty heights.

In 83 seasons prior to Spurrier's arrival, Gator football teams had never won an official Southeastern Conference championship, nor a national championship. They had never won more than nine games in a season, they had experienced just three Top-10 finishes in the Associated Press poll, they had played in just three major bowl games and they owned an overall winning percentage of .579 (452-322-29).

Fast forward after 12 seasons under Spurrier.

The Gators captured six SEC championships and one national championship. They won 10 or more games in nine seasons and won nine each in the other three. Spurrier teams had 10 Top-10 finishes in the AP poll, the Gators played in eight major bowl games and the team had an overall winning percentage of .819 (122-27-1).

Spurrier addressed the media three days after his resignation and spoke frankly about his reasons for leaving.

"If you study coaches, study history and cycles of coaches," he said, "most of them hang around long enough until the job chews 'em up and spits 'em out.

Every coach at Florida, I think the last 75 years, has been shoved out the door. I think Gen. VanFleet was the only one. He coached two years and got a reassignment of his ROTC position somewhere. So he left on his own.

"But the rest of them have been pretty much asked to leave, or something another. And hopefully, that's something that's always been very important to me. To be able to walk out on your own instead of somebody shoving you out and somebody paying you two or three years to do nothing. I don't ever want to, hopefully, ever be in that situation. I don't plan on being paid for sitting around because I got a big contract and got fired. Some people say, 'Coach, they'd never fire you.' That's not the point. If it ever starts going downhill pretty good, you have to make changes. That's part of our coaching profession. We all know. So I hope to try and move on before it ever goes down."

Spurrier expressed frustration at the stress of continuing to produce at the high level now expected by Gator fans.

"Some people say 'he could stay at Florida and win 10 games every year,'" Spurrier said. "It's not as easy winning 10 games every year as a lot of people think. Everybody's gotten a lot better than they used to be. The SEC wasn't quite what they are now back in the early '90s. As most of you know it was a running league. Run the ball and play defense. And now everyone is pitching it all over the place, and they're pretty good at it, too. There's a lot of good offensive coaches in our league now, whereas in the early '90s, there weren't too many, as you probably know."

Spurrier's intentions were clear: he wanted to coach in the NFL.

After a suspenseful week, the *Washington Post* reported Redskins coach Marty Shottenheimer had been fired and Spurrier would be the new coach, signing a five-year contract worth $25 million.

Redskins owner Dan Snyder saw enough of what the Redskins' future might be with Spurrier and decided to eat the remaining three years on Shottenheimer's contract, which cost him approximately $7.5 million.

"I need to learn a lot," Spurrier said when introduced to the media as the Redskins' new coach on January 15, 2002. "I need to learn who all the players are, and the organizational part of it. The playbook? I've got a playbook. We've got plays we can run up the middle all day or we can scatter out and throw it. We got plenty of plays. That won't be a problem. Learning about the NFL is something I'm looking forward to."

And about that Spurrier swagger. . . .

The Head Ball Coach let Redskins fans know the hated Dallas Cowboys already were in his crosshairs. Heading into the 2002 season, the Redskins had lost nine straight to their archrivals.

"I've already told Dan Snyder that the first game ball I'm going to give him is when we play the Dallas Cowboys," Spurrier said, then looking at Snyder on the podium. "That's the first one you're going to get. We should, can't make any guarantees, but we will be ready to play the Dallas Cowboys. I've learned that that's a game our fans really want to win. And all I can say is I'll try my best to do my part along with everybody else to beat those Dallas Cowboys this coming season."

One thing comes to light when trying to understand the complex Spurrier: he lives in the present, which is why he thinks about beating the Cowboys rather than aggrandizing about past glories at Florida.

"Oliver Wendell Holmes once said, 'What's most important in life is not where you are, but what direction you're moving,'" Spurrier said. "I'm always trying to get better, always trying to look forward to the next challenge. The most important game of your life is the next game. Yesterday and years back were just good memories."

Spurrier likes to study and recite motivational quotes and credits them for inspiration over the years. He knows he has been successful, but seems to temper his success with caution when looking toward the future.

"Winston Churchill once said, 'Success is never final,'" Spurrier said. "And I think that is so true."

2

THE FOUNDATION

John Graham Spurrier's life's work came to him during his senior year of high school in Charlotte, North Carolina.

Steve Spurrier's father needed one additional credit to graduate and selected a class in Bible study. Christianity had been involved in his life, but his faith had not been his life until he experienced an epiphany about his life's calling while taking the Bible study class.

John Graham's father worked the Carolinas selling flour and found such success he had to take occasional breaks when the company could not keep up with all the orders he was selling.

While John Graham's father successfully sold flour until his death in a car accident around the time John Graham began seminary school, John Graham would successfully sell religion.

John Graham met Marjorie Orr at an interdenominational youth group in Charlotte in 1938. He was in the midst of his studies to become a Presbyterian minister; Marjorie played piano for the church. They were married two years later, in 1940, a year coinciding with the beginning of John Graham's nomadic pursuit as a minister.

In 1942, the couple had their first child, John Graham Spurrier III, while John Graham preached at a church in Eudora, Arkansas. John Graham's next assignment was St. Albans, West Virginia, and the couple had their second child, Sara Kathleen Spurrier, in 1944. From there, they headed south to Miami Beach, where Stephen Orr Spurrier was born April 20, 1945, at St. Francis Hospital. The couple's decision to name their third child Stephen was in honor of the first Christian martyr.

Franklin D. Roosevelt, the thirty-first president of the United States, died eight days before Spurrier was born, with the United States and allied forces perched on the brink of victory in World War II. Harry S. Truman assumed the presidency on the day of Roosevelt's death. Benito Mussolini, the "Father of Italian Fascism," was shot with his mistress and 11 others eight days after Spurrier was born, and Hitler committed suicide in Berlin two days later. By May, the Germans had surrendered unconditionally.

Steve weighed 8-pounds, 14-ounces and was nicknamed "Little Mutt" by the nurses at St. Francis.

After two years in Miami Beach, the Spurriers moved their three children, ages five, four and two, to Mars Hill Presbyterian Church in Athens, Tennessee, just north of Chattanooga. From Athens they moved to Newport, Tennessee, before rooting down in Johnson City in 1957 when Steve was 12.

Johnson City rests at the foothills of the Appalachian Mountains, near the North Carolina and Virginia borders, in a part of Tennessee known as the "Tri-State" area. The city had a population of approximately 25,000 along with a quality athletic history.

Graham Spurrier III viewed the constant moving as a positive in their lives.

"We did [move a lot]," Graham said. "My dad ministered several churches. Each time we moved, we'd have to make new friends and get on to other sports-related teams and that nature, and new schools. Meet new people in our churches. But it probably, in the end, was good for us, because I think it helped us meet new people and to assimilate into other teams easier when we moved around."

Steve first got interested in football while in Athens, home to Tennessee Wesleyan. Steve and Graham attended the team's practices and were allowed to fool around on the field from time to time; the school won the National Junior College title in 1951. Steve was in first grade and the team embraced him as its mascot. Hanging around athletic fields aided Steve's sports development. He watched and imitated athletes, including his brother, in learning how to play the different sports.

"I don't know if I really taught him [how to play sports]," Graham said of his brother. "He just sort of tagged along and learned to watch and then learned by doing."

Graham played Little League baseball on a team his father helped organize in Athens. Steve was too young to play, but not to watch. When the Spurriers moved to Newport, the Rev. Spurrier and some other men helped start a basketball team at the elementary school his boys attended; Steve was on the jayvee team.

"Steve was probably like in the third or fourth grade," Graham said. "That was his first organized sport and my second, after Little League."

Steve began playing football in the sixth grade. Organized sports were just a small part of the brothers' sports education.

"We always had a hoop out in the yard," Graham said. "We'd shoot baskets and stuff. Dad would always play with us there. He'd always throw baseball with us. He'd throw grounders and high pops, or we'd just throw. Then when football came around, we'd go out and throw the football with him. He was always involved with our sports. He never forced us to play, but he always made it available. Once we started playing organized sports, he never missed any games. And he would always sort of critique us when we got home, a constructive critique. He never really jumped on us for not playing well, which sometimes you do. He critiqued us and gave his input. It was usually pretty wise what he said."

The Rev. Spurrier had been a "pretty decent athlete during his day," according to Graham.

"And it sort of carried over to us," Graham said. "He just made [sports] available to Steve and I and we both pursued athletics. Steve was a lot more successful than I was, but I like to think I helped him a bit being I was a little older."

Joe Biddle, a childhood friend, who is now a sportswriter in Nashville, Tennessee, grew up in Johnson City playing sports with both brothers and remembers how the boys in Johnson City quickly learned about Steve Spurrier.

"When he first moved to town, we'd heard about him," Biddle said. "Elementary school was [grades] one through six, and they had elementary school basketball league games, and we heard about this kid who was scoring like 25 to 30 points a game [in elementary school]. And remember, that's when our teams were hoping they could get 25 or 30 points a game."

Spurrier scored 40 of his team's 44 points during a fifth grade game. In sixth grade his basketball team went undefeated, and he pitched and played shortstop to lead his Little League team to an 18-1 mark.

"He was so far ahead of everyone," Biddle said. "In fact I thought he was a better basketball player in high school than he was a football player. He was, I thought, ahead of his time. He was doing all that behind-the-back dribbling while going down the court, dribbling between his legs and stuff. He could play all three positions on the basketball court, great shooter. In the clutch he'd always come up with something. You always thought you had a chance with him in the game. He pulled out a lot of games just on his own athletic ability."

Biddle played against Spurrier in Little League and Babe Ruth League baseball.

"And his dad, 'The Reverend,' coached him in Little League and Babe Ruth League," Biddle said. "He's where Steve gets his competitive drive."

A well-circulated story tells about the elder Spurrier asking for a show of hands among the boys he coached to identify those believing the object of the game was not to win or lose, but how you played the game. Once he looked at all the raised hands he informed the boys nobody would be keeping score if the object wasn't to win and that an athlete may as well stay home if he wasn't competing to win.

"He said, if you keep score, you're out there to win," Graham said. "That's a true story. It was all about winning. If you keep score, if it was sandlot ball or whatever, you're out there to win."

The Reverend's words did not fall on deaf ears with Steve.

"[Steve] didn't take [losing] well then, doesn't take it well now, and probably won't take it well with the Redskins," Biddle said. "You know, he just hates it and he's miserable to be around if he loses. . . .

"The Reverend was very competitive, too. Hated to lose. Didn't take it well at all. Always had an excuse. Always wanted to blame somebody else why they lost. So Steve gets a lot of that honestly."

Graham called his father "very competitive" but said he tempered the competitiveness with sportsmanship.

"You know, he didn't like to lose," Graham said. "We don't either. He taught us early to learn how to lose, to be graceful when you lose. But you're there to win. That's what it's all about. He did teach us to lose gracefully if we did lose. That's part of being a good winner I think. He taught us that."

While much of what has been written about the Rev. Spurrier paints the portrait of a competitive man, little is said about his other side.

"He was a real God-fearing man, he was very strict," Graham said of his father. "There were no movies for us. There were no dances for us. There was no ball playing on Sunday for us, until we moved [to Johnson City] and started slipping off, because we lived a block away from a city park, Kiwanis Park. And we started slipping off on Sunday. And he finally realized it was hopeless to keep us away."

Rev. Spurrier never did change in his approach to Sunday, even after his boys began playing regularly on the Sabbath. He stuck to his guns even after Steve went to the NFL, watching his son's Sunday games on TV, but never attending.

Even if Rev. Spurrier's sons snuck out to play sports Sunday afternoon, they could be found in church on Sunday mornings. Steve had a 13-year record of perfect Sunday school attendance.

Marjorie Spurrier played the role of supportive wife and served as a counterbalance to her husband with the couple's three children.

Graham Spurrier died in 2000, but Marjorie is still alive and well, living in Green Cove Springs, Florida.

"She just kept everything together," Graham said. "She left the disciplinary stuff to Dad, except for my sister. Mom took care of the shopping and money matters and the buying and all that stuff. How she did it I'll never know. We never wanted for anything, we never had anything extra much, but we always had what we needed, and she always saw to it that we had it."

Biddle remembers the youngest Spurrier being consumed by sports and little else.

"He didn't spend a whole lot of time on books," Biddle said. "He was not highly motivated in school. He did enough to get by."

Kiwanis Park provided an idyllic setting for the development of a young athlete with fields for football and baseball as well as basketball courts.

"Steve, Graham and I used to go down there and umpire games in the summer," Biddle said. "Played pickup games of football. That's where [Steve] learned how to punt. He and Graham punting to each other by themselves there at Kiwanis Park."

Steve remembers the games they played.

"We'd punt back and forth, play that kick-back game where you'd punt it and catch it," Steve said.

Steve showed a lot of talent early.

"I punted the ball well, too," Graham said. "But [Steve] started banging them past me at an early age. He worked hard at it. He never lacked for every day getting out there and working on something."

Spurrier competed against the older boys at Kiwanis Park in many a sandlot game.

"We'd bring [Steve] down there at first," Graham said. "Since he always punted the ball well, he started punting for both sides for the older guys. When the guys his age started playing he would quarterback both teams because he threw it better than everybody else."

Graham said his brother "absolutely" benefited from playing against the older kids but said his brother had an unmatched love for athletics.

"He got a little kicking tee one Christmas," Graham said. "That was when we were here in Johnson City. And he'd take that sucker out. It was his favorite Christmas present, a little old plastic job. He'd put that ball up there and kick it over a tree. And I don't know how many times he'd do that every day."

Steve remembered the tee fondly.

"I was probably eight or nine years old," Steve said. "I got a yellow plastic kicking tee. I think it cost 50 cents, and that was my best toy. We had one or two old footballs, and I mean they were old ones, and I'd put it on a tee and kick it over a tree that was about the height of a goal post."

Competitiveness caused fights between Graham and Steve.

"We fought a lot," Graham said. "Usually when we fought it was over getting beat in something. Early on, I could take him in about everything. Then he got taller than me. I'm about five-ten, and he grew up to be about six-two, so he started passing me height wise. Then, when he started beating me at whatever we were playing, I'd get mad and end up fighting with him because I was the older brother, and getting beat, that didn't sit real well."

Steve calls the relationship he had with Graham "a typical brother relationship" and recognizes Graham's contribution to his athletic development.

"I think he was important in that he was three years older," Steve said. "I was always trying to keep up with him. Playing one-on-one basketball, it was tough to beat him, of course, being three years younger. Then I finally caught him. I got about as tall as him. . . . Trying to beat him in one-on-one forced me to try and get better."

Graham, who played basketball and baseball in high school before playing college baseball at East Tennessee State, knew Steve was going to be special.

"Everything he did he did well," Graham said. "But he worked on it. He had a lot of talent and God-given ability, but he worked on it also. And that's why he really was good. He just was a winner. A lot of times he wasn't the quickest, or the fastest, or the tallest, or strongest. But he just found a way to win. And that's been true playing and his coaching also."

Steve was in junior high when he began serving messages to his brother, who was in high school; humbling lessons taught by a better athlete.

"Scout Hall, where they held Boy Scout meetings [in Johnson City] was right behind the house, indoor gym with a really low ceiling," Graham said. "We had a key to it. And every day when it rained or it was too cold outside, we'd go in there and shoot hoops. We'd even throw the baseball and football. But I remember Steve really started to take it to me in basketball. And, like I say, I was a pretty good high school player and he was still in junior high. Personally, that right there was when I knew he was really going to be something special. In high school, when he really did start playing basketball, you could see it. He was just a winner. I don't know how many games he'd bring them from behind in football, basketball, or even baseball, too."

Steve recalled when playing football came together for him.

"Kermit Tipton, my high school coach, is the one who really helped me," Steve said. "It was between my sophomore and junior year, when I began to grow and got the baby fat off. I began to play ball about the sixth game of my junior year in high school."

Tipton called Spurrier "easy to coach."

"Because he always wanted to do the best," Tipton told the *Tampa Tribune*. But Tipton called Spurrier "slow and awkward" as a sophomore.

"He couldn't get to the tackle hole fast enough to make a quickie handoff," Tipton said. "But Steve spent a lot of time at home working on his techniques. He wasn't born to become a Heisman Trophy winner. He worked hard on his own."

Spurrier's friends didn't think football would be his game, and neither did Spurrier.

"By all means and rights I should have quit football," Spurrier said. "My buddies said I'd quit, because I was better in baseball and basketball. Those sports were more natural to me, the eye and hand coordination, hitting and throwing. Whereas in football, I couldn't run very fast and I wasn't very strong. There wasn't much I could do in football but hang in there and get banged around like everybody else. I guess it was inbred in me to not quit anything I started, so I stayed.

"Between my junior and senior years I grew a little, got tall, got to working out better as far as some of the agility drills. Football became my game."

An odd variable to Spurrier's development showed up at Science Hill High in the form of Chicago Bears quarterback Billy Wade.

"Billy Wade was preaching out at East Tennessee State," Spurrier said. "They had a thing every year called 'the preaching mission.' Athletes come through and so forth, and go by the high schools. And he spoke at the high school, then came by and watched spring football practice one day and gave Coach a few little pass patterns, like a little hitch, a little sideline, a little streak. We didn't have any of that stuff. We just sort of ran the old dead T, two tight ends, a few little play-action passes. He told our coach, 'That kid Spurrier, he can throw. And you've got some good little receivers out here that can catch, you know, here's the way to go about it.' That got our coach to say, 'Hey, let's throw the ball a little bit.'"

Had Wade not influenced Tipton to balance the offense with more passing, Spurrier's passing skills might have gone unnoticed.

Spurrier's development in football did nothing to deter other fields of competition; pickup basketball games were a part of daily life in Johnson City.

"A lot of people from town had goals in their driveways," Biddle said. "The one across the street from me was lighted. So we had some ferocious pickup basketball games. Plus, prior to integration, there was an all-black high school called Langston High School. And they had a black recreation league at the community center. We would go over there and play those guys. They had unbelievable basketball and football teams. We'd play those teams at the rec center during the summer and, man, that was some of the finest basketball ever seen in that town, with no referees or anything like that. We got to be pretty good friends with them. We'd go to their games when we didn't have games."

Football, basketball and baseball were the main sports, but Spurrier loved them all.

"Anything that had competition to it, he was in for it," Biddle said. "He wanted to win whether it was pitching pennies against the wall or whatever."

Spurrier's love affair with golf began in high school.

"He'd go out to the country club when the caddies had their day to play and he'd play with the caddies," Graham said. "We couldn't afford to be playing at any country club or anything, so that's where he started playing. Never took any lessons."

Steve managed to get into the Johnson City Country Club more often than just caddy's day.

"Steve came up with a 3-iron somewhere," Biddle said. "And we got some old golf balls, and probably stole them out of the putt-putt if the truth be known. And we would climb over the fence of the Johnson City Country Club on occasion. Steve tried to teach me how to hit that 3-iron. And we started playing holes. All we had was a 3-iron and a bag and some stolen golf balls. It was kind of funny. We would have to dodge the real golfers out there."

Spurrier's competitiveness could wear thin on those he competed against, even when it came to something as innocent as a game of pool.

"If you were going to shoot a game of pool, he would start with all those psychological mind games," Biddle said. "We were too naive and stupid back then to know what it was. He probably was, too. But he would do that, like, 'There ain't no way you can win this game' before you even started playing. He was one of those, if you beat him, and I usually beat him at pool—one of the few things I could beat him at—he'd kind of want you to stay there until he won. So you either lost or you had to stay there all night. That's the way he was, so competitive. He just found ways to win. Steve didn't lose much."

Steve wasn't the stereotypical hell-raising preacher's kid. Sports were just fine for the son of Rev. Spurrier.

"He didn't smoke, he didn't drink, he didn't cuss and he wouldn't be around anybody who did for any length of time," Biddle said. "His father was pretty strict on him.

"I never had a drink until I went to college. And he didn't either. So it wasn't a thing where he was a PK [preacher's kid] who went off on a wild tangent or anything."

They were typical kids growing up in a city Biddle called "a good place to grow up." Johnson City was dry. It had two theaters, a pool hall and a downtown where everybody went on Saturdays and saw everybody else. Spurrier, Biddle and the rest of the group they ran around with took part in all the typical activities of anybody else their age.

"The Reverend had an old blue Buick," Biddle said. "That's back when Buicks weighed about 18 tons. So when Steve got a driver's license, he'd alternate with Graham on who got to drive the thing. More than once we double dated and went to the drive-in movie or whatever. I think we pushed that thing further than we ever drove it, because it was always breaking down. We called it the 'Blue Bomb.'"

Biddle hung out with Spurrier but said Spurrier has never been the "life of a party type of guy."

"Steve's always preoccupied with what's on his mind," Biddle said. "He doesn't care a whole lot about what's on anybody else's mind. He doesn't let a whole lot of people get very close to him, get to know him. But he's always been like that. You could be talking to him and you'd realize he doesn't hear a word you're saying. Or his mind is 50 miles away wondering what he's going to do next."

Spurrier's style of play made him look arrogant even back at Science Hill High School, particularly in basketball.

"He'd take the ball around his back, between his legs and he was a really fine shooter," Graham said. "He could shoot the ball awfully well. Real good ball handler. Of course he worked on that."

Biddle added: "As you can imagine, he wasn't very well liked by people at the other schools and other communities. He was seen as cocky and aloof and all those other things, which he probably is."

Biddle laughed recalling an incident after Spurrier led a Science Hill basketball victory against an arch rival.

"One time they were playing Kingsport Dobyns-Bennett, that's where Tennessee Eastman, Eastman-Kodak, had a big plant over there," Biddle said. "We always accused them of recruiting the best athletes from wherever and their parents ended up working at Tennessee Eastman making more money. Imagine that.

"Anyway, they played Kingsport, and I think Steve scored like 30 points that night. He was in one of those zones and [Science Hill] beat them on their home court. That didn't happen very often so whatever media was around back then wanted to talk to [Steve after the game]. Meanwhile, the rest of the team got showered and dressed and got on the bus. Steve was running late. Coach comes back to the locker room, doesn't see anyone, gets back on the bus and they drive back to Johnson City. Steve was in the shower at the time. So he didn't know the team had left. He gets dressed, walks out of the locker room and he's stranded. He doesn't have a way home or anything. And that was pretty funny unless you were him."

A Dobyns-Bennett track coach, who had been a junior high coach in Johnson City, happened to drive by and picked up Spurrier, giving him a ride back to Johnson City. Biddle notes the incident probably didn't bother Spurrier a bit.

"People would yell all sorts of things at him and he didn't care," Biddle said. "He'd have that letter jacket on with letters all over the place, you know how you do it in high school. He didn't care. That just motivated him more."

Graham takes exception to his little brother being called arrogant, even back in the days when Steve appeared to be showboating on the basketball court.

"[The crowd] would a lot of times get fired up," Graham said. "Because they thought he was showboating. And that's part of, you know, how people say he's arrogant. Steve's not arrogant. He's a confident guy. He knows he does a good job and he's just confident. And I think there's a lot of difference between being arrogant, which a lot of people call him, and that's people who don't know him, and being confident and successful."

If anything, Spurrier defined athletic success, winning all-state honors in football, basketball and baseball at Science Hill High School, and he was a prep All-American in football in 1962. Science Hill won two straight state baseball titles in Spurrier's junior and senior seasons, and in three seasons of pitching he never lost a game. His athletic prowess was well known in the Tri-State area, but news of the three-sport star traveled to other parts of the country as well.

"Everybody in the country wanted him," Graham said. "He had letters from everywhere. Alabama, Ole Miss, they were all hot on him, basketball as well. I think [the University of Tennessee] would have offered him a basketball scholarship just to get him to come down there and play."

Both Spurrier boys were fans of the Southeastern Conference and specifically the University of Tennessee, which sat approximately 100 miles away in Knoxville.

"[Steve] always wanted to go to Tennessee and play football there," Graham said. "When Dad could scrape up some freebee tickets, we'd go down and see them play probably a couple or three times a year back when we were younger."

Steve seemed to glow when asked about the trips.

"It was a thrill . . . it was an exciting time," Steve said wistfully.

Graham said his brother would have gone to Tennessee, but they still ran the single-wing.

"He couldn't have been a tailback because he didn't have the speed," Graham said. "Of course he could throw and punt. But he didn't have the speed to be a runner. And if you're a tailback in the single-wing, you've got to run the ball."

Pepper Rodgers, now a vice president with the Washington Redskins, was an offensive coach at the University of Florida when Spurrier was recruited and explained the nature of the single-wing.

"Well, [the quarterback] is not a quarterback," Rodgers said. "He's a tailback. There are a lot of guys playing the single-wing today and they call it the shotgun. One guy runs the ball. One guy passes the ball. One guy kicks the ball. Basically that's what it was. You have a wingback outside the tight end and you had a blocking back between the guard and the tackle. You had a fullback about two and a half yards off the ball and you had the tailback about five yards. So the ball would be snapped about 95 percent of the time to the tailback and he would either run or pass the ball. Then once in a while, they'd snap to the fullback, the short guy.

"Now they do that with the quarterback, handing him the ball out of that spread. The one person did it all. There was no quarterback up under the center, just one guy. Steve was obviously a wonderful passer, a wonderful kicker, but I wouldn't consider him one of the top running quarterbacks in America."

Steve recognized that his skills did not suit the single-wing.

"The single-wing was something I could not play, although they tried to tell me that I could have," Steve said.

Tennessee also was in a transition period with their coach; popular Doug Dickey had not yet become the Vols' coach.

"If they'd been running the T and Doug Dickey had been the coach and he'd recruited me, gosh, I'd have probably gone to Tennessee," Steve said.

Tennessee and the single-wing were scratched from the list of schools Spurrier wanted to attend. During the early part of 1963, Spurrier visited Alabama and Mississippi and enjoyed both visits. But he chose to direct his attention to the basketball season at Science Hill rather than focus on his scholarship decision, which he put on hold.

Alas, the University of Florida got wind of Spurrier's existence. Florida coach Ray Graves, with the help of his offensive assistant, Rodgers, was interested in installing a pro-style offense and had no interest in running the single-wing. In a pro-style offense, any running by the quarterback, other than scrambling out of the pocket, was not a part of the offense.

Today the recruiting of high school athletes has become a creature of media hype and the big business of college football, creating a cottage industry for information about what 18-year-olds are being recruited by the various colleges and universities. Internet sites such as BorderWars, Max Emfinger,

Tom Lemming and PrepStar provide information on what recruit is leaning in the direction of what colleges as do 1-(900) recruiting hot lines. National Signing Day, which is the first day athletes may sign binding national letters of intent, is now one of the more visible college football stories each year.

Recruiting didn't have the same flavor in the early 1960s. And the argument could be made that recruiting has taken a step backward from those days given the crazed diligence by alumni and fans, who follow the huge crapshoot of signing an 18-year-old football player as if they were following their team's regular season. In the 1960s, recruiting athletes from far away geographically wasn't prevalent as it is today.

"Unless you knew somebody, who knew somebody in maybe North Carolina or Tennessee, you pretty much stayed around home," Graves said.

Graves became aware of Spurrier because of his brother.

"My brother, Edwin, called me when Johnson City played my old alma mater, Central High School there in Knoxville and beat 'em something like 28-7," said Graves, who was from Knoxville and attended the University of Tennessee. "[Edwin] was postmaster and he said 'have you ever heard of Steve Spurrier?' And I said, 'No, I haven't.' He said, 'Well, he's from Johnson City and beat Central High last night. He does everything. Kicks extra points. Punts. Passes. Pretty good prospect.' I said, 'Well, I'll drop him a note and try to find out a little more about him.' So I did."

Graves pursued Spurrier without seeing a single clip of film showing him playing high school football. Instead, he did his homework on Spurrier.

"I called the coach up there and got acquainted with him," Graves said. "[Spurrier] was playing basketball at the time when I tried to get him down for a visit. My brother said I might have a chance because his daddy was a preacher and our daddy was a preacher. Anyway, it sounded pretty good. I made the contact, but I couldn't get him down because it interfered with his schedule for basketball."

Seasons changed and Spurrier traded in his basketball sneakers for baseball cleats and still had not made his visit to the University of Florida.

"Once he got into baseball, I went up to Greenville [Tennessee] and saw him play a baseball game," Graves said. "He played shortstop and pitcher. He did everything. He was an athlete. I always tried, with every player I recruited, to find out from the players, the coach and the parents if they had leadership. You've got to have leadership on the field and off the field. He was a leader. They recognized him as their leader on and off the field. That sold me on him as much as his ability.

"I was talking to some people around there and they said 'listen, he's a winner, he's an athlete, he can do it all.' He was being pretty highly recruited with

Ole Miss, Tennessee, Kentucky and Ohio State. He was considering, I think, all of them. I found out later Ohio State called him about every other night. Anyway, we finally got him down for a visit."

Spurrier had an eventful visit to the Florida campus.

"While he was here visiting, we showed him the place," Graves said. "Then we went out and showed him the golf course that we just bought. The Athletic Association bought it because the university couldn't buy it. I told him we bought the golf course and he said 'I've kind of gotten interested in golf a little bit.' And I said 'let's go out and take a look at it.' We went out there, got him a bucket of balls. Hit a few. To this day, I've asked him how much of an influence that had on him coming to Florida. He says, 'I don't know.' I kid him about it."

Spurrier caught the flu during his visit, which afforded the Gators the opportunity to demonstrate how well they could take care of a young man away from home.

"I think he scared them real bad," Graham Spurrier said. "He got real sick down there, either the first or second day he was down there, and they had to check him into the hospital. He had a bad case of the flu or something. Coach Graves checked on him most of the night, and I think that made him feel like the guy really cared and would take care of him when he went down there."

Spurrier flew back to Johnson City in a private plane accompanied by one of the Gators' coaches.

"He was not feeling well, but when he got back his mother called and thanked us for taking care of him and getting him back," Graves said. "She said he got better attention [in Gainesville] than he would have gotten [at home]."

However, Spurrier heading to Florida wasn't a done deal just yet.

"We communicated some on the phone and I was realizing then that he was a pretty top prospect," Graves said. "Finally, it all turned out and he said he was coming to Florida."

Graham believes part of his brother's decision was based on his looking toward the future.

"I think Steve thought when he got back up here he wanted to be somewhere, after he got out of school, where he could retire,'" Graham said. "Somewhere where he could really enjoy himself and the weather was conducive to the outdoors. Golf and stuff like that. I think that entered into it also. He couldn't have done any better. He made the best choice, no doubt."

Graves believes Spurrier looked at Florida as a challenge.

"To this day I think it was a challenge to him," Graves said. "He'll accept a good challenge any time, and I think that was a big challenge to come down and have a good record here. And I think we might have sold him on our offense at the time. What we were trying to do. I tried to tell him the kind of football we were trying to put in here. We were trying to have a balanced offense. Passing and running as well. It's a running conference here [in the SEC], but I said you've got to be able to throw the ball if you're going to win. And I think he was impressed with the way we had been playing and the offense we had been using. Finally he said to come on up [to Johnson City], he was ready to sign. I was really excited about it. I think everybody at Florida was, too. It was late [for signing a recruit], end of May, after the baseball season."

Tom McEwen, longtime sports columnist for the *Tampa Tribune*, said Spurrier told him he chose Florida for three reasons.

"One, to throw the football," McEwen said. "Two, Graves was also the son of a preacher. He liked that tie-in. And to play golf. He liked the weather to play golf. Those were the three reasons."

One theory on why Spurrier chose Florida suggests he wanted to be away from the strong influence of his father.

"Yeah, that's right, I think that is true," Graves said. "I think Kentucky tried to get him; they offered him a basketball and football scholarship. But I think that might have been a big factor."

Graham McKeel, a fullback who grew up in Lakeland, Florida, and entered Florida in Spurrier's freshman class, also believes Spurrier wanted some space.

"You know, in my own mind, I think he came to Florida to get a little bit farther away from his father," McKeel said. "His dad was pretty domineering. And I think he used it as an opportunity to get away."

Graham Spurrier didn't put any stock in his brother choosing Florida to be farther away from his father.

"Nah, I don't think that's true," Graham said. "He had a real good visit to Florida and he was into golf. Steve said he couldn't believe how nice the weather was in Florida during his visit."

Looking back to his recruiting experience, Steve said, "I didn't know if I'd even be good enough to play football in college."

"I was always much better in basketball and baseball than football," Steve said. "Wasn't really until my senior year in high school that I started to think, 'Hey, I'm going to have a chance to get a scholarship in football instead of basketball.' Fortunately there was no time limit on when to sign.

"Now they have the signing limit in February. I was able to go ahead and play high school basketball and wait until that season was over. Then I visited Florida. Florida didn't really recruit me until January when they figured out there was this kid up there that hasn't signed with anybody, so, 'Hey, let's go recruit him.' So Coach Graves came up two or three times and it just seemed like the place to go."

Spurrier liked Graves' honesty.

"He was nice, and he didn't say I would start as a sophomore as others had," Spurrier said. "He said I'd have to earn it.

"I wanted to stay in the South. I almost went to Ole Miss. They were one of the best passing teams in the '60s and they were usually fighting for the conference championship with Alabama. Somebody once told me, though, that you ought to go to the school in the state where you'd like to live. Well, I didn't want to live in Mississippi and I figured there must be a reason why everybody up North is saving their money so they can retire in Florida.... Then Coach Graves visited us several times. He made no wild promises. But he did say it was a pass-oriented offense Coach Rodgers had, and I could see that. Also I think it helped that his dad was a minister and so was mine. I chose Florida because of the passing, the SEC, the weather and Coach Graves."

Once Spurrier decided on Florida, a party was set up to commemorate his signing with the Gators.

"I got up there [to Johnson City] and there was a party at the restaurant there," Graves said. "His family and some news people, they had a nice dinner set up. Shrimp cocktail and the works. And his daddy was sitting up there at the head of the table and said 'Coach, did you know we haven't blessed this food yet?' And I thought 'I've come all this way up here and set up this dinner and I lose him because I didn't say the blessing.' I apologized. I got close to his mother; I think she had a lot of influence on him. Of course, his daddy had been his coach since he was a little kid. And he listened to his daddy. He was his first coach. I talked to both parents and I think we got along pretty well. I finally got that signature and it started a little romance with the University of Florida."

Spurrier's father ended up relocating to a church in High Springs, Florida, just north of Gainesville, when Steve was a freshman.

"His dad followed him down here," said McKeel, who became Spurrier's roommate. "I don't know the family situation, but I don't think Steve was real crazy about that. You could tell [Steve's father] wanted to be around Steve. Steve kind of wanted to be out on his own, which he obviously did, and make his own mark."

3

A HISTORY
OF FOOTBALL
FRUSTRATION

If Steve Spurrier looked at bringing respectability to the University of Florida's football program as a challenge, the idea was well founded.

From the beginning the University of Florida looked jinxed.

On November 22, 1901, Florida Agriculture College in Lake City, Florida, played Stetson at the Fairgrounds in Jacksonville, Florida; FAC would become the University of Florida in 1906 after moving 50 miles south to Gainesville. The first game came to be known as the first "unofficial" game of Gator football and seemed to set a template for years of bad fortune. Stetson led 6-0 late in the second half when FAC drove the ball to the Stetson eight and got stumped, literally. A stump in the field interfered with play, causing the ball to be relocated to the other side of the field. Accounts of the game say the new position played to Stetson's advantage in stopping the drive and preserving their victory.

In 1904, FAC lost all five games by a margin of 224-0.

The Gators' current media guide does not acknowledge that football began for the university until 1906 when they played Rollins on a baseball field located north of where Florida Field currently sits. The Gators won that game 6-0 and posted a record of 5-3 under coach Jack Forsythe, whose teams followed with records of 4-1-1 in 1907 and 5-2-1 in 1908.

Halfback Willie Shands, who later became a senator and had the Shands Hospital and Clinics at Florida named after him, starred on the 1908 team before G.E. Pyle coached the Gators in 1909.

Under Pyle, the Gators went 26-7-3 in five seasons, good for a career winning percentage of .763. Included in Pyle's tenure was a 144-0 rout of Florida Southern to open the 1913 season and an appetite to play tougher competition such as Auburn, Clemson, South Carolina and Georgia Tech. Pyle also led the Gators to their first postseason football, which consisted of two exhibitions in Havana, Cuba.

The first of those contests saw the Gators take a 28-0 win over the Vedado Club of Havana. But in the second contest, Pyle didn't like the officiating and called his team off the field. The move upset Cuban officials, who maintained forfeiting a game in front of paying customers was against the law. Cuban police arrested Pyle, who made a plea at the police station then fled with his team back to Florida an hour before his trial was scheduled.

Pyle left following the 1913 season, giving way to Charles McCoy, who went 9-10 in three seasons and A.L. Busser who went 7-8 in three seasons. Included on Busser's resume was a 7-0 loss to Florida Southern in 1919, representing a 151-point turnaround from the lopsided win over Florida Southern in 1913.

William Kline enjoyed moderate success from 1920 to 1922, posting a 19-8 record, which laid the groundwork for the successful tenure of Gen. James A. VanFleet.

VanFleet was a classmate of Dwight Eisenhower and Omar Bradley at West Point in 1915 and played fullback on an undefeated Army team as a senior. In addition to being the head football coach at Florida, VanFleet was the senior officer of the school's ROTC program from 1921 to 1923 and again from 1932 to 1933. VanFleet served under Black Jack Pershing during the Mexican Revolution and led the 17th Machine Gun Battalion in World War I. He further distinguished himself as the leader of major campaigns in World War II and the Korean War. Along the way he earned three Distinguished Service Crosses, four Distinguished Service Medals, three Silver Stars, three Bronze Stars and three Purple Hearts. The ROTC building on the Florida campus now bears his name.

Gator teams went 12-3-4 under VanFleet for a .737 winning percentage, including a memorable 7-7 tie with Georgia Tech, the premier Southern football team at the time. VanFleet also coached one of the biggest upsets in Gators history in 1923 when they beat Alabama, coached by the legendary Wallace Wade.

All-Southern back Edgar Jones scored all of Florida's points that day, but much of the credit for the victory went to VanFleet, who instructed his team to remove their soggy socks at halftime after playing the first half on a muddy field and trailing 6-0. No longer weighted down, the Gators scored 16 unanswered points in the second half. Wade was so mad about VanFleet's tactic he never spoke to him again, but he did employ the tactic in future Alabama contests played in poor weather.

In 1928, the Gators coached by H.L. Sebring led the nation in scoring, en route to an 8-0 start. Then the Gators traveled to Knoxville, to play the University of Tennessee, which had a 7-1-1 record. A victory would have given the Gators their first Southern Conference championship and earned the team a berth in the Rose Bowl.

Clyde Crabtree played quarterback on the 1928 squad, leading the Gators' "Phantom Four" backfield, and the team had end Dale Van Sickel, the Gators' first All-America selection.

Unfortunately for the Gators, the Vols grabbed a Crabtree lateral and returned it 70 yards for a touchdown and the Gators came up short on both of their conversion attempts, losing the game 13-12.

Florida went 8-2 in 1929 and did not experience another seven-win season for 23 seasons.

In December 1932, during a meeting in Knoxville, Tennessee, the 13 most western and southern members of the Southern Conference broke away to create what is now the Southeastern Conference. Charter members were: Alabama, Auburn, Florida, Georgia, Georgia Tech, Kentucky, LSU, Mississippi, Mississippi State, Sewanee, Tennessee, Tulane and Vanderbilt. The new league began to compete for the SEC title in 1933.

The Gators found frustration from the outset of their new association. Florida students personified this frustration in the early 1940s when they hurled coach Tom Lieb into a lake.

New coach Raymond B. Wolf didn't exactly get off to an auspicious beginning in 1946 when the Gators went 0-9. Wolf had a 13-24 record in four seasons, triggering a need recognized by the state of Florida's governor.

Gov. Fuller Warren understood the futility of Gator fans. During his 1948 campaign he promised to make winning football at Gainesville a priority.

"Fuller Warren was elected governor on two planks," Tom McEwen recalled. "One was to get the cows off the highway. Florida was an open-range state. If you ran into a cow back then, it was your fault. So they had to be fenced in. No more open-range. That, plus a winning football program at the University of Florida. And I'm not shittin' you. I talked to Warren about it and he said 'That's what we're going to do.'

"I talked to him about it on an airplane. It was absolutely important and what he thought he had to do to get elected. So what he did was he went and got Bob Woodruff at Baylor. He was a smart sumbitch, as an athletic director."

Florida hired Woodruff to be the coach and athletic director. He brought financial stability to the program by coming up with the idea to start the Athletic

Association and pull it away from the university, where the Athletic Association could raise all of its own money.

While Woodruff laid a solid foundation for future years of Gator football with his work as athletic director, his work between the white lines proved mediocre. Woodruff was an ultra conservative coach whose strongest suit was defense.

Under him the Gators were known as a smash-mouth team. Woodruff's teams boasted of All-America linemen like Vel Heckman, Charlie LaPradd and John Barrow. And the Gators went to their first-ever bowl game on Woodruff's watch.

Florida's first bowl came after the 1952 season when they played Tulsa in the Gator Bowl in Jacksonville on January 1, 1953. Running back Rick Casares, who would go on to NFL fame, powered the Gators that season and they took a 14-13 victory over Tulsa by virtue of Tulsa kicker Tom Minor's missed point after touchdown, the first missed PAT of Minor's career.

Woodruff's Gators made a return trip to the Gator Bowl in 1958 and lost to Mississippi 7-3. Disappointment followed when the Gators went 5-4-1 in 1959, which became Woodruff's final season; he finished with a mark of 53-42-6.

Ara Parseghian was the name at the top of Florida's list of coaches to replace Woodruff, but a "communications snafu" nixed a deal with the man who would coach Notre Dame to two national championships. Ray Graves took a pay cut to leave his assistant coaching job at Georgia Tech and take over for the Gators prior to the 1960 season.

"They hired Graves," McEwen said. "He's the one, in the 'Silver Sixties,' took the program up a notch. He took them national. Took them to the Orange Bowl. Never done that sort of thing before. He had good players and good teams."

Graves was 41 when the Gators hired him away from coaching legend Bobby Dodd. Graves brought with him an offensive mind and an element of fun instilled by Dodd. It's not a stretch to look at Graves and link some of Spurrier's coaching mindset to passed-down philosophies from Dodd. Like going home once all the work is done instead of working just to work, which is a rampant practice in the coaching profession.

"I learned that from Coach Dodd," Graves said. "He'd run us home. We'd try to stay there looking at film. He liked to say, 'You'll never make a right decision after 10 o'clock.' So I think a lot of my philosophy spilled over from Coach Dodd, which was sort of passed on to Steve.

"Dodd believed you had to get [the coaches] home, where they'll be fresher tomorrow, so they can be better coaches on the field. Bobby was like that. He'd call off a meeting in the middle of the afternoon to go play tennis. He'd get all of us to play tennis with him. But it was fun there at Georgia Tech. That was 13 of the nicest years I've had."

Dodd counseled Graves, advising him to take the Florida job, even though the schools had four games left on a contract. In addition, Dodd's son, Bobby Dodd, Jr., was on scholarship at Florida; the Georgia Tech coach did not want to put his son in a position of having his father as his coach.

Graves visited alumni groups and Gator fans prior to his first season, assuring all the Gators would be putting on an offensive show. Pepper Rodgers came over from the Air Force Academy to become an integral part of the staff that would create such an offense.

Rodgers had been a cocksure quarterback and kicker at Georgia Tech. Rodgers' most famous moment came as a sophomore in the 1952 Orange Bowl when Georgia Tech played Baylor. A crowd of 66,000 watched Rodgers break a 14-14 tie with 2:56 remaining by kicking a 14-yard field goal that proved to be the winner, preserving Tech's undefeated season. Rodgers loved pressure and had a winning aura.

The new regime proved to be the antithesis of Woodruff's in the third game of his first season when the Gators played Georgia Tech on October 1, 1960, in Gainesville. The Gators were sizeable underdogs entering the contest that would test Graves' team against his former mentor's. Georgia Tech still played in the SEC and was one of the conference's powerhouses.

With Bobby Dodd, Jr. and Larry Libertore splitting time at quarterback, the Gators found themselves trailing the Yellow Jackets 17-10 with the ball on their own ten and five minutes left in the game. Facing a fourth and goal at the one-foot line with 32 seconds left in the game, Libertore pitched the ball to Lindy Infante, who barely stayed in bounds to score and cut the lead to 17-16. After the touchdown, Graves sent a signal to his offense that became a famous picture in Florida football history. Wearing a white shirt and tie, Graves held his left hand in the air showing two fingers. The message was clear: he wanted his offense to go for two points. Gator fans went nuts. Graves' decision felt like a breath of fresh air in light of decisions by Woodruff.

A year earlier the Gators were tied 13-13 with Rice late in the game and Woodruff had his team run out the clock rather than risking a fumble or interception. Afterward, Woodruff explained: "I'll gamble to win, but I'll never gamble to lose."

Going for two was a given according to Graves.

"There was never a question," Graves said. "There was no decision to make. We were going for the win. I wish that had been the toughest decision I ever had to make at Florida."

Libertore completed a pass to convert the two-point try against Tech en route to an 18-17 win and a grand opening to a new era.

"It was a must [win] you know," Graves said. "Me being from Tech, and Bobby Dodd, Jr. on the team, and Pepper Rodgers and things like that. Dodd had recommended me for the job. I had to prove he was right. The truth is I think some games you are meant to win and some you are meant to lose. It was our destiny that day at Florida Field to beat Georgia Tech. That win set me off on my career and Larry Libertore on his way to a place in my heart."

Dodd called the game "one of the most exciting games I have ever witnessed."

"The buildup, of course, was so great, with the family involvement, and unlike so many times when games like that turn out dull, this one didn't," Dodd said. "The result probably was a great thing for everyone concerned, particularly Coach Graves and his new staff. It meant a great deal to them getting started at Florida, and gaining the confidence of the Florida people. As for us, I guess we could stand another loss, and as you know, we evened things up the next couple of years." Tech finished out the contract with the Gators with three wins by a cumulative score of 46-0.

By the end of Graves' first season, the Gators had a 9-2 record, including victories over FSU, LSU, Georgia and Miami. They finished the season with a 13-12 win over Baylor in the Gator Bowl.

Graves followed with records of 4-5-1 in 1961 and 7-4 in 1962. The Gators finished the 1962 season with a Gator Bowl victory over No. 9 Penn State.

Spurrier's decision to attend Florida looked like a challenge given the history of the program. However, given the Gators' new direction, the decision to embrace the challenge under Graves and his wide-open offensive philosophies must have looked intriguing and worthwhile.

4

GATOR BEGINNING

Graham McKeel went to Gainesville in August 1963 and remembered a different climate for incoming freshmen than the one existing today.

"Players weren't as touted back then," McKeel said. "You didn't have as much information as you do today. [Florida] recruited so many running backs that year. Today, I probably wouldn't have gone to Florida because there were too many running backs. I mean there were 10 or 12 running backs ahead of me. I'm like 'What the hell am I doing here?' But they all of a sudden began to drop like flies, getting hurt. My time came."

Sparse information allowed room for surprises, like Spurrier. McKeel knew nothing about Spurrier until he got to Florida. Once McKeel got to know Spurrier, he felt himself drawn to him like everybody else.

"The guy was so laid back and casual," McKeel said recalling his first impression of Spurrier. "And he was a natural leader. He was just the kind of a guy everybody liked. He was called Orr. Everybody had nicknames. He was just one of the guys. He didn't make himself special at all. That goes as far as I can remember back. Steve always fit in with everybody."

Spurrier's competitiveness could be seen from the outset.

"It's an art," McKeel said. "[Spurrier] was laid back. But when he got into the game, he was incredible."

Norm Carlson went to Florida in 1963, after being SID at Auburn, and also thought Spurrier had something special.

"I think during his freshman year there was just a presence he had about him," Carlson said. "He was very mature, very sure of himself. And you could tell in a hurry it rubbed off on the players around him. He quickly became the guy."

Quarterbacks had more responsibilities in the 1960s than they do today.

"Back then the quarterback ran the show," McKeel said. "The quarterback called all the plays. He did everything. He didn't look to the sidelines. So from day one, Spurrier was the quarterback."

Freshmen were not eligible to play varsity sports in 1963, leaving Spurrier and McKeel to play on Florida's junior varsity team. The more McKeel got to know Spurrier, the more competitive a person he saw.

"He could beat you in anything and he would," McKeel said. "He hasn't changed much today. I could go on and on forever with the stories about how competitive he is. A guy here in [Tampa, where McKeel lives], was a real hotshot ping-pong player. He had a room with a ping-pong table. Nobody could beat the guy. Spurrier beat him. He's just a player.

"In tennis, we play these 'Silver Sixties' tennis matches. (Silver Sixties is a group of Florida football players from the 1960s who remain close; they have a yearly outing.) He never looked good. He doesn't have a beautiful swing, but he gets the ball back. Like his golf swing. I told him one time, 'That's the worst looking golf swing I've ever seen in my life.' He goes, 'Watch this. I'm going to draw this thing in. See how the green's sloped? I'm going to bring it right in here.' And he does it. You can just see [the competitiveness] in certain people, naturals who can do anything. Spurrier taught himself to play golf. He was out there on the practice range during the spring and he'd just hit balls. Before he left school he was a scratch golfer."

And there was the jock softball team on which Spurrier played center field.

"This guy hits a shot out to center field and Spurrier catches the ball behind his back," McKeel laughed. "It was incredible."

McKeel disputes the idea Spurrier is not fun to be around because he is so competitive.

"He is as down to earth, friendly, knows everybody, speaks to everybody," McKeel said. "How you doing? How is everything? I don't know, this impression he gives from the playing field [coaching today] is not the impression I had when I was a player with him."

Spurrier impressed Ray Graves during his freshman season. When the freshman team scrimmaged against the varsity, Spurrier looked like the future of the Gators' offense.

"Even as a freshman you could see Spurrier never looked as sharp in practice as he did in the game," Graves said. "He could step it up. I think he was more a rhythmic quarterback in practice, and you wondered if he was going to execute what he was running. But he was thinking all the time."

Carlson saw in Spurrier a player with a strong belief in his ability to play well under pressure.

"And he was always looking at the positive side," Carlson said. "He would never dwell on negatives, even at that age. No matter what happened or what someone would say, he would always find a positive."

Spurrier brought to mind players from another era.

"I was there when [Spurrier] came in," Pepper Rodgers said. "Steve is a throwback. All those guys, like Bobby Dodd, came from that era where they could punt the ball. Steve was a wonderful athlete.

"There was no question he could do it all. Punter, he could kick it. He was one of the last guys who could kick the ball out of bounds like they did in the old days when Tennessee and all of them kicked on third down all the time. And he also was obviously a wonderful quarterback. Had all the confidence in the world in himself as a player, and he was very smart. And also, to be a great player, you have to know your limitations and also how to play your strengths, and Steve did all of the above."

Rodgers noted coaching Spurrier was a pleasurable experience because he was fun to be around, relaxed and nothing seemed to bother him, making for the perfect recipe for a quarterback capable of leading a team when the game was on the line.

"Everybody makes mistakes, but it's the guy who worries about the last mistake that ends up making more mistakes," Rodgers said. "I remember Jack Nicklaus once said in golf, 'Everybody hits bad shots. It's the guy who worries about the last shot who hits another bad shot.' Steve never worried about the bad shot he made. He always hit the next one well."

Florida's varsity finished 6-3-1 without going to a bowl game in 1963, but there were some bright spots, like the 10-6 victory over No. 3 Alabama on October 13 at Tuscaloosa. Joe Namath was the Crimson Tide's quarterback that day, but when the game was over, Graves was carried off the field on his players' shoulders. The Crimson Tide did not lose again in Tuscaloosa until 1982. Tommy Shannon was the quarterback who engineered that upset. Few thought he would be challenged for the starting job after the 1963 season; he was cagey and had earned a reputation as a winner after leading the Gators' 17-7 Gator Bowl victory over Penn State in 1962. Shannon's presence would allow the Gators to bring along Spurrier slowly in his sophomore season.

Spurrier's first break at Florida came in the spring of his freshman season when Shannon, who was All-SEC in baseball, played baseball instead of participating in spring football practice.

"Steve had the opportunity to run the first team all spring," Shannon said. "I think that helped his confidence tremendously. That was good for him and good for me because I really liked baseball better than football anyway. Steve had the

opportunity to work with the first and second team all spring. We were just trying to get the team better. And I think we had a helluva team my senior year."

Spurrier's competitiveness drew attention early.

"It didn't take long to see what a great competitor he was," Rodgers said. "It
was very easy. Of course, he was a highly recruited athlete. Everybody wanted
him. We signed him and it took about halfway through his sophomore year for
him to become the regular quarterback. And we had a quarterback who had
done very well the year before named Tom Shannon. It's always tough to bring
down an older quarterback and put in a young one. But Steve was different. He
was just better than most of the guys playing the position at any school. Not just
Florida."

Shannon started the 1964 season as the Gators' quarterback in a 24-8 opening win over Southern Methodist at Gainesville. However, it didn't take long for
Spurrier to show his stuff. Spurrier entered the SMU game in the second quarter and promptly hit Jack Harper for a 56-yard completion; the Gators scored
on the next play. Spurrier had engineered a touchdown drive on his first series
as a Gator, setting the stage for him to share time with Shannon throughout the
1964 season. The competition created a difficult choice for the coaching staff.

"Just checking the film of the practices and everything [choosing between
Spurrier and Shannon] was a real hard decision," Graves said. "Finally we put
[Spurrier] in as a sub, second string, and he executed real well, took them down
the field.

"I don't know what it was [that made the decision to add Spurrier to the
quarterback mix]. It might have been a gut feeling. As a staff we talked about it
and finally decided."

Graves admits that part of his decision to play Spurrier more was motivated
by a look toward the future. He had a quality group of sophomores on the team,
and the idea was they could develop together with Spurrier, who executed the
offense well.

"From the first pass he completed, he knew what he was doing on the football field," Graves said. "And the sophomore versus the senior, if they're even,
you're saying to yourself 'he's got three years and the other has one.'"

Competitive, yet respectful, Spurrier felt uneasy about his situation.

"To tell you the truth, I felt a little bit uncomfortable starting ahead of [Shan-
non] since most of the guys were his teammates he'd started with for two years,"
Spurrier said. "So we sort of rotated and I think that worked out best that way."

Graves agonized about what the team might think, so he talked to Shannon,
who made the decision easier for Graves to make. Graves complemented Shannon's leadership for doing so.

"That could have been a big factor with those seniors, but I think we were lucky it worked out," Graves said. "We got through that hurdle pretty well. [Spurrier] and Tommy are best friends."

Spurrier was more of a passer, equipped to run a wide-open offense; the left-handed-throwing Shannon brought another dimension to the offense.

"I probably was more of an option, rollout quarterback," Shannon said. "I probably never threw the ball standing still in my life. Keep in mind the changes that were going on at this time. There was a very big transition going on. When [Spurrier] was a sophomore, we didn't know he was going to win the Heisman Trophy two years later, so the revelations that occurred the next two years were pretty strange. We were barely having men in motion and one wideout or half-back set out behind the tight end."

Shannon emphasized the prevailing conservative climate of the era by pointing to the numbers from his junior season.

"I literally played 99 and a half percent of the offensive plays and my [passing] record that year was 56 for 100, something like that," Shannon said. "One hundred attempts the whole year. That was in 1963. In 1969, I went to [the Auburn–Florida game] and saw [Florida quarterback] John Reaves throw 66 passes in one ballgame. That's how much football changed. A lot of stuff was going on. You're just getting over the Army, the late '50s, early '60s was the lonesome end."

Florida started off the 1964 season 4-0 with wins over SMU, Mississippi State, Mississippi and South Carolina. Ranked at No. 9 in the polls, they traveled to Tuscaloosa on October 24 to play No. 3 Alabama, which also was undefeated and eager to avenge the previous year's upset to the Gators.

Though the Gators lost to Alabama, the game was Spurrier's stage to shine in his first-team debut.

The Gators' first three possessions ended with punts by Spurrier, who put on a remarkable display, leaving one punt dead at the Alabama nine another at their 11, and he kicked the third out of bounds at the Crimson Tide's nine.

Namath, who already had a history of knee problems, reinjured his knee on a fumble that gave the ball to the Gators. Spurrier drove the Gators to the Alabama nine before hooking up with Randy Jackson in the end zone for a 7-0 lead.

Spurrier led a 61-yard drive to give the Gators a 14-7 lead early in the second half. Alabama answered with a touchdown early in the fourth quarter, then David Ray kicked a 21-yard field goal to make it 17-14 Alabama with 3:06 remaining in the game.

The ensuing kickoff went into the end zone, making the 20 yard line the starting point for the Gators' final drive.

Spurrier looked cool completing critical passes of 16 and 19 yards en route to the Alabama 45 with 2:30 left before hitting Charles Casey for a 20-yard gain to the 25. Spurrier got sacked for a five-yard loss then threw a screen pass to Don Knapp that took the ball to the Alabama 12 with 1:15 to go.

After two incomplete passes, Spurrier scrambled to gain five yards to put the ball at the 7. But the run left Spurrier dazed and confused. He called a plunge on the next play that lost two yards. With 10 seconds remaining, a hurried Gators squad managed to get just 10 players on the field for a field goal attempt that went short and to the right as the final gun sounded.

"I misjudged the 7 yard line for the 2," Spurrier told the *Tampa Tribune*.

The sophomore mistake, though costly, couldn't diminish what Spurrier had accomplished in the marquee contest. He completed 9 of 14 passes for 141 yards and ran 19 times for 43 yards.

Legendary Alabama coach Bear Bryant complimented the Gators afterward.

"This is my finest team ever," Bryant said. "And I never had a greater effort or greater concentration from one of my teams. Florida is the best offensive team I've ever seen."

Spurrier wrote about the 1964 Alabama game in a 1970 column for the *Tampa Tribune* entitled "Passing Thoughts."

. . . It was my first start in college football and if I'd have known then what I knew at the end of the season, maybe we would have won or tied.

Spurrier relieved Shannon in the FSU game after Shannon took the blame for a botched snap the Seminoles recovered at their own goal line to stop an early-game drive.

"There was a big fumble that wasn't Shannon's fault," McEwen said. "And [Shannon] was irate about it, too. It was Bill Carr, the center's fault, because Jack Shinholster was on the nose [for FSU] and he knocked the shit out of him." McEwen paused to chuckle. "Jack Shinholster was maybe the meanest son-of-a-bitch, maybe, who ever lived. He just knocked the shit out of Carr, so he didn't get the snap to [Shannon]. But it looked like it was Shannon's fumble. So Spurrier went in."

Trailing 13-0 in the fourth quarter, Spurrier led a drive capped by Jack Harper's six-yard touchdown run with 9:03 remaining to make it 13-7. The Gators appeared to still be in the game until their onside kick failed. FSU started a drive at the 50 that resulted in a field goal that iced the game and FSU had a 16-7 victory, their first of the storied series.

Differences in styles existed between Spurrier and Shannon, but Shannon called their competition "friendly" and he spoke of one trait that has stayed with Spurrier since he has known him.

"He's honest," Shannon said. "I always say that the honesty comes out in a brashness, if you will. Whether you should be honest at some times, he just says it anyway. For example, if you said to me, 'Tom, do you like the way I've combed my hair?' And I said, 'It looks like shit.' I wouldn't say that to you probably if I didn't like it. I'd probably say, 'It looks okay.' He'd probably say, 'It looks like shit.' I don't think he understands diplomacy. I don't know where that comes from. I don't know if it's in class or what. He's a different kind of guy when it comes to that. But I will tell you, he's honest. And he's got a very high level of integrity."

The Gators finished the 1964 season with wins over Miami and LSU, but there was no bowl game, writing a disappointing final chapter for what appeared to be a promising season. Shannon would be gone in 1965, leaving the Gators' offense to Spurrier alone.

5

AN EMERGING FORCE

Spurrier finished the 1964 season with 65 completions in 114 attempts for 943 yards and six touchdowns. Not the kind of off-the-chart numbers Spurrier's quarterbacks would post once he became a coach, but they were outstanding numbers for his era and good enough to show he belonged.

"When we moved in as sophomores and [Spurrier] took over as a junior, he was leading the team," McKeel said. "And he had the aura of, 'We're going to win this game. Stick with me and we're going to win it.' And he did and we did."

Graves, who felt it was important for his players to look to their quarterback for leadership, grew more enamored with Spurrier the more he watched him and rewarded him by making him the first quarterback he allowed to call the signals by himself.

"I realized after a few games, probably the end of his sophomore season, that he was quite a football mind," Graves said.

Graves constantly quizzed Spurrier about his thought process, which convinced him how immersed Spurrier was in the game.

"I asked him, 'What do you think about when you're back there? Are you wondering what date you've got tonight, or what's going on?'" Graves said. "He said, 'I'm looking at the other side to see if anybody is injured or limping, substitutions and changes. Also, get the down and distance, if the play is going to work.' You find a lot of that out from your players. I believe it was the LSU game, the one postponed after a hurricane. I believe it was Graham McKeel, the fullback. We had a play for him and he was wide open on the first one. He came back and told Steve 'I'm open every time.' So every time it was third and eight or ten, [Spurrier] would hit him. The players had a rapport with him. He was trying to get the players and challenge them to make the key block or whatever it took. He was always thinking on the football field. By his junior season, I realized he was a coach on the field. He was somebody who kept all the fans there until the game was over. He pulled a few games out in the fourth quarter during the last two or three minutes."

Pepper Rodgers left Florida to go to UCLA prior to Spurrier's junior season, in 1965. Ed Kensler was put in charge of the offense; Spurrier continued to excel.

The Gators opened against Northwestern on a hot day in Evanston, Illinois. Spurrier connected with Charles Casey for the first touchdown and the Gators led 24-0 by the end of the third quarter in a 24-14 win.

Mississippi State upset the Gators in the second game, then Spurrier led the team to victories over LSU, Ole Miss and North Carolina State. Spurrier set school records in the Ole Miss game by completing 18 of 31 passes for 245 yards. Against North Carolina State, Spurrier broke his own record by completing 21 of 39 passes for 259 yards. Casey continued to be Spurrier's favorite target and hauled in two touchdowns against the Wolfpack.

Spurrier rallied the Gators from a 14-10 deficit against Auburn on the road, leading the offense 80 yards to take a 17-14 lead on a 20-yard touchdown pass to Casey. But the defense couldn't hold, and Auburn rallied to take a 28-17 win.

Florida had a 4-2 record heading into their meeting with heated rival Georgia. Florida fans had begun referring to the time late in the game as S.O.S. time, or Stephen Orr Spurrier time. The Georgia game played October 6, 1965, at Jacksonville's Gator Bowl found the Gators trailing 10-7 with 4:06 left in the game. Spurrier and the Gators' offense took the ball at their own 22 and stared out at a prevent pass defense. "S.O.S. time" and Spurrier answered the call by connecting with Casey, who took the ball to the Georgia 19. Spurrier finished off the drives with a 19-yard touchdown pass to Jack Harper and the Gators had an improbable 14-10 win.

"It was one of my high points," Spurrier said afterward.

Georgia coach Vince Dooley had a different perspective.

"It is a game I would like to forget," he said.

Spurrier threw three touchdowns the following week to lead a 51-13 victory over Tulane in Gainesville and entice the Sugar Bowl to extend the Gators a bid to play in the New Year's Day bowl even though they had games remaining with Miami and FSU.

Graves proclaimed his excitement at reaching a major bowl, which was one of his two initial goals when he became coach of the Gators, the other being an SEC Championship. Meanwhile, history would show that the Gators were the beneficiary of a black eye received earlier in the year by the city of New Orleans.

The American Football League All-Star Game had been moved from New Orleans to Houston because black players had been refused cab service and admittance to some French Quarter nightclubs.

New Orleans' better establishments were not guilty as the New Orleans restaurant, hotel and motion picture associations agreed to accommodate all. Nevertheless, some of the less-than-mainstream spots did not find it necessary to extend such courtesy, prompting the change of cities.

New Orleans was scorned, particularly by the northern press, giving the city a bad image that likely extended to the selections for the 1966 Sugar Bowl.

Late in the 1965 season, many top teams were still in the hunt for the top spot in the Associated Press poll, prompting the AP's decision to name its national champion after the bowl season. Based on this decision, the top teams looked to be paired for the best possible match-up that would aid their chances to get voted into the top spot if they won on New Year's Day. The Sugar and Orange Bowls were available to accommodate the marquee game, Alabama–Nebraska, but due to the AFL walkout, Nebraska would have no part of New Orleans. Thus, Alabama and Nebraska headed for the Orange Bowl, where Alabama defeated Nebraska 39-28 to claim the national championship.

Florida was one of several teams being considered for the Cotton and Sugar Bowls. After several hypothetical situations played out, the Gators received their Sugar Bowl bid.

Unlike bowl bids of today, the Gators and the Sugar Bowl didn't immediately announce the New Year's Day pairing against Missouri, delaying the announcement until after the following week's 16-13 Gator loss to Miami, which would go down as one of Spurrier's poorest performances.

He completed just eight of 22 passes and made several costly mistakes. A Spurrier interception led to the field goal that ended up being the difference in the game. And when Spurrier had a chance to atone, leading the Gators to the Hurricanes' 15 in the waning moments of the game, he was called for intentionall grounding and the drive stalled.

The Gators' record fell to 6-3 with Florida State heading to Gainesville to end the season.

FSU brought a 4-4-1 record into the game, but the record didn't seem to matter when the Gators found themselves trailing 17-16 with 2:02 left; FSU had trailed 16-3.

Spurrier remained cool after the 'Noles' go-ahead-score, telling Graves not to worry just before the Gators took over at their own 29.

"I'd never seen anything like Spurrier," Graves said shaking his head when he recalled the moment.

Spurrier threw incomplete on the first play before he connected with Casey for 10 yards. Harper then hauled in a deep pass to give the Gators the ball at the FSU 43 with 1:32 left. Spurrier ran for five yards, called time out, then threw to Casey for 13 yards to the FSU 25. Spurrier's improvisation skills were put on display on the touchdown pass that followed.

"He changed Casey's route," Graves said. "Ball was snapped, he rolled out and gave Casey a hand signal and threw a touchdown to him. That was the winning score."

Spurrier later called the pass his favorite of all the passes he threw at Florida.

"I rolled to my right and Casey was to juke, then go straight down the sideline in front of me," Spurrier told the *Tampa Tribune*. "As I moved right, two important things happened. Don Knapp made a great block on the Florida State end to give me more time to fool around, and I saw that the FSU middle guard had jumped offsides. That would give us five yards and get us closer for [kicker] Wayne [Barfield] to try the field goal if other things failed. Casey was in front of the defender, Billy Campbell, but with the time I had, I motioned for him to go deeper and I kept threatening to run. Coach [Fred] Pancoast had told me from the booth that the object was to get close for the field goal, but to play it by ear. Campbell stood his ground as Casey went by him, and I threw at Charley. He caught it in the end zone. I won't forget that one."

Allen Trammell put the game away for good when he returned an interception 46 yards for a touchdown to make the final score 30-17, and the Gators would head to the Sugar Bowl with a 7-3 record rather than an embarrassing 6-4.

"Steve was a winner and I think the players believed anything he called was going to work, it would be a winner," Graves said. "I think he gave everybody confidence, the players and the fans."

Spurrier's legend had grown during the '65 season on the wings of the 148 passes he'd completed in 287 attempts for 1,893 yards and 14 touchdowns. He also ran for 230 yards and had a 41-yard punting average to earn first-team All-America honors. All of Spurrier's regular-season heroics would pale in comparison to the show he put on in Tulane Stadium during the 32nd Sugar Bowl.

Florida extended Graves' contract by five years, through the 1970 season, prior to the 1966 Sugar Bowl; the Gators came in as 1½ to 2 point underdogs to Missouri, which had lost a close one to Nebraska, 16-14.

A bad omen came when Albert V, Florida's alligator mascot, arrived in "The Big Easy" with a bloody nose. He'd banged his snout against his specially constructed cage during his station wagon ride to New Orleans.

From the outset, the game appeared to be a Missouri massacre in the 78 degree temperatures.

Missouri coach Dan Devine, who went on to coach the Green Bay Packers and Notre Dame, tried to stop the Gators' explosive offense by putting more pressure on Spurrier with a "wide tackle six," which translated to an eight-man line. Devine felt confident in the strategy since one of Missouri's strengths was a defensive secondary led by All-America safety Johnny Roland and safety Skip Grossnickle.

"It couldn't have worked better," Spurrier told the *Tampa Tribune*. "For a while I couldn't breathe out there."

Missouri so overpowered Florida in the first quarter that the Gators had the ball for a measly seven plays while the Tigers had the ball for 28, en route to a 17-0 lead at the end of the first quarter. The Gators didn't do much better in the second quarter on offense and went to the dressing room trailing 17-0 at the half.

"We were just dead out there in the first half," Spurrier said.

Florida coaches adjusted at the intermission. The half back was moved wide as a receiver, and Spurrier was instructed to roll away from the pressure and look for receivers in the flats. The Gators' offense didn't get any results in the third quarter, but they did get a break when a holding call forced Missouri to kick a field goal after they had been inside the Gators' 10.

"When we didn't get into the end zone in the first half, I knew we were going to have a hard time staying in the game," Graves said. "We finally got the feel of their offense in the second half and started to slow them up."

Missouri led 20-0 after three quarters.

"We figured we could only score three times in the last quarter," Spurrier told the *Tampa Tribune*. "What we had to do was keep Missouri from getting a touchdown. But they might have gotten close enough for a field goal, which would have given them 23 points. So to win, we would have needed 24 points."

Missouri seemed to be wilting in the heat in the fourth quarter; Spurrier began to enjoy great success rolling out.

Spurrier led the Gators 86 yards on six plays—all completed passes—finding Harper for a 22-yard touchdown to make it 20-6 early in the fourth quarter. Florida's coaching staff elected to go for two points despite the fact the team had not gone for two points following a touchdown the entire 1965 season.

"When you are behind that far, you need a shot in the arm," Graves told the *Tampa Tribune*. "And I thought a two-pointer would give us a boost."

Spurrier's pass to Richard Trapp fell incomplete and the two-point conversion failed, leaving the Gators 14 points behind with time running out.

Tom McEwen said the Florida coaching staff was thinking more about not getting embarrassed than winning the game.

"The Gator coaches sat right behind us in the press box," McEwen said. "Suddenly it's 20-6 and the guys said go for two. And everybody in the press box is like, 'Why are you going for two?' They thought 20-8 would look better than 20-6."

Graves confirmed McEwen's story.

"I thought eight points would look better than six, since we hadn't scored any touchdowns," Graves said.

Missouri ran one play after taking the kickoff and fumbled at their 10.

"That looked like manna from heaven," Spurrier told the *Tampa Tribune*.

Three plays later Spurrier scored on a quarterback sneak, and once again the Gators went for two. This time Harper threw an incomplete halfback pass into the end zone and the score was 20-12 Missouri.

Missouri made one first down on their next possession before the Gators forced a punt, giving the Gators the ball at their own 19. Spurrier led the Gators up the field on an 81-yard drive that would culminate with his second touchdown pass of the game.

Spurrier spotted Casey and tried to loft a pass over Grossnickle into the end zone. The Missouri safety covered the play well, deflecting the pass, but Casey dove outstretched and parallel to the ground to get his hands on the ball. The ball bounced into the air then Casey pulled it close to his chest for a 21-yard touchdown with 2:08 remaining.

Now the Gators were forced to go for two points to tie the game. Spurrier tried to hit Barry Brown, but once again the ball fell incomplete and the Gators trailed 20-18.

Florida had one last chance when they got the ball back at their own 3 with 50 seconds left in the game. Even though the S.O.S cry went out, Spurrier could only get the Gators to their own 32 as time ran out.

"If we had just kicked the three extra points, we would have won," Graves said. "We never tried a two-point conversion play all year, but I thought we could make it this time."

All kinds of records were broken that day. Missouri set a Sugar Bowl record for the most points scored in a quarter in the first quarter with 17; the Gators broke that record with 18 points in the fourth quarter. But most of the records set that day belonged to Spurrier.

Davey O'Brien, the 1938 Heisman Trophy winner from Texas Christian completed 17 passes in the 1939 Sugar Bowl; Spurrier completed 27. Spurrier also attempted the most passes, 45, for the most passing yards, 352, and he led the Gators to the most total yards on offense while participating in the most plays, 52.

Quarterbacks just didn't throw for over 300 yards in a single game in the 1960s. Spurrier became the first player from the losing team to be named the game's most outstanding player in the Sugar Bowl.

"Some of the things he did, he was something," Graves said. "He was one player in the first half and another in the second.

"Missouri was a good football team. A lot of those boys went into the pros. But in the second half, [Spurrier] just took us up and down the field like we were in practice. The first time we went for two and didn't make it, I don't know if Steve heard me or not, I said, 'How the hell can you go 80 yards and not be able to make it three yards [for the two-point conversion]?' That game definitely was a spring board for his senior year."

6

EVERYBODY'S ALL-AMERICAN

Spurrier entered his senior season in 1966 facing two new aspects to his life. First, he married Jerri Starr on September 14, 1966. Second, after two years of success as a college quarterback, he was a candidate to win the Heisman Trophy, college football's most prestigious award.

Being a Heisman hopeful in the 1960s didn't translate into the kind of media hype Heisman candidates endure today. Cable television with its all-sports stations did not exist and most cities received just three or four TV stations. As a result, only a minuscule portion of games were televised, leaving accounts of the games to the print media. Most of the Heisman voters were sportswriters, but few, if any, were able to see all of the candidates play. Thus, Heisman winners normally carried their region and a smattering of votes from writers around the country.

Having played for two years, Spurrier's name was out there among those being considered for the Heisman. If he was to have a chance at winning the award, he needed to add another solid season to stay in the running. But his performance wouldn't be graded in a weekly Heisman watch familiar to today's candidates.

"I had a good idea he was a Heisman candidate heading into his senior year," Tom McEwen said. "We had talked about it before the season, or early in the season when [the Gators] won a few games and it looked like they were going to have a good season and he was going to be good enough.

"First of all, [Spurrier] had to do what he did. Have the winning season and be the extraordinary player that he was. But our fear was that [Bob] Griese at Purdue, and whomever else was in the race, would carry the Midwest and Northeast so strongly because [the Gators] hadn't been on the national scene that long and the Southeastern Conference in those years was Alabama, Auburn and Georgia. [Florida] didn't have a reputation in any way. We were all afraid that there was going to be such a block vote in the Midwest that it was going to be difficult [for Spurrier to win the Heisman]."

Ray Graves knew he had a Heisman candidate in Spurrier but says they weren't hounded by the media to address Spurrier's chances; having a candidate never became bothersome.

"We just didn't talk about it much," Graves said. "It was just something that happened at the end of the season in New York. Neither Steve nor anybody was thinking about that. We were trying to win a conference championship, and it seemed like Georgia or somebody else knocked us out every year. That's about the way it was. We didn't talk about it much, and there wasn't much written until late in his senior year when he began to get some publicity."

Teammates saw no changes in their leader.

"Spurrier was just a regular guy," Graham McKeel said. "He could take all that Heisman stuff and he just didn't let it affect him."

McEwen held a Heisman vote, which he would cast for Spurrier. In addition, he planned to do what other writers around the country were doing for their candidates: lobby.

"Norm Carlson really helped as the public relations man," McEwen said. "[The Heisman race] was small, with less people back then. And back then you had contacts. It was nothing to talk about candidates with other people in other parts of the country. I covered Steve. I knew him well enough, and Jerri, because they were sweathearts all those years. I did as much as I could to help him get the Heisman."

After the Sugar Bowl, Carlson recognized Spurrier would have a shot at winning the Heisman.

"Everything was different back then," Carlson said. "Back then you didn't have ESPN Game Day. Steve's senior year we weren't even on television. We never had a game on TV. You didn't have all those shows voters could see to watch in person and see how good he was doing. That was the problem we had to try and overcome."

Carlson tried to gain attention for Spurrier by sending out a lot of film clips.

"Not video, obviously," Carlson said. "I think it was three or four plays to show his versatility; one throwing the ball, one punting it, one placekicking, one whatever else. We sent them all over the country. Then about midseason, the governor, Hayden Burns, his office called and asked how they could help promote Spurrier."

Carlson requested they pay to send out updated film clips from Spurrier's senior season.

"You couldn't do that now because the Tourism Bureau wouldn't approve it, it would be too political," Carlson said. "Hayden Burns was a Gator and he said the Tourism Bureau was going to do it, so they sent these film clips all over the country to the same stations we had sent them to originally in the middle of the year and they got a lot of play. One of the plays here, one of the plays there, and it wound up giving him a lot of exposure. And it was very important because we weren't on TV."

Graves called his 1966 team the smallest-sized squad he'd had since he'd been at Florida, but he also said they were the best physically conditioned team he'd ever had.

"Never have I approached an opening with, truly, as little an idea about what might happen," Graves said prior to the 1966 season. "I just don't know what to expect from this club. They've been anything from terrible, to not so terrible, to fair and OK to good."

Florida opened the season against Northwestern at Florida Field. Spurrier's favorite receiver, Charles Casey, had graduated, but Richard Trapp, McKeel and Paul Ewaldsen were back, and they were joined by sophomore running back Larry Smith.

Smith who had been a highly sought All-American from Tampa, stood 6-foot-4, 213 pounds and had a bruising running style that would eventually make him a first-round selection by the Los Angeles Rams in the NFL draft. Smith was a sophomore in 1966, making him eligible and giving the Gators more balance on offense.

Smith recalled traveling by bus from the team hotel just outside Gainesville to Florida Field before the 1966 Northwestern game, the first game he ever played at the University of Florida.

"I looked over [at Spurrier] and he was sound asleep," Smith said. "He was always a cool customer. He never lost his composure. I think that's the thing that always impressed me the most. He always stayed cool no matter what the circumstance."

Smith called Spurrier the "unquestioned leader" of the team.

"That was pretty clear [coming in as a sophomore]," Smith said. "He was the quarterback and quarterbacks usually are the unquestioned leaders. I don't remember any specifics of things he did in the huddle [as an anecdote to personify his leadership]. Maybe it's because I'm too old. But he was clearly the leader. He clearly knew what was going on on the field. We had great confidence in him. For example, whenever he got the ball back and we were behind, we felt like it wasn't going to be a problem. We just knew he'd move the ballclub. I thought he did a good job of selecting plays. He seemed to have a real feel for the ebb and flow of the game."

Spurrier experienced an eventful week leading up to the Northwestern game. Not only had a writer and photographer from *LIFE* magazine followed Spurrier around, he and sweetheart Jerri Starr slipped off on Wednesday to a Methodist church in Kingsland, Georgia, where they were married. The couple had known each other since Spurrier was a freshman and Jerri was a "little sister" at his fraternity, Alpha Tau Omega. Starr hailed from Fort Lauderdale and was the niece of former Penn State coach Rip Engle.

The guy from *LIFE* "was here to interview Steve," Carlson said. "I think that was going to be the first interview of several. But Steve wasn't here. And so, as is typical with [Spurrier's] timing and outright luck, that made it a better story than it would have otherwise been because they were so enamored with 'here's the star quarterback and the sorority queen bouncing off to Georgia to get married.'

"They had decided they wanted to [get married] before the season got started. They had a good friend, Fred Goldsmith, who later coached at Duke, he and his wife had gotten married that summer in Folkston, Georgia, so they were all 'this is the thing to do, be cool.' And they followed [the Goldsmiths] up there and Goldsmith got lost and they wound up in Kingsland, Georgia. Therefore, they were very late getting back. And [Spurrier] missed practice and she missed sorority rush. It was a big to do, kind of humorous. That was the start of the season. The fact that *LIFE* was here kind of typified Spurrier with his outright luck and timing."

Spurrier remained cool in the opener leading the 6½-point favorite Gators against Northwestern.

Northwestern switched defenses continuously and Spurrier countered by checking off at the line of scrimmage most of the day. Spurrier hooked up with Trapp on a 19-yard touchdown early in the first quarter then connected with Ewaldsen for a 10-yard touchdown in the second quarter. Spurrier completed his third touchdown pass of the day with a 53-yard strike to Trapp in the third quarter.

Lost in the rout were Spurrier's field goals of 25 and 42 yards. Neither Smith nor McKeel remembered Spurrier kicking a field goal in the Northwestern game. Graves remembered, because unbeknownst to many of Spurrier's teammates, he'd worked on his placekicking during the special teams portion of practice. Graves was a stickler about keeping his special teams sharp.

"Special teams, I'll tell you, I learned that at Tennessee under Coach [Bob] Neyland," Graves said. "Every close game seemed like it came down to the kicking game. That always seemed to be the difference in the ballgame."

The Northwestern game provided the perfect opportunity to test Spurrier, Graves' special teams' wildcard.

"We'd gotten our manager to fit him with a [square-toed] zip-up shoe that he could put on quickly," Graves said. "He stayed out late after practice [to work on punting and placekicking].

"Steve kicked extra points and field goals in high school. Told me about some kick where he won a game. But I had [Wayne] 'Shade Tree' [Barfield]. He was second in the nation in field goals. [Kicking field goals] was always in the back of [Spurrier's] mind."

Not only did Spurrier display his kicking toe against Northwestern, he also showed a talent for finding and exploiting defensive weaknesses.

With Florida leading 19-7 after a safety, Northwestern kicked off and George Grandy made the return for the Gators. Spurrier noticed how Philip Clark and Dennis Coyne each got up slowly after bringing down Grandy; both were starters in the Wildcats' secondary. On the next play, Spurrier threw to Trapp out in the right flat, a territory primarily defended by Clark and Coyne. Trapp caught the pass, dodged Clark and scooted 53 yards for a touchdown.

"He misses nothing," Ed Kensler said. "He picks on people. Always has the game under control."

Spurrier was selected to the United Press International's National Backfield of the Week. On the same Saturday, Griese threw three touchdowns against Ohio University in a Purdue victory; the Heisman race had begun.

Florida followed their victory over Northwestern the next week with a 28-7 win over Mississippi State to avenge the previous year's defeat to the Bulldogs. Spurrier led an 80-yard touchdown drive in the second quarter and later threw a 13-yard touchdown to Ewaldsen to complete the rout.

Spurrier threw touchdown passes of 22 and six yards in a 13-0 win over Vanderbilt in Nashville to improve the team's record to 3-0 before they headed to Tallahassee to play FSU on October 8.

FSU brought a 1-1 record into the game, having lost to Houston in a heartbreaker before beating Miami 23-20 the previous week. The Gators had plenty of offensive weapons, but so did the Seminoles with quarterback Gary Pajcic and talented receiver Ron Sellers.

And the game lived up to its expectations.

The lead changed several times before midway in the fourth quarter when the Gators found themselves trailing 19-14 as they took over on their own 21. Graves sensed the offense was worn down and opted to send in the second-team, except for Spurrier. They proceeded to march the ball to the FSU 22 before stalling. But the blow seemed to spark the starting unit.

"That was the first rest for our offensive team," Graves said. "Well, it kind of showed the first team up a bit."

Rested and snorting after having to sit, the Gators' first-team offense had a different look upon reentering the game on the next possession. Spurrier completed a pass for 20 yards then found Smith all alone on the next play for a 41-yard touchdown to make it 20-19 Gators. Trapp caught a Spurrier pass for two points, putting the Gators up 22-19 and setting up one of the most controversial finishes in the rivalry's history.

The scoreboard showed 2:46 left to play when Pajcic began the Seminoles' final drive at their own 13. Pajcic guided the team up the field to the Gators' 45 with 17 seconds remaining when he rolled right, dodged a defender, then spotted Lane Fenner streaking down the sideline toward the end zone. With Gator defensive backs Larry Rentz and Bobby Downs draped on Fenner, the FSU receiver caught the ball as he fell to the ground. The play appeared to be good for a go-ahead touchdown, but the official on the spot ruled Fenner out of bounds. Afterward Fenner said, "I was in."

Instead of taking a 26-23 lead, FSU still trailed 22-19. Then with 10 seconds left in the game, Pajcic hit a pass that took the Seminoles to the 32 to set up Pete Roberts' 48-yard field goal attempt that fell short and to the right.

Pictures seemed to validate FSU's claim that Fenner had possession of the ball in bounds. Meanwhile, FSU coach Bill Peterson's words the day before the game seemed prophetic.

"Remember, I think I was one of the first coaches in college to use the pro-set [wide-open offense] and here, this, with Spurrier, just may be the very thing that will beat me Saturday," Peterson said.

Spurrier gave Gator fans heart palpitations again the following week in Raleigh, North Carolina, against North Carolina State.

The Wolfpack led 10-3 in the third quarter when Smith scored from the one to tie the game at 10. Spurrier then led the Gators 77 yards for the go-ahead score, a 31-yard touchdown to Trapp, for a 17-10 win. It should be noted Spurrier attempted, and missed, a 30-yard field goal against the Wolfpack.

Adding to the Spurrier lore in the North Carolina State game was the dialogue in the huddle when the Gators faced a critical third-and-short situation during the drive toward the winning touchdown.

"Steve turned in the huddle to our guard Jim Benson and said, 'Truck, what do you call here?'" said Bill Carr, the Gators' All-America center, in an article appearing in the 1989 *ACC Football Yearbook* published by Four Corners Press. "Old Truck was a little stunned, but he called the right play, we got the first down and eventually scored to win.

"Steve always used the huddle as showtime. There was a method to his madness. He would instill confidence in us and loosen things up a bit."

Benson wasn't the only teammate to take part in the unique huddle maneuver by Spurrier.

"Right there in the middle of the huddle, in front of 60,000 screaming fans, he'd say to one of our wide receivers, 'DT, if I throw it to you are you going to do something with it, or are you going to fall down?'" Carr said. "He has a way of relating to you personally that it puts the individual at ease. It makes the other person feel relaxed and special. It's a way of welcoming you to his world that says he's noticed you and that you count."

After two close ones, the Gators enjoyed a laugher in Baton Rouge against LSU. Spurrier capitalized on a Tigers' fumble at the LSU 14 and hit Smith for an eight-yard touchdown three plays later. By halftime the Gators led 21-0 as they cruised to a 28-0 win.

The LSU victory gave Spurrier a three-year sweep over coach Charlie McClendon's Tigers.

"[Spurrier] had a sixth sense that all great athletes have when they get crowded," McClendon said. "In a couple of very clutch situations we put enough of a pass rush on him to force him to run, and he would start to run and get to the line of scrimmage and throw. When you get that type of performance with the pressure on you, you usually win games."

By beating LSU, the Gators ran their record to 6-0 while improving their standing in the national rankings to No. 7. Spurrier was named the United Press International's SEC Back of the Week for the third time that season after completing 17 of 25 passes for 208 yards and two touchdowns against LSU.

"I'm running out of adjectives to describe him," Graves said.

Auburn loomed next on the horizon.

While Florida had waltzed in Baton Rouge against LSU the week before, Auburn had struggled against Texas Christian to run their record to 3-3.

Texas Christian had scored first to take a 6-0 lead. The Horn Frogs' kicker, Bruce Alford, entered the game having kicked 65 consecutive extra points; against Auburn he missed. In the second half, Auburn scored a touchdown and added the PAT to take a 7-6 win.

Oddsmakers installed Florida as a 16-point favorite to beat Auburn before a homecoming crowd at Florida Field. Graves dismissed the spread, noting he thought the game would be a defensive struggle.

"I think two TDs will be enough for a victory," Graves told the *Tampa Tribune*. "[The point spread] is too much. The way I see it, 16 points will win the game."

Auburn coach Shug Jordan played the aw-shucks routine familiar to Southern coaches.

The Gators are "awesome," Jordan said. "I've been coaching against and playing against Florida teams since 1928. This is the finest I ever saw."

The Gators might have entered the game a tad overconfident, including Spurrier, who was photographed at breakfast by a wire service photographer. In the photo, Jerri Spurrier poured her husband's cereal—Tiger cereal.

Any overconfidence on the Gators' part was understandable given their 6-0 start and the team's well-founded confidence in their leader. After a practice during the week of the game, Trapp was heard teasing Spurrier: "Here comes Batman, holy touchdowns!"

Spurrier carried a .657 completion percentage into the Auburn game, establishing himself as the most efficient passer in the nation.

If the pressure of a big game wasn't enough, an Associated Press story reported Spurrier would be headed to the NFL's New York Giants after the season. The AFL and NFL were merging and Spurrier looked like the top prize for the worst team. Atlanta Falcons owner Rankin Smith was quoted in the story about the chances of Spurrier going to the Giants and said, "I'd say it's a good possibility."

Adding fuel to the report was the presence of Giants head coach Allie Sherman in Gainesville. The Giants had an off week, so Sherman watched Spurrier practice and also made arrangements to attend the Auburn game.

Legend has it that during the team breakfast on the morning of October 29, 1966, hours before the 2 P.M. kickoff against Auburn, Spurrier spoke of a premonition.

"He told someone at breakfast that he had a dream that he was going to kick a field goal to beat Auburn," Graves said.

Spurrier laughs about his alleged prophesy today.

"My buddy Gene Peek, he was like a backup receiver," Spurrier said. "Seemed like every pregame meal I'd say, 'Peeker, I think I'm going to kick a field goal to win the game today.' Jiving around. Then one day it happened. So [after it happened] he says, 'He told me he was going to do it.' But I'd jive around with him. Things like that."

Scalpers were getting $30 a ticket outside of Florida Field, an exorbitant price for the 1960s considering Florida lobster sold for 79 cents a pound and a pound of Folgers coffee went for 69 cents. Inside, a record crowd of 60,511 prepared to watch the biggest game in Gators history.

Only 1:41 had passed when Spurrier hooked up with Trapp on a nine-yard touchdown. Auburn answered by returning the ensuing kickoff for a touchdown.

Spurrier and Smith continued to pass and run the ball all over Florida Field, but stubborn Auburn wouldn't go away. The score was tied at 7 after the first quarter and Auburn grabbed a 17-13 lead by halftime. Florida tied the game at 20 by the end of the third quarter only to find themselves tied 27-27 in the fourth quarter with less than four minutes remaining.

"We had run Auburn up and down the field," McKeel said. "But they came back, came back, and we were behind. . . . Auburn always is a strange game. I was exhausted, because we'd been moving it up and down the field. We moved down for a touchdown, then they'd get a kickoff and score."

Auburn had scored touchdowns twice on plays that defied the odds; Larry Ellis returned a kickoff 89-yards and Gusty Yearout returned a fumble 91 yards. Any kind of fumble return was an oddity in college football during that era since college rules prohibited advancing a fumble once it touched the ground. Unfortunately for the Gators, Yearout plucked Gator running back Tommy Christian's fumble off the back of one of the Florida linemen then rambled for the score.

But Auburn could not stop Spurrier. After the touchdown pass to Trapp, Spurrier scored on a keeper and engineered drives capped by McKeel's one-yard plunge and Smith's two-yard run. Spurrier completed 27 of the 40 passes he attempted for 259 yards and punted five times for a 46.9-yard average; he finished the game with 442 yards of total offense compared to Auburn's 159. Yet the Gators' unblemished record looked in jeopardy when they began a drive at their own 26 with time running out.

Spurrier masterfully guided the Gators to the Auburn 20, where he was called for intentional grounding. The penalty called for a loss of down and five yards to be marked off against the Gators from the spot of the foul, pushing the Gators back to the Auburn 39.

Spurrier responded with a 15-yard completion to Jack Coons. Then the Gators stalled.

"It came down to third and long," Graves said. "Called a pass to Jack Coons, fake a block and curl in. Steve overthrew him by about three yards. He was open."

Facing a fourth and 13 at the Auburn 24, Spurrier called time out.

"He goes over to the sidelines and we all just hang out, sitting there waiting," McKeel said. "Then he comes back. I was just thinking the only shot we had was 'Shade Tree' coming in to kick a field goal. Although it was a little bit farther than he could normally do it. We had no other shot."

Graves recalled talking to Spurrier about Barfield.

"I never figured Steve was going to try and kick it," Graves said. "We talked about the wind factor, I guess. I don't know what we talked about, but it wasn't Steve kicking the field goal. I was going to send Barfield in, but [Spurrier] waved him off. And he can do that. Team captain can wave off a substitute if he doesn't want him in. I didn't have time to do anything else. Just watch what happened."

Spurrier felt confident.

"It was a long field goal," Spurrier told the *Tampa Tribune*. "It was out of Wayne's range. I pointed to my chest, looking at Coach Graves, indicating I wanted to kick it, and he nodded to go ahead. . . . I definitely wanted to kick it."

After the time out "he comes back onto the field and says 'I'm going to kick it on three,'" McKeel said. "First of all, I didn't ever realize he kicked. He apparently had done some practice with Coach Graves. Coach Graves was a field goal practice guy. I didn't even know he kicked field goals and I thought to myself, 'you've got to be kidding me.' I said, 'You're going to kick this?'"

Conceding there was nothing he could do, Graves said he was "concerned or flabbergasted."

"I was thinking, 'What's he going to do, fake the field goal and pass it?'" Graves said. "He's thought of something. You couldn't ever question him. I thought it was going to be a fake."

Normally Spurrier would have been on the field when the holder, Rentz, ran to the huddle carrying Spurrier's zip-up kicking shoe. Trapp, who wasn't part of the field-goal team, would then carry Spurrier's regular right cleat off the field to complete the shuttle system. Since Spurrier had just been on the sidelines for the timeout, such a maneuver wasn't necessary.

The Gators set up for a field goal with Spurrier prepared to kick from the right hashmark, which was not an ideal spot for a straight-on, right-footed kicker. The snap hit Rentz in the hands, he set the ball down on the 30 and Spurrier connected.

"We get up on the line and the sumbitch kicks it right through the goddamned uprights," McKeel said. "I couldn't believe it. He apparently told Coach Graves he was the only shot we got because Barfield can't kick 'em that far. He could only kick them like 20 yards. He was an extra point guy. I think that cinched the Heisman for him. If there was any doubt between him and Bob Griese, it had to be that kick. I think if anything iced it, that was it."

Smith, who can be identified in photographs of the historic kick on the left side of the line blocking a rushing Auburn lineman, thought the kick was out of Barfield's range.

"I don't think Shade Tree could have kicked it that far," Smith said. "So there really wasn't much of a debate. Steve was the only one who could get it there. Everything just sort of came together. So it was sort of remarkable he was able to make such a kick under such pressure.

"My recollection was it was a pretty good kick. But it didn't clear [the uprights] by a lot. I mean it was a pretty good kick as I recall. And that was the old straight-forward kick."

Spurrier was mobbed by his teammates as he ran off the field.

"That's one thing [Spurrier] said after he kicked it," Graves said. "He said, 'I figured it was a little too long for Barfield. And I figured if I kicked it they're going to think it's a fake and they aren't going to rush me.' It didn't go over but by about that much." Graves held his hands six inches apart. "That got him the Heisman. That's for sure. It was well covered by all the media."

Jordan confirmed Spurrier's thinking.

"We sort of anticipated a pass in place-kicking formation," Jordan told the *Tampa Tribune*. "We knew Spurrier hadn't been kicking field goals much. I watched him kick it. It was wobbly, and the trajectory was low. In other words, it was not a good place-kick, but it went through, and it was worth three points, and it won the ball game."

Graham Spurrier and some of his college buddies at East Tennessee State had driven from Johnson City to watch the game. Florida sat fans in chairs on the field back in the '60s, and Graham was camped in prime position to watch his brother's kick.

"Of course, that's probably the most exciting game I've ever seen him play," Graham said. "And it won him the Heisman Trophy. I just remember the kick, really. I wasn't privy to what all went on with he and Coach Graves before he went in and kicked it, but I do remember the kick. I was sitting on that end and I remember seeing it go through, barely clearing the goal post."

Graham is asked the question: Did his making the kick surprise you?

"Not really, no."

Of course, making the kick and being successful was what people expected from Spurrier. He'd conditioned them to think he could do no wrong.

"I think if there had been no goal posts and the official had said, 'Steve, you'll have to kick it through my upraised arms,' Steve would have done that," said Forrest Blue, the Auburn center.

Spurrier never had any doubts about making the kick, which suited his competitive personality perfectly.

"The posts are wide enough," Spurrier told the *Tampa Tribune*. "If you kick it right, it'll go through."

Spurrier might have been sure, but Graves said the general nature of his team's season-long habit for late comebacks was wearing on him.

"These fourth quarter rallies [Spurrier] originates are great for the fans, ticket sales and so forth," Graves said. "But they let this one a little close to suit me."

Graves added: "If I could give him two Heisman Trophies, I would. He's the greatest pressure player I have ever seen."

Which Spurrier's teammates believed ever more after the Auburn game.

Auburn "got some lucky breaks," middle guard Jerry "Red" Anderson said. "But when you have a great quarterback like Spurrier, it makes it easier to come back the way we did."

Joe Durso of the *New York Times* called Spurrier a "Real-life Frank Merriwell."

John Logue of the *Atlanta Journal* wrote, "Spurrier, with his hands tied behind his back and facing a firing squad, would be favored to escape."

Talk about timing, Spurrier's final heroics in the Auburn game might rank as the most opportunistic timing in the history of the Heisman Trophy. Ballots had been mailed out to the approximately 1,300 voters the previous week and were due back the following week. Spurrier's excellent timing coincided with a day in which Griese threw a 32-yard touchdown to win the game against Illinois, but he also threw five interceptions.

7

HEISMAN BOUND

While the dust settled after Spurrier's heroics against Auburn, Ray Graves chose to compliment Spurrier about an area in which he had done a superlative job, yet didn't receive much notice for: his punting.

"Steve could make a good living in pro football just as a kicker," Graves said. "Even if he couldn't do all the other things he does. He's a great punter, long and very accurate. . . . The best thing about Steve's punting is he aims his kicks so high that they can't be run back."

If ever there was a time to give Spurrier accolades, it was the week before the Georgia game. With Spurrier, the Gators felt as though they could always find a way to come back and win, even against Georgia, which had long bullied the Gators.

Gator players, coaches and fans alike pointed to the Georgia game as the biggest game of the season. The Bulldogs were 6-1 overall, having lost 7-6 to Miami, and they had a 4-0 mark in the SEC.

Georgia is "far and away the best team we've faced all year," Graves said the week of the game.

Graves looked at his smallish Gators squad and no doubt saw the possibility of problems going against the physical Bulldogs. Particularly sophomore defensive tackle Bill Stanfill, who had size, speed, great range, quickness and he was competitive.

"I don't see how the boy [Stanfill] can miss being one of the great all-time defensive linemen in the SEC," Graves said.

Graves assessment proved accurate. Stanfill went on to win the Outland Trophy as the nation's top lineman as a senior in 1968; was All-SEC each of his three varsity seasons; and played with the Miami Dolphins from 1969 to 1976, earning All-Pro honors four times.

Georgia coach Vince Dooley talked about what he felt would be the key to the Florida game.

"No one has put a really great pass run on [Spurrier] yet," Dooley told the *Tampa Tribune*. "And we know that is what must be done to stop him. . . . Spurrier has the receivers, but to stop Florida we must have the best pass rush we have had all season."

The chances of Georgia putting together such a pass rush seemed to dwindle with the reports that Stanfill had a neck problem and might not play; his status was listed as questionable.

Georgia–Florida was the biggest game in the nation on November 5, 1966. At stake were the SEC championship, national rankings, Spurrier's Heisman Trophy chances and the possibility of earning a spot in the Orange, Sugar, Cotton or Gator Bowls. And at 7-0, the people in Gainesville were starting to believe the 1966 season might just be the year the Gators went undefeated.

A record-setting sellout crowd of 62,800 packed inside Jacksonville's Gator Bowl for the game. National media crowded the pressbox where 37 leased Western Union wires were hooked up to newspapers.

The game didn't live up to the hype.

The Gators scored all of their points in the first 16:02 of the game and took a 10-3 lead into the half; the second half was a different story. Stanfill, who played the entire game, helped the Bulldogs' defense to totally shut down the Gators' offense in the second half en route to a 27-10 Georgia win.

"They got a little lead on us at halftime," Stanfill said. "But we wore them out in the second half."

The Gators were limited to 26 offensive plays in the second half.

"Controlling the game in the second half was really the difference in the game," Dooley told the *Tampa Tribune*. "We rushed Spurrier better than anyone has so far this year and we intercepted more of his passes than anyone combined has. We intercepted three and he'd only lost two all year. . . .

"We dropped our double coverage of Trapp in the second half to give us a better rush on Spurrier."

The Bulldogs held the Gators' offense to five yards rushing in the second half. The Gators were forced to pass, resulting in Spurrier having to run for his football life all afternoon and forcing him to throw early and often wild. Spurrier completed just six of 15 passes in the second half, including an interception to Lynn Hughes, who returned his theft 31 yards for a touchdown. For Hughes, the play provided redemption after wearing goat horns in the 1965 game as the defender who failed to bat the ball away from Jack Harper, who caught the winning touchdown in the Gators' 14-10 win.

"Georgia put the first rush on Spurrier that anyone has during his career," Graves said. "Steve had few opportunities to throw like you would hope for. This was due to the tremendous pressure from the rush."

Georgia's defensive coach, Erk Russell, called all the right signals for stopping Florida's offense. But he admitted Spurrier had worried him.

"Now, that Spurrier is not just a great player, he's a cool operator," Russell said. "Spurrier read our defense real good at the line of scrimmage and even after we thought we concealed them. He checked off at the line and went to the running and ate us a new one."

The blitzing Bulldogs eventually were too much to handle.

"Oh, we blitzed," Russell said. "We blitzed as many as seven at a time. We blitzed 80 percent of the time. We blitzed with the object of getting to the passer. Now we had the advantage of having the tall linemen, and that forces the quarterback to throw a little higher or quicker."

Spurrier complimented the Bulldogs for gambling and gambling correctly.

"Everything they did was right," Spurrier said. "They rushed up the middle, contained their tackles and, when I tried to throw to the deep man, they covered him with the safety."

When the clock ran out, Spurrier went to one knee, the picture of frustration.

"My worse [defeat]," Spurrier said. "My absolute worst."

Georgia's victory killed Florida's hopes for an SEC championship and a national championship, but a trip to a major bowl still was within reason. Next up was Tulane. And like the previous season, a bowl bid hung on the outcome.

Spurrier and the Gators bounced back against Tulane to take a 31-10 victory at Florida Field. His passes accounted for 288 yards and the running of Graham McKeel and Larry Smith gave the offense the necessary balance to dispose of the pesky Green Wave.

Orange Bowl committee members attended the game and liked enough of what they saw to extend the Gators a bid on November 21 to play Georgia Tech on January 2, 1967, in Miami. The next day Spurrier was announced as the winner of the 1966 Heisman Trophy.

Each year the Downtown Athletic Club of New York City, Inc. presents the Heisman Memorial Trophy Award to honor the outstanding college football player in the United States. The club occupies a 35-story building built in 1930 and looks out over the North River and lower harbor. Inside are hotel rooms, banquet rooms and various workout facilities.

The Downtown Athletic Club wanted to make a display of its devotion to sports and came up with their award in 1935. In conjunction with their decision, the Club Trophy Committee enlisted well-known sculptor and National

Academy prize winner Frank Eliscu to create, in bronze, a muscular looking player holding a football and plowing for yardage.

Eliscu first made a clay model, which the Downtown Athletic Club approved, before enduring the scrutiny of Jim Crowley, who was one of Notre Dame's legendary Four Horsemen and, at that time, the Fordham football coach. Crowley's players looked the sculpture over, offering suggestions. A famous photograph shows Crowley observing running back Warren Mulrey striking a pose in front of Eliscu's clay model, which he modified for more authenticity.

Initially, the award was called the Downtown Athletic Club Trophy, but was named in honor of John Heisman the following year.

Heisman had been a legendary winning coach from 1892 to 1927 at Auburn, Oberlin, Clemson, Georgia Tech, Akron, Penn, Washington and Jefferson, and Rice. Heisman was a historian of the game as well; several of his suggestions triggered innovations to college football. He became the first athletic director of the Downtown Athletic Club in 1930. When he died of bronchial pneumonia in 1936 the award was renamed the Heisman Memorial Trophy.

Electors are composed of club members, sectional representatives from the press, radio and television media, and a representative from each of the 50 states. The state representative keeps the file up to date on all eligible electors in his state.

Each elector must vote for three players according to the Heisman voting guidelines. His first choice receives three points; second, two points; and third, one point. The player receiving the greatest number of points is the winner.

Spurrier received 433 first-place votes, 150 second place and 80 third for 1,679 points. Bob Griese finished second with 615 points, Notre Dame's Nick Eddy was third at 456, and UCLA's Gary Beban had 318 to finish fourth.

Griese held a grudge about not getting the award according to Tom McEwen.

"Frankly I don't think Griese's ever forgiven us, really," McEwen said. "I think it took Griese a long time on the air [doing color for college football games] to be as exuberant about the University of Florida as he probably should have been."

An element of suspense is part of today's Heisman Trophy ceremony, which is consistent with TV becoming more involved. Three or four candidates are invited to attend the ceremony and the results of the balloting are hush-hush, lending the feeling of the Academy Awards, except they are jocks. In fairness to TV and the Heisman Trophy, the award grew into an event due to public interest.

In Spurrier's day, the production was far less complex. The Downtown Athletic Club notified the winner and the results of the voting were announced. In early December the winner was flown to New York, along with his coach and dignitaries from the winner's school.

Spurrier was notified he'd won by a telephone call from the Downtown Athletic Club at 12:45 P.M. on November 22. The progression to get Spurrier to receive the call typified his laid-back manner.

Jerri Spurrier received a call from the Downtown Athletic Club around noon.

"They called, but I didn't know where he was," she told the *Tampa Tribune*. "I knew one thing, I knew he'd be home for lunch. He never misses lunch."

Spurrier returned home around 12:10; he had been watching film of the Gators' next opponent, Miami.

Jerri served her husband vegetable soup and a chicken sandwich but was nervous about the Heisman and forgot the potato salad. A representative from University of Florida President Dr. Wayne Reitz's office showed at 12:20 to tell Spurrier they needed to be at Dr. Reitz's office to receive a 12:45 call.

Jerri marveled at the calm of her husband.

"Why he even picked up the paper and read it after he finished [lunch] and turned to get the man interested in what he was reading about something somebody had done in a pro game Sunday," Jerri said. "The man and I kept looking at each other, nervous and all. It was about 12:30 or maybe later when he finally left, after I made him change his pants. But he still forgot to put on socks."

Spurrier made it to Dr. Reitz's office on time and received the news he had become the South's first Heisman Trophy winner since LSU's Billy Cannon won the award in 1959.

"I knew I had a chance; a pretty good chance," Spurrier said. "But I was really surprised at the margin by which I won. I guess I knew [I'd won] when the man from the president's office came over."

Florida Gov. Hayden Burns announced Spurrier had won the award during his November 22 cabinet meeting and the room burst into applause.

"This is the greatest acclaim that has ever been earned by a Floridian and one representing the universities," Burns said.

A press conference for Spurrier came together in which the Gators' leader thanked all.

"I know it would not have been possible without the fine blocking of Jim Benson, John Preston, Bill Carr and everybody," Spurrier said. "And our fine backs and our defensive unit. This whole team is all for one. . . . I'm glad I could bring this home, back to the South, and do a lot for this part of the country."

Florida still had one game remaining on its schedule, against Miami. Would Spurrier winning college football's most prestigious award add motivation to the 'Canes' effort? Not to Spurrier's way of thinking when the question was posed to him.

"They've been after me before, so I don't think there will be any extra pressure from Miami or Tech just because they're playing against the Heisman Trophy winner now," Spurrier said.

Miami didn't need the extra incentive. The fact they had lost twice, despite having a talented team, proved to be sufficient motivation.

The 'Canes brought a 6-2-1 mark to Gainesville for their November 26, 1966, meeting with the Gators. Along the way they had beaten Georgia and Southern Cal, but they appeared to be beatable since they lost to FSU and LSU, teams Florida beat.

Coached by Charlie Tate, Miami earned a bid to the Liberty Bowl in Memphis.

"I think they were the best team in the country that year," Larry Smith said. "Georgia was good and all, but you felt like they just had a great game plan and executed it well to beat us. Miami just seemed loaded. I don't know how they lost two games. Like I said, I thought they were the best team in the country. They were huge."

Included on the Miami roster was Ted Hendricks. Known as "The Mad Stork" due to his 6-foot-7, 220-pound body, Hendricks later enjoyed a Hall-of-Fame career in the NFL.

Miami built a 21-3 lead before Smith threw a touchdown to Richard Trapp and Spurrier hit Paul Ewaldsen for another. But with the clock running down in the fourth quarter at the Miami 30, Spurrier couldn't get his team to the line quick enough to run one final play and the clock ran out with the Gators coming up short 21-16. According to the story by McEwen, Spurrier "flung the ball to the turf and wept."

Graves rarely made excuses for his team. However, he later confessed he believed the 30 or so interviews Spurrier gave after winning the Heisman had been a distraction for his quarterback.

Spurrier, who normally didn't complain, griped after the Miami loss.

"The awards don't mean much when you lose," Spurrier said. "But things just didn't go our way. I was racked up twice while watching my receiver make the catch. Those were both obvious roughing the passer violations."

Tate called Spurrier "the finest quarterback in the country."

"You're just on pins and needles all the time with Spurrier in there," Tate said. "Florida is so explosive, so dangerous anytime you give them the football."

Florida faithful gave Spurrier a heartfelt ovation after the game when his No. 11 was officially retired. He had set 16 records while calling the signals for the Gators including SEC season records for most pass attempts, completions and passing yardage; he was the SEC's most valuable player in 1966.

Another award Spurrier received was academic All-America. Norm Carlson chuckles recalling the circumstances of Spurrier receiving the award and points to the story as the personification of Spurrier's honesty and how black and white he is when asked a question.

"Steve's always been a guy who said his honest opinion when he was asked a question," Carlson said. "Sometimes he wasn't so tactful because he was extremely honest. The funniest thing, they used to have the academic All-America team and the only rules that were set down were that the grade point average from the previous semester was used. It could have been summer or spring or whenever the previous semester was. The rules didn't say anything about how many hours you had to take or anything. And he made an A in a four-hour class, football course in PE in the summer before his senior year. So I nominated him for academic All-America and he made it as the first-string quarterback. So I told him, 'Steve, when this thing comes out and they ask you about it, all you need to say is what an honor it is, that kind of stuff.' And he's like, 'Okay, okay.'

"Well, the first guy who talks to him is our beat writer for the *Miami Herald*. When he asked Steve about it, Steve said, 'Well, I don't know how that happened. I only took one course. It was in football. It was four hours.' Then he wasn't content with that and he adds: 'And the guy favored football players, maybe that's why he's no longer employed at the PE school.' And they ran that all over the country. Typical Spurrier, and it was true."

Spurrier appeared on *The Ed Sullivan Show* with other college All-America honorees the Sunday following the Miami game.

CBS began running Sullivan's variety show in 1948 under the name *The Toast of Broadway*. In 1955 the name of the show was changed to *The Ed Sullivan Show* in honor of the show's host. Sullivan had a knack for booking talent as witnessed by those who made their American TV debuts on his show. A lineup including Bob Hope, Lena Horne, Jerry Lewis, Dean Martin, Dinah Shore, Irving Berlin, Fred Astaire and the Beatles. An endearing part of Sullivan's celebrity was his penchant for botching introductions and monologues. Spurrier became one of the many introductions Sullivan botched when Sullivan introduced Syracuse running back Floyd Little to the audience as Spurrier. When the producers discovered the mistake, Spurrier was called back on stage and, again, Sullivan made a blunder when he told his audience Spurrier played for the University of Miami.

"We knew he'd made a mistake and when we left the stage to go up to the balcony, all of the team, everybody kidded me about it," Spurrier said. "Then a guy tapped me on the shoulder and said I had to go back on. I went down and they pushed me out on the stage. I never heard him say anything about Miami at all. Didn't know about the error until later."

Complaints from angry Gator fans flooded the network's New York switchboard. The next week Sullivan's mistake was rectified when a clip of Spurrier's appearance the previous week was shown and Sullivan told the audience "For all those undergraduates at the University of Florida, here is the Heisman Trophy winner Steve Spurrier."

Spurrier had been awarded the Heisman Trophy three days earlier, on December 1 in New York.

Steve and Jerri arrived in New York for the ceremony on Wednesday, November 30, 1966, and were whisked away to the 21 Club, where they noted seeing 1964 presidential candidate Barry Goldwater.

The following day Spurrier had a noon press conference then spoke to 75 high school "Heisman" trophy winners, telling them to do whatever they pleased, but do it well. By 6 o'clock he was at a pre-dinner party and said to be running out of energy, but never did he show signs of nervousness. A friend asked him if he was uneasy about addressing the large audience and Spurrier replied, "I'm fine, just have to make a little ole speech."

A large contingent accompanied him on the trip including his parents; his brother; Ray Graves; three Florida assistant coaches; the mayor of Jacksonville, Florida; Hayden Burns; Doyle Carlton, Florida secretary of agriculture; Dr. Wayne Reitz; and Spurrier's attorney, William C. O'Neal. In addition, a contingent from the New York Giants attended the ceremony as the rumors they would be drafting him continued. Giants representatives included Allie Sherman; Jim Lee Howell, head scout; and Ray Walsh, general manager.

Spurrier, his father and O'Neal spent much of their time leading up to the ceremony addressing the possibility of Spurrier playing for the Giants.

At the time the rules for the fledging NFL–AFL player draft had not yet been hammered out. But word had leaked that even though the expansion New Orleans Saints would have the first choice, the Giants would be empowered to trump the Saints if they wanted to draft a quarterback with the first pick. This was rumored to be a part of the pending merger agreement between the two leagues.

Both leagues recognized the need for a unified draft, which would prevent a player from pitting teams from each league against one another to bid for the player's services. Players entering the league could not expect to get the same kind of money players had received the year before because of the new agreement, which led to posturing and bluffing by college seniors. Some threatened to go to the Canadian Football League and other shoddy pro leagues. Spurrier's contingent played it coy in New York regarding future plans.

Spurrier's father stated the obvious to the *New York Times*:

"If the leagues were bidding against each other this year the way they were last year, I honestly think he might have got $1 million."

O'Neal told the *Times*, "Someone who said he was indirectly representing a Canadian team said they would give Steve $500,000 to sign. A Continental League team has indicated a willingness to give a fairly good-sized bonus plus stock in the club. We haven't had any direct offers from National or American teams yet."

O'Neal further told the *Times* he felt like Spurrier should "at least get as much as Joe Willie Namath got from the New York Jets." Two years earlier, Namath had signed an unprecedented three-year deal worth $427,000.

The questions to Steve related more to his preferences for the NFL. Asked about the possibility of playing for the Giants, Steve replied, "Would I prefer playing in New York? Well, it's a good place to play but down South is a good place, too. I really don't get a choice."

All three Spurrier men wore tuxedos for the occasion. Jerri wore a pink dress with an orchid on her shoulder and beamed about her husband.

"I read all these things all this time about Steve doing this and that and about how good he was," she told the *Tampa Tribune*. "But really, not until now does it hit you between the eyes."

A crowd of 1,400 watched the night's activities at the Downtown Athletic Club. The eighth-floor gymnasium hosted 1,000 in reserved chairs placed about the room in a semicircle facing the two terraces of speaker tables. Another 400 watched the presentation via closed-circuit TV in the Heisman room one floor below.

Everyone attending the ceremony was given an orange and blue ribbon to wear on their lapels and a University of Florida banner hung behind the speaker platform.

With a nationally radiocast presentation covering the event, emcee Al Hofler kicked off the evening by announcing to the audience: "We gather here in acclaim for you, Stephen O. Spurrier of the University of Florida."

Graves followed and gushed about being a part of the ceremony.

"It is with pride and humility that I am one of the 32 coaches ever to sit on this dias," Graves said.

And Spurrier's coach beamed about his prized quarterback.

"I'd like to say I brought Steve a long way from Johnson City," Graves said. "But I'll have to say he brought me a lot further."

Dr. Reitz then spoke.

"The more than 18,000 Florida students, the faculty and the people of the state are proud of Steve Spurrier and we have taken him to our hearts. The greatest joy is to do something extremely well. Steve has done this and he also lives beautifully."

When Gov. Burns awarded him a gold seal of Florida plaque, which had previously been awarded only to astronauts, he told the audience: "[Spurrier] is the greatest field general since Robert E. Lee."

Past Heisman Trophy winner Pete Dawkins spoke about the award, which led up to the actual presentation made by Downtown Athletic Club President Joseph F. McGoldrick. Upon receiving the award, Spurrier turned to Dr. Reitz and said, "I want to give this back to the University of Florida and to the people of Florida for what they have done for me."

Spurrier's gesture brought him a huge ovation and helped change the way the Downtown Athletic Club handled the award in later years. The Heisman Trophy Committee voted to begin awarding two trophies each year in 1968, one for the athlete and one for his university.

Spurrier thanked his friends, the university, his coaches, his family and the press for the good things that had happened to him. Humbly he said the way he won the trophy was by letting "Larry Smith run up the middle, Richard Trapp score a touchdown and by following the blocking of Bill Carr and Jim Benson. With these people it wasn't very hard."

Not forgetting he was in New York and the fact he might be playing football in the city, Spurrier told the audience toward the end of his speech, "And if there's a chance that I return here to play football, I promise to do my best."

Spurrier remained gracious throughout the proceedings, but ever the competitor, he looked forward rather than back. Spurrier told friends, "I know [the Heisman] is something, and in later life I'll begin to appreciate it more I'm sure. But right now the wins we had over FSU, LSU, and Auburn, and the one we hope to have over Georgia Tech [in the Orange Bowl] mean much more."

The Orange Bowl pitted the Gators against once-beaten Tech and provided an emotional forum for Graves. Not only would the game mark Spurrier's last appearance in a Gators uniform as well as marking the Gators' first-ever Orange Bowl appearance, Graves also would be going up against Bobby Dodd, who would be coaching his final game.

"Oh yeah, it was quite emotional for me," Graves said. "[Dodd and I] were just like brothers. I'd rather beat him and he'd rather beat me than anything, same way in fishing or whatever. But that was a big one."

Graves opted to hold closed practices after the team's 12-day layoff leading up to the game. By doing so Graves hoped to prevent distractions like the ones Spurrier endured prior to the Miami game.

Meanwhile, there was a great deal of excitement about the game, which had been sold out since October 30.

"We could have sold 130,000 tickets," said Ernie Seller, Orange Bowl executive vice president.

Tech's defense, dubbed "Carson's Raiders" for defensive coach Bud Carson, had allowed just 81 points in 10 games and 23 of those had come in the team's 23-14 season-ending loss to Georgia. Tech's Lenny Snow was the leading rusher in the South, just ahead of Florida's Smith. The Yellow Jackets entered the game ranked No. 8 in the polls and they were a 1½ point favorite over the Gators.

Each team would receive $260,000 for participating in the game. Tech, which left the SEC after the 1963 season to become an independent, would keep all of their bowl money, while Florida would keep just $115,000 with the remainder being split with other SEC teams.

On January 1, 1967, the day before the Orange Bowl, the NFL's Green Bay Packers beat the Dallas Cowboys 34-27 in the NFL Championship Game to earn a spot in the first Super Bowl against the AFL's Kansas City Chiefs.

There seemed to be some bad blood between the Florida and Tech players. Florida's last practice was open and attended by several Tech players, who razzed Spurrier for an autograph.

Some reports said Spurrier went into the game with a sore arm; Spurrier said his passing was affected by poor mechanics.

"I think I was releasing the ball too quickly," he said. "It just didn't feel good."

Nevertheless, Spurrier managed the team well in the Gators' 27-12 victory on a steamy night in Miami. He completed 14 of 30 passes for 160 yards to bring his college career to a close with 435 completions for 5,363 yards and 38 touchdowns in 32 games.

But Smith stole the spotlight in Spurrier's final game as a Gator.

Tech trailed 7-6 late in the third quarter but was threatening when the Gators intercepted one of quarterback Kim King's passes. On the ensuing drive, Smith burst off tackle and went 94 yards for a touchdown, his pants falling down as he finished his sprint to the end zone.

"That was our lead play that we would run off tackle where [fullback] Graham McKeel would lead block," Smith said. "It was our standard bread and butter play. We were on the six-yard line and we were just trying to get a little bit of room to punt, get further away from the end zone. They knew we were going to do that and I think they had like a goal line defense in there. So when I popped through the line, there weren't any defenders left to stop me, they were all bunched up at the line of scrimmage."

Smith finished with 187 yards rushing and Orange Bowl MVP honors.

"Larry Smith hurt us more than Steve Spurrier," Dodd said.

The victory registered high with Graves.

"You'll have to say it was the greatest victory for me in my coaching career," Graves said after the game. "I have all the respect in the world of Bobby Dodd. He's one of the greatest. That's why it's so sweet."

An interesting side note to Smith's success was the link between his performance and the kickoff of Gatorade, the noted sports drink.

Dr. Robert Cade, a physician in the University of Florida's College of Medicine, had been questioned about why players didn't need to use the restroom during games, which led to his research indicating players lost all of their fluids through sweat. As a result of this research, Cade and a research team developed a drink to help the body prevent dehydration caused by hot temperatures and physical exertion. In 1965, 10 members of the Gators' football team served as Guinea pigs for the experiment. Choosing the football team showed sound logic since the players seemed to wither in the heat in the second half. The research team believed using their drink for rapid fluid replacement would benefit the players by replenishing carbohydrates and electrolytes.

The chosen Gators players sampled different flavors from milk cartons provided by the university's agriculture department.

"Some days it tasted good and some days it wasn't so good," Smith said. "But we were happy to participate because it meant we could drink something during practice. Back then, they didn't let us take breaks for water.

"They'd take [the players] blood everyday. [Participating players] would wear rubber gloves out to practice so they could analyze their sweat. See how much fluid was lost."

Stokely-Van Camp was negotiating to buy the rights to Gatorade at the time of the Orange Bowl and chose to monitor Smith during the game.

"They said they wanted to see how much [Gatorade] he drinks during the game," Graves said. "They told me after the game he drank two gallons. It was a hot night and he was running pretty well in the fourth quarter."

After the game Dodd teased with reporters: "We didn't have Gatorade . . . that made the difference."

Dodd's quote ran in *Sports Illustrated* and the sports drink was well on its way toward becoming a billion-dollar product.

Five months later, Stokely-Van Camp purchased the rights to produce and sell Gatorade.

8

GOING TO THE NFL

Spurrier left for Hawaii after the Orange Bowl to participate in the Hula Bowl, an all-star game featuring the best college seniors. Such games weren't as meaningless in the 1960s as they are today since TV exposure was rare and fewer games were shown during the season. Scouting combines, in which players demonstrate their abilities, were only a twinkle in the eyes of NFL scouting directors. All-star games were some players' only avenue to show what they could do in front of an audience of NFL scouts and coaches.

The buildup for the game focused on the matchup between Spurrier, who would quarterback the South squad, and Bob Griese, who would quarterback the North.

Spurrier did nothing to hurt his standing in the North's 28-27 victory. He rallied the South from a 16-0 deficit by completing 17-of-32 passes for 281 yards and one touchdown. Griese also performed well, completing 14-of-21 passes for 279 yards and three touchdowns.

Purdue coach Jack Mollenkoff obviously drew more from the showdown than most as he declared his quarterback, Griese, to be far and away superior to Spurrier.

"Griese was quicker afoot and threw the ball quicker and better," Mollenkoff said. "A pro coach told me [Griese] was the greatest third-down quarterback he'd ever seen."

Despite Griese's endorsement by his former coach, Spurrier maintained his status as the most coveted quarterback eligible for the upcoming NFL–AFL draft, even if the date for the draft had yet to be decided upon.

Spurrier continued to live large while waiting for his fate to be determined by an as-yet-to-be-known professional football team. *SPORT Magazine* named

Spurrier its top college football performer. The editors of the magazine noted about him:

"Though the merger of the NFL and AFL clouded Spurrier's bonus hopes, he still played football as if he were worth a million dollars."

Spurrier went to Johnson City and was given a special day in his hometown.

The Tennessee senate made a special proclamation that January 12, 1967, was "Steve Spurrier Day."

Spurrier seemed touched by the attention when he spoke to an adoring crowd.

"Coach Tipton once told me you have to have a dream," Spurrier said. "And ever since then, in the back of my mind, I felt I might be an All-America.

"I've always had confidence in my abilities and, of course, I've been fortunate to have good coaching and a lot of help from my teammates."

Spurrier's parents, Jerri and others from his family were on hand to see him get honored. Science Hill High held a banquet for their returning hero, which gave the locals a chance to honor him and fueled speculation about which team would draft Spurrier. An appearance by former Giants running back Frank Gifford at the banquet made most feel the Giants would be the team.

Spurrier lived with daily questions about becoming the Giants' selection in the draft, even in his hometown. He answered tactfully.

"If the Giants draft me, I think it would be a great challenge to play for them," Spurrier said. "I look on pro ball as just another step up in football. I think it is just a matter of improving in all phases of the game."

Spurrier would be joining a changing NFL.

The NFL recognized a need to merge with the AFL when it finally acknowledged the fact the new league appeared to be on firm financial footing, thanks in large part to NBC signing the AFL to a $36-million television deal prior to the 1965 season. The reality of the situation prompted Tex Schramm, the president of the Dallas Cowboys, to contact Lamar Hunt, the owner of the Kansas City Chiefs, to set up a meeting to broach the subject of a merger between the two leagues.

While Schramm and Hunt worked to bring the leagues together, Al Davis had other ideas. Davis replaced Joe Foss as AFL commissioner and set forth to instigate a player war with the NFL. Davis wanted to beat the NFL and become *the* primary professional football league.

Buffalo kicker Pete Gogolak, the first soccer-style kicker to play in the NFL, played out his option to sign with the Giants prior to the 1966 season. Gogolak's defection to the other league added fire to Davis' cause. AFL teams got to work, trying to entice star NFL quarterbacks Roman Gabriel and John Brodie, among others, to consider jumping leagues.

Schramm and Hunt recognized the negative effects of having their respective leagues bidding against one another for talent. Given the climate, NFL Commissioner Pete Rozelle gave Schramm and Hunt the go-ahead to work out a merger agreement. In June 1966, the two leagues announced they would become one league in time for the 1970 season. The arrangement called for all of the AFL teams to become NFL teams, creating a two-conference, four-division setup where the champions of both leagues would meet in a championship game at the end of the season, which would come to be known as the Super Bowl. The merger upset Davis so much that he resigned as commissioner.

Despite the agreement between the two leagues, many loose ends remained.

The coming NFL–AFL draft continued to be cloaked in mystery. Before a date was finally settled on and the draft actually occurred, many external factors arose that affected Spurrier's future.

On February 11, 1967, Rozelle confirmed what had been rumored for some time: Even though the expansion New Orleans Saints held the first selection in the draft, the Giants could trump the Saints when it came to drafting a quarterback. New York, which was the worst team in the league, might have held even more power in the 1960s than it does today when it came to the power structure of the league. The gist of the Giants having the unusual power to take the first pick if they so desired stemmed from their reluctance to agree to the merger without being compensated. According to the terms of the NFL–AFL merger, the Giants were given the privilege of picking first, even ahead of New Orleans, if they were to choose a quarterback. The option was good for 1967 or 1968.

Meanwhile, trouble brewed in Minnesota.

Vikings quarterback Fran Tarkenton spoke out, telling the media he no longer wanted to play for the Vikings. A day later Vikings head coach Norm Van Brocklin resigned.

Tarkenton, who was just 26 at the time, was known widely by NFL fans as the scrambling quarterback. He had been the first such quarterback to consistently scramble out of the pocket to buy more time to find open receivers. Tarkenton was not happy with Van Brocklin, who benched him on two occasions during the 1966 season.

Even after Van Brocklin resigned, the Vikings wavered on whether they wanted to continue with Tarkenton as their quarterback under new head coach Bud Grant.

Vikings general manager Jim Finks conceded, "It will be difficult for [Tarkenton] to come back."

Rumors began to circulate about Tarkenton being shopped around by the Vikings. Among the teams rumored to be interested were the Giants.

In Spurrier's camp there was nothing to do but wait. Spurrier's lawyer, Bill O'Neal, still believed the Giants would be drafting his client, whom O'Neal represented without charge.

"I don't think rumors of big offers from Canada—which were totally unfounded—have scared the Giants," O'Neal told the *Tampa Tribune*. "And of course, I'm in no position to demand anything. All I will do is advise the boy as I have done with commercial companies. All we do is wait.

"Now I don't know if it will continue, but it is my understanding in the past a club planning to draft a boy will get in touch with him before the draft to see if he has any fixation against going to that city, or that part of the country. San Francisco doesn't want to draft a boy in South Carolina who simply won't play in California. I assume that will happen again. And no, I don't think Steve has his heart set on any club."

While Spurrier waited, O'Neal negotiated him an endorsement deal with Wilson Sporting Goods. The belief was many such endorsements would follow.

NFL owners met in Honolulu in the middle of February. Among the topics discussed was the date to hold the draft. They settled on a two-day draft that would begin on Tuesday, March 14, 1967.

Once the date for the draft had been settled, teams began to maneuver and negotiate for possible moves to improve their clubs. The Saints made the first major move on March 6, 1967, when they traded the No. 1 pick of the draft and veteran center Bill Curry, who had been selected in the expansion draft, to the Colts for quarterback Gary Cuozzo.

Cuozzo backed up Colts star quarterback Johnny Unitas and generally was regarded as the best back-up quarterback in football. The Saints, like many teams in football, believed Cuozzo could step right in to a starting position if given the chance.

The Saints–Colts trade began to fuel speculation the Colts would draft Spurrier in the event the Giants deferred exercising their option to draft a quarterback with the No. 1 pick until the following season.

The Giants continued to be the wild card in the whole situation.

Given the climate in New York, the Giants desperately needed a marquee quarterback. Joe Namath was winning the hearts of New York football fans, swaying them to Shea Stadium, home of the Jets.

Namath, and the entire AFL, were gaining on the old-guard NFL. The AFL had a wide-open reputation that Namath only helped to perpetuate.

Namath's nickname was "Broadway Joe." He had sex appeal, made a lot of money and continued to improve on the football field. After winning AFL Rookie-of-the-Year honors in 1965, Namath continued to blossom in 1966.

Memorable was a classic between the Jets and Boston Patriots in Shea Stadium on December 17, 1966. The Buffalo Bills and the Patriots were contending for the Eastern Division championship; Buffalo was 8-4-1 while the Patriots held a slight edge at 8-3-2 heading into the final week of the season.

The Jets had been knocked out of contention weeks earlier, but still had a chance to have a .500 record. Namath played brilliantly, throwing for 287 yards and three touchdowns with no interceptions to give the Jets a 38-28 victory in front of 58,921 fans.

"Joe learned, at last," Jets coach Weeb Ewbank said afterward. "He learned when to throw and when not to throw. When Joe's going like that, we're really rolling."

The Jets' victory gave the team a 6-6-2 record.

After the season Namath's popularity continued to improve on the wings of his leading the AFL All-Star team to a 30-19 victory over the AFL champion Bills. Two years later the Jets would become the first-ever AFL team to win the Super Bowl, when they beat the Baltimore Colts 16-7 in Super Bowl III.

Namath's success equated to the Giants' disaster.

The Giants entered the 1960s as one of the more successful NFL franchises but had evolved into a team in transition by 1966. They reached the NFL Championship game in 1961, 1962 and 1963 before experiencing a rash of injuries and retirements, leaving the team wallowing in mediocrity until it reached the bottom in 1966.

The Giants' 1966 season began on a high note when Earl Morrall threw a 98-yard touchdown to Homer Jones, but they could muster only a 34-34 tie with the Pittsburgh Steelers. The Giants lost their next four games before beating the Washington Redskins 13-10, then eight consecutive losses followed to give the team a 1-12-1 mark.

The Giants needed a quarterback to counter Namath's popularity to help stave off the migration of fans to Shea Stadium.

On March 7, 1966, the Giants traded three top draft choices to the Vikings for Tarkenton, the quarterback they believed could go toe-to-toe with Namath when it came to the fans.

"I knew [the Giants and Vikings] were dickering," O'Neal said. "I knew they were trying to get Tarkenton, but frankly I thought the Giants would end up drafting Steve, then trading him for a quarterback with some experience."

With the Giants out of the picture, the rumor mill had the Vikings selecting Griese with the first pick and the Colts following by taking Spurrier with the second. Next came the rumors the Atlanta Falcons were considering trading the No. 3 pick in the draft to the Packers.

Atlanta would have suited Spurrier fine, given the city's location. And, no doubt, he would have been a popular player. However, the Falcons already had Randy Johnson and Steve Sloan, both young quarterbacks who had shown promise.

The Falcons–Packers trade rumors continued on the Sunday and Monday before the Tuesday, March 14 draft.

"I thought I was going to Green Bay," Spurrier said.

Sound logic since Packers incumbent Bart Starr only had a couple of years left, which would give him time to groom Spurrier as his replacement. The Falcons wanted two linemen, the Packers would offer just one.

On March 14, 1966, Spurrier arrived at O'Neal's Gainesville office at 9:50 in the morning to wait for draft news. Approximately 35 minutes passed before a wire service newsman called to give Spurrier the news: "San Francisco."

Michigan State defensive end Bubba Smith went first to the Colts and Smith's teammate, Clint Jones, went to the Vikings on the second pick. From out of nowhere, the Falcons pulled the trigger on a deal with the San Francisco 49ers.

The Falcons surrendered the No. 3 pick of the draft for flanker Bernie Casey, guard Jim Wilson and end Jim Norton.

"San Francisco, huh?" came Spurrier's surprised response.

O'Neal also sounded as though he'd been caught off guard. "It comes as a complete surprise to me and to Steve. But not an unpleasant one."

The 49ers' quarterback situation made Spurrier an attractive choice. Brodie, their starter, was holding out for $1 million, and his backup, George Mira, wanted to be traded.

Spurrier left O'Neal's office, attended a class and was preparing to go to Jacksonville to attend a high school banquet when he heard from Lou Spadia, 49ers co-owner and general manager.

"[Spadia] said he'd be down next week and we'd talk," Spurrier said. "He also said that he was looking forward to me spending 20 years or so with them. So I don't guess they're going to trade me.

"I've never been [to San Francisco]. There's no smog, is there? That's in Los Angeles, huh? Well, as long as I get to play, that's all. And Jerri, she likes it OK, too."

Ironically, Griese was selected by the Dolphins, who had the No. 4 pick. Spurrier had bested the Purdue quarterback at every turn to that point, but Griese beat Spurrier in an area where neither of the quarterbacks had any control. Timing.

Had the 49ers opted to draft Griese instead of Spurrier, there is no telling how history might have been altered. Griese went on to lead the Dolphins to three Super Bowls; Spurrier went on to a lackluster professional career. Had Spurrier been on the Dolphins when Don Shula took over, would he have been the guy to lead them to a 17-0 mark? We'll never know.

9

YEARS OF
FRUSTRATION BEGIN

John Brodie joined the 49ers in 1957 after a standout career at Stanford, where he became a consensus All-American in 1956 after leading the nation in passing. However, he didn't become the starting quarterback until his fifth season, after Y.A. Tittle was traded to the Giants prior to the 1961 season.

Then 49ers coach Howard "Red" Hickey decided to commit to Brodie after watching Brodie and Tittle run the 49ers' offense from the shotgun formation. Brodie stood out in the system where the quarterback received the center snap from five feet away.

Brodie set a 49ers record in 1965 when he threw 30 touchdowns; the team averaged 30 points a game that season under third-year coach Jack Christiansen. Brodie led the league in pass attempts, completions, yards and touchdowns. But the 49ers finished just 7-6-1. The following year Brodie threw 22 interceptions and the team posted a 6-6-2 mark.

Despite the missing championships, there were few questions about Brodie's abilities, which made him an attractive player for AFL teams to put on their wish list of players to steal from the NFL by virtue of huge bonuses and salary increases.

Brodie parlayed an offer to play for the AFL's Houston Oilers into a new deal with the 49ers, leveraging a four-year, $827,000 deal to remain with the 49ers. A deal coinciding with Spurrier's arrival and one that didn't bode well for the rookie quarterback.

"They had Brodie and they had Mira and I didn't see myself getting much of a chance," Spurrier told the *Tampa Tribune*. "And I had other troubles. They use a bigger ball than we had in college, and my hands aren't very big, so I had difficulty with that. And I had to get used to different center snaps.

"In college I took snaps from the same center—Bill Carr—for three years. Shoot, I was already starting back to throw before Carr snapped the ball, I was so used to his snap, but it was different as a pro. . . . I'd find myself hesitating a second to be sure I had a good grip on the ball."

With Brodie at the helm, the 49ers got off to a fast start in 1967, winning five out of their first six. But the injuries mounted and the team lost six straight games before winning its last two to finish a disappointing 7-7. By the end of the season the fans at Kezar Stadium were booing Brodie and yelling for Spurrier to get his shot.

"I'll never forget my rookie year; after a game, I was running off the field," Spurrier said. "We'd been beaten. John Brodie was ahead of me, running, and John David Crow in front of him.

"I saw Crow pull out of the line and wait for Brodie to go by and I stopped and asked him if he was hurt and he said, 'No, but I refuse to run off the field close to Brodie. There might be a crazy sniper up there trying to take pot shots at him.'"

The voice of the fans was answered in the team's final two games when George Mira started both games, which were 49ers victories.

After the season, Christensen was fired and Dick Nolan was named head coach.

Brodie once again was the starter in 1968 and responded to Nolan's vote of confidence by leading the league in passing.

Spurrier had gone from college hero to bench-warmer and part-time punter during his first three seasons with the 49ers.

Graham Spurrier believes the fall from grace hurt his brother.

"It was hard on him, but I think he accepted it," Graham said. "And I think in the long-run, and he'll tell you, sitting over there on the sideline he really got to learn more. He got to see things on the field. He got to see how defenses play. And I think he learned a whole lot.

"At first I think it kind of wore on him, but then, as time went on, he learned to use his time well. And he knew he wasn't going to play unless Brodie got hurt. So he just put his mind to learning the defenses and how players react to different things. Plus, it didn't hurt his body any either. He's happy about that now, looking back."

Spurrier did finish the 1969 season as the starter and played well in a defeat of the Baltimore Colts. San Francisco finished the season with a 4-8-2 mark, fueling speculation Spurrier would be the starter in 1970. Spurrier spoke about what playing in San Francisco was like at the time.

"Funny crowds in San Francisco," Spurrier said. "But, they've been known to cheer.

"I guess it would be all right if we'd win some more games. But it got so bad there for a time that when the club gave an Easter egg hunt for the players' children, some of the fans showed up and booed the kids that didn't find any eggs."

Brodie entered the 1970 season at age 35. Ten years his younger, Spurrier believed he could compete for the starting job, and he didn't waste time thinking about what could have been had he gone to a team closer to home, or one without talented quarterbacks the likes of Brodie and George Mira.

"I'm happy with San Francisco and there's no time to think about where I'd rather be," he said.

Spurrier had adjusted to the NFL game ball as well as 49ers center Forrest Blue. And 49ers management finally accommodated Mira's wishes to be traded by sending him to the Philadelphia Eagles. Rusty Clark, a quarterback out of Houston, had been the only quarterback drafted by the 49ers, but he signed to play in Canada, making the competition for the 49ers' starting quarterback job a mano a mano duel between Brodie and Spurrier.

"The coaches tell me I'll get a really fair shot at winning the starting job this year," Spurrier told the *Tampa Tribune*.

Spurrier was in the final year of his initial four-year deal with the 49ers, but unlike today's NFL, where players can become free agents, thereby enjoying the freedom to change teams, Spurrier's options were limited. NFL players could play out their option, but it wasn't without baggage; unwanted baggage most teams weren't willing to carry.

Playing out your option "doesn't work so well anymore," Spurrier said of his situation. "For one thing, the team you eventually make a deal with must send one of its players along in a trade, and the commissioner seems usually to insist that the second player be better than the first."

Such actions by the NFL created a strong governor for restricting free-agent mobility, which would have driven salary prices upward.

Spurrier did not beat out Brodie for the starting job in 1970. Early in the season he started a controversy by stating in the "Passing Thoughts" column he wrote for the *Tampa Tribune* that he had considered asking Nolan to trade him. Spurrier then addressed his comments in his next column.

Before I get branded as Billy Bigmouth, let me say that I did not ask to be traded by the San Francisco 49ers.

Spurrier explained how the episode had been a misunderstanding between Nolan and him, and Nolan had actually apologized to him for not notifying him that Brodie would be the quarterback in a game against Denver and he would not play. Spurrier ended his column by noting he did not want to be labeled a troublemaker and managed to find some humor in the situation.

So I'm still not completely happy about the whole thing, but there's not much I can do.

My teammates have been ribbing me—calling me another George Mira.

One thing they'll have to agree on about us quarterbacks from the state of Florida—we don't play much, but we sure talk a good game.

Controversy over, Spurrier went back to the bench, save for his punting duties, and Brodie had what might be remembered as his finest season in 1970.

Led by Brodie, the 49ers posted a 10-3-1 record in 1970 to claim the NFC Western Division title, the team's first title of any sort in their 25-year history.

The 49ers had the best offense in the NFL. Brodie led the league in passing and Gene Washington in receiving yards and touchdowns.

Once in the playoffs, the 49ers defeated the favored Vikings 17-14, thanks to two Brodie touchdown passes in the fourth quarter. The Cowboys ended the run by beating the 49ers 17-10 in the NFC Championship Game.

Brodie was voted the NFC player of the year and Nolan coach of the year to put an exclamation point on another frustrating season for Spurrier.

In 1971, the story line was much the same.

The 49ers left Kezar Stadium to play their home games in Candlestick Park. Once again Brodie led the potent 49ers' offense en route to a 9-5 record, which was good enough to claim the franchise's second-consecutive NFC Western Division title. After beating the Redskins in their opening playoff game, the 49ers fell to the Cowboys in the NFC Championship as they had the year before, losing 14-3.

Spurrier finally got the chance to demonstrate what he could do in the NFL when Brodie hurt his ankle in the fifth game of the 1972 season.

"I'd played so little when I went in and our record was 2-3-1, well, everybody had some thoughts on what would work," Spurrier said. "The tackle said come over him, the receiver said he could get open and the running back said give the ball to him. We decided to let the bench call them. Oh, I called all the plays [at Florida], except for special situations. We had a game plan and went with it. . . . Brodie has always done that. But he's been playing all those years."

Spurrier led the team to five wins in their final six games to claim their third-consecutive NFC Western Division title. Under Spurrier the team went 6-2-1, but he didn't kid himself about his standing.

"I know I wouldn't be playing if Brodie hadn't hurt his ankle," Spurrier said. "I'm only here through circumstances."

Along the way Spurrier earned the praises of coaches like Green Bay's Dan Devine after the Packers squeaked by in a 34-24 win on November 5, 1972, in Milwaukee.

"I've always had a lot of respect for Spurrier," said Devine, who had been Missouri's coach during Spurrier's memorable Sugar Bowl performance his junior year at Florida. "He can kill you with his passes."

Spurrier completed 19 passes in 31 attempts against the Packers for 315 yards, including touchdown passes of 62 and 34 yards. Two weeks later he threw for five touchdowns against the Bears in Chicago.

Tight end Ted Kwalick caught touchdowns of 2 and 16 yards in the first half, then Gene Washington, Vic Washington and Larry Schreiber caught touchdowns of 43, 9, and 64 yards in a 34-21 49ers win.

Schreiber's reception came while the 49ers were protecting a six-point lead. Spurrier scrambled around in the pocket, managing to dodge the Rams' rush before tossing a "dump" pass to Schreiber at the line of scrimmage; the 49ers running back then went the distance.

Spurrier completed 17 of 27 passes for 275 yards. The five touchdown passes equaled a team record shared by Frankie Albert and John Brodie. Spurrier downplayed his feat.

"Circumstances [allow a quarterback to throw five touchdowns]," he said. "Who knows that Schreiber is going to run 64-yards with a little dump pass or that Ted [Kwalick] is going to make those great catches? . . .

"We haven't thrown many screen passes all year. They blitzed a lot and when they jump around and have to run back, sometimes they don't get back where the ball is and you can throw short. Sometimes they don't get back far enough and you can beat them deep."

Four days later, on Thanksgiving, Spurrier led a 31-10 victory over the Cowboys at Texas Stadium, the Cowboys' first loss in 15 games inside their $21-million football palace.

NFL coaches were taking note of Spurrier and the extra dimension he added to the 49ers' attack. Prior to the Rams' December 4, 1972, contest against the 49ers on Monday Night Football, Rams coach Tommy Prothro talked about the difference in preparing for the 49ers without Brodie.

"[Brodie] is a known factor, predictable," Prothro said. "Spurrier, we just don't know that well. I'll say this, from what we have noticed in films and from what our scouts tell us, Spurrier's a pretty cool young man and he has been hitting his [receivers] about as well as any quarterback in the league."

Despite the accolades, Spurrier couldn't lead his team to victory against the Rams, who took a 26-16 win. Three sure touchdowns of considerable length were dropped by 49er receivers; one resulted in one of Spurrier's three intercepted passes.

"I think Steve threw well," Nolan said.

Spurrier did manage to connect on two touchdown passes.

"I hit a few and I missed a few," Spurrier said. "We just didn't play well."

While Spurrier enjoyed his finest stretch with the 49ers, the 1972 season might have been his most disappointing as well. He started the 49ers' final game of the season against the Vikings needing a win to put the 49ers in the playoffs. A healthy Brodie stood on the sidelines as he had the previous two games until late in the game with the 49ers trailing. The veteran promptly threw two fourth-quarter touchdowns, the final one coming with 19 seconds remaining, and the 49ers won 21-17.

Nolan decided to start Brodie against the Cowboys in the playoffs the following weekend.

Famed oddsmaker Jimmy "the Greek" Snyder favored the 49ers on the basis of the veteran Brodie returning to the lineup.

San Francisco players felt confident of the quarterback situation heading into the playoffs.

"It's great to have two fine quarterbacks like Spurrier and Brodie," Blue said. "John of course is the classic quarterback. Spurrier doesn't look so good sometimes. But he gets the job done. He was a winner at Florida and he's still a winner. It's a good situation."

Brodie completed 12 of 22 passes for 150 yards, but he also threw two interceptions, which enabled Cowboys quarterback Roger Staubach to bring his team back from a 28-13 deficit to win 30-28.

Spurrier finished the 1972 season as the fourth-ranked passer in the NFC, completing 147 of 269 passes for 18 touchdowns; Brodie completed 70 of 110 passes for 905 yards and nine touchdowns, once again putting Spurrier into a familiar position entering the 1973 season: Brodie had to be beaten out in order for Spurrier to start.

Brodie continued to have the job Spurrier wanted on the football field and continued to top Spurrier off the field as well.

Spurrier normally went off to training camp with a finely tuned golf game.

"By the end of summer," Spurrier said, "I can get down to a 2 or 3 handicap, then comes football and no more golf."

But a low handicap didn't put Spurrier in the same league as his quarterback competition; Brodie played golf well enough to compete in a few tour events.

"I've beaten John a couple of times," Spurrier said. "But he's better than I am. He plays all the time."

Spurrier damaged his knee during an exhibition game in Tampa, leaving him gimpy for the 1973 season. Brodie began the season as the starter, but was benched after a slow start, giving way to Spurrier and Joe Reed.

Spurrier figured he was the heir apparent to Brodie and later in the season voiced his displeasure with Nolan's choice to start Reed against the Rams without telling him until after he had told sportswriters.

"I've played one full game this year and I set a team record for completions and threw for 323 yards [in a 17-14 loss to Minnesota]," Spurrier said. "If I'm not going to play, I wish he'd tell me about it. I'd go ahead and get my knee cleaned up. I have some loose cartilage and it needs minor surgery."

Nolan's response: "I intended to tell Steve but you guys [writers] beat me to it."

The 49ers finished the 1973 season a dismal 5-9 and Brodie announced his retirement.

Spurrier had what he called "a major knee job" to his right knee immediately following the season. The surgery was known as a "Slocum" operation, which tightened up the ligaments.

"The truth is I first hurt my knee the spring after my sophomore year at Florida when I kicked an extra point and Steamboat Scales fell on me," Spurrier told the *Tampa Tribune* prior to the 1974 season. "It was put in a cast then, but no operation.

"[During the 1973 exhibition season] in Tampa in the game against the Jets, I was on about the 40, went back to pass and my right foot slipped out from under me. It looked like I was sacked. I fell and took myself out. That, as it turned out, almost tore a ligament in half."

The successful operation meant Spurrier would enter the 1974 season with healthy legs and ready to compete for the starting quarterback job.

"[Nolan] has said that he is going to pick a No. 1 quarterback and play him in the exhibition games and in the regular season like [Cowboys coach] Tom Landry did in Dallas," Spurrier told the *Tampa Tribune*, drawing a comparison to the competition between Cowboys quarterbacks Craig Morton and Staubach. "It'll be my job to win the No. 1 spot and I'm ready to go for it. I'll have to give it full dedication all the time, even at practice."

Spurrier mentioned practice in relation to his acknowledged lackluster practice performances, which had always been the case, even at Florida. Spurrier was a rare athlete, who looked bad in practice but could turn up his performance a notch during games.

Spurrier also felt good about the prospect of going to camp and not seeing No. 12, Brodie, ahead of him on the quarterback depth chart.

"No doubt about the fact that it'll be a good feeling knowing John's retired and there's only me and Reed," Spurrier said. "And there's the good feeling my legs are sound again. I'll be 29 but I've played so little so far I should be able to play until I'm 50."

The upstart World Football League went into business in 1974 and Spurrier, like many NFL players, was contacted about the possibility of playing in the rival league. Spurrier had been signing year-to-year contracts with the 49ers, which made signing with the WFL an option. He talked to the Jacksonville Sharks but never had any serious discussions.

"Maybe they [WFL] weren't interested in me," Spurrier said. "But by the same token I'm pretty happy where I am."

Spurrier felt as though he'd more than paid his dues in San Francisco.

"I've been waiting too long for the shot I think I'll have in 1974 to be talking about going anywhere else," Spurrier told the *Tampa Tribune*. "I don't know of any place that would be better for me to do at last what I've felt like I could do for seven years."

Spurrier signed a six-figure, three-year contract and continued to feel like the starting job was his to lose as he entered training camp.

"Brodie's gone, I have a pretty good contract and all those things considered, I'm pretty happy," Spurrier said. "[In the past] the only time I was really the quarterback was when [Brodie] was hurt. But, they always treated me well and the opportunity was there. It seems like it all worked out well. There were varied opinions on who the quarterback should be. It's hard not to play a guy who has played as well as he has."

Spurrier appeared to have the starting job under wraps when the 49ers played the Los Angeles Rams in their final exhibition game on September 8, 1974, a week before the start of the season. Unfortunately for Spurrier, the Rams' defense ended his hopes for starting after swarming him and throwing him down on his right shoulder. Spurrier suffered a separation and was operated on September 9, which caused him to miss most of the season.

The 49ers used five different quarterbacks, experiencing a seven-game losing streak at one point, and finished the 1974 season with a 6-8 record. Spurrier appeared in two games and completed one pass in three attempts.

While the season had been a disaster, what happened afterward seemed like a blessing after Spurrier and Jerri escaped serious injury in a head-on collision in Gainesville.

Jerri had two teeth knocked out and had cuts on the inside of her mouth, on her chin and face. Steve suffered minor facial cuts and a bruised chest.

Jerri, who was driving, spoke of the accident in the *Tampa Tribune*.

"We had been to dinner with the Willie O'Neals and were coming home on 39th Avenue. I was driving. Steve was taking his customary nap. I was going 55. I always do. I am very careful. I saw this car coming at me and saw it move over into my lane. I figured the driver had gone to sleep. I even had time to check my lights to see if they were bright. I had a decision to make. I decided to try to go to my left since he was veering right, but apparently he moved as I did. It almost was head on. The police said Steve's right shoulder apparently hit the post between the side window and front and kept him from going into the windshield. That was the recently operated on shoulder. I got cut up, but wasn't knocked out. We didn't turn over, but we were still in our lane. The other car went into the ditch."

Jerri took the worst of the accident.

"I counted 50 stitches on one and 15 stitches on my chin cut," Jerri said. "I haven't been able to count the stitches in my mouth yet, but it's sure sore. The doctor said the skin inside my mouth somehow was pulled loose from my jawbone. Steve was really lucky. He's hardly hurt. But then he was asleep."

The other driver stayed in the hospital several days with contusions.

Looking at the two cars after the accident, Jerri question how nobody was killed.

"No my face doesn't worry me," Jerri said. "It will be fine. The thing is that we are alive and there were seconds when I didn't think we would be."

Spurrier began the 1975 season as the 49ers' second-string quarterback, backing up veteran Norm Snead. He got his first start in early November when the 49ers played the Rams.

"I just felt we had to make a change," Nolan said. "Steve's throwing the ball better than he ever has."

Spurrier proceeded to lead a 24-23 upset victory over the Rams, who had won their previous 10 games against the 49ers. Having received another chance to start, Spurrier forgave all after the game.

"I'm not bitter about my years here," Spurrier said. "We have a first-class organization and everyone has treated me very well. . . . I've looked around the league and I still feel the opportunity here is as good as anywhere."

The 49ers had taken a 2-5 record into the Rams game and were greeted by loud booing from the San Francisco fans.

"When you're 2-5, you have nothing to lose," Spurrier said of the situation. "[He and his teammates decided to] start playing for fun, rather than in fear."

Spurrier threw three touchdown passes, including a 68-yarder to Gene Washington.

"There isn't a pass I'm afraid to throw now," Spurrier said. "I'm throwing better than at any time in my life. I think the wide receivers like me because I'm more daring."

The 49ers ended the season with a 5-9 record. Nolan lost his job, and Spurrier had played his final game as a 49er.

10

EXPANSION FOOTBALL

On April 24, 1974, NFL Commissioner Pete Rozelle awarded NFL franchises to Tampa and Seattle during a press conference inside the Drake Hotel in New York. Originally the Tampa franchise was awarded to Philadelphia businessman Tim McCloskey, but he withdrew, affording Hugh Culverhouse, a Jacksonville, Florida, attorney and real estate magnate, the opportunity to buy the team for $16 million.

By October 1975, the team had chosen a name, the Tampa Bay Buccaneers, as well as team colors, orange and white with red trim, and they signed coaching legend John McKay from the University of Southern California to a five-year contract on October 31, 1975.

On March 30, 1976, the team selected 39 players in the "veteran-allocation draft" held in New York. Like most teams drafting players in such a draft, the Bucs did not pick any real keepers. Which is why the general connotation "expansion team" evokes negative imagery of comical players with little athletic talent. A hard truth of professional sports is expansion teams normally play like expansion teams. Judging from the talent they received from the allocation draft, the Bucs realized they would be hard pressed not to be a big loser. Recognizing this fact, they decided they needed to find a draw, a popular player with novelty value. Trade rumors circulated that Ron Wolf, the Bucs' director of operations, was looking to land such a draw. Spurrier fell into the rumor mix along with ex-Gator quarterback John Reaves, former Florida State quarterback Gary Huff, and ex-USC quarterback Pat Haden, who had played for McKay in college and was a Rhodes Scholar in England at the time.

Spurrier held great popularity in Tampa, a city partial to the University of Florida given its location; Tampa is approximately 120 miles south of Gainesville, site of Spurrier's greatest glory. The Tampa sports community remembered Spurrier's college heroics with grandeur. If the Bucs were to bring in a draw to help add to their season-ticket sales, which stood at 34,000 at the time, Spurrier fit the bill perfectly.

"We talked [Bucs owner] Hugh Culverhouse into signing Steve," Tom McEwen said. "Me and some others. Because he'd sell tickets, we thought, and he was a name. They had to have someone here. We didn't know what was going to happen with pro football. I'm not so sure that [Bucs head coach] John [McKay] wanted that."

On April 2, the Bucs made the franchise's first trade, sending wide receiver Willie McGee and linebacker Bruce Elia, plus a second-round draft pick, to the 49ers for the 31-year-old Spurrier.

The 49ers had their eyes on trading for Jim Plunkett, the Heisman Trophy–winning quarterback from Stanford, who played for New England. Talks about trading Spurrier were initiated two months earlier by incoming 49ers coach Monte Clark, who contacted Wolf by telephone.

"At the time, I didn't give it much thought," Wolf told the *Tampa Tribune*. "But all the time we were interested in quality football players.

"At the conclusion of the allocation, I heard from Monte Clark again. We had been on the telephone constantly since then and consummated the deal just this morning."

The Bucs put a lot of thought into the decision to trade for Spurrier.

"There was a lot of examining and soul searching on our part," Wolf said. "I honestly do not feel we could have come up with a better quarterback at this time. We obviously feel it was a good trade or we wouldn't have made it."

The Bucs also signed Bill Cappleman of Florida State and Jim Foote of Delaware State to join the quarterback competition. No guarantees were issued to Spurrier that he would start.

"You have to have a backup," Wolf said. "You can't play with one quarterback . . . the two quarterbacks signed as free agents have proved they are capable players. I can't say that Spurrier is No. 1. He still has to win it."

Nevertheless, Spurrier, who lived in Gainesville with Jerri and their two daughters, seemed happy with the trade.

"It is the best thing that could have happened for me and my family," Spurrier said. "I look forward to helping the Buccaneers open their first season and playing in a state and before people who have meant so much to me for so many years.

"I have been given a new start in pro football. It's like being reborn, I guess. It's like coming home. I think we'll surprise some people."

Days after acquiring Spurrier, the Bucs began to put a positive spin on the deal, defending their new quarterback against the raps against him.

Bucs offensive coordinator John Rauch, the former head coach at Oakland and Buffalo, addressed the perception Spurrier could not throw the long ball and could not drop back quick enough. He recalled watching film of Spurrier playing against the Rams the previous season when Spurrier had led the 24-23 upset.

"His three touchdown passes were long ones," Rauch told the *Tampa Tribune*. "No quarterback could have put the ball to an area more perfectly than he did."

Expansion teams normally have bad offensive lines, which brought up the question whether Spurrier would be mobile enough to handle the lack of protection.

Spurrier "certainly is not in the image of a Fran Tarkenton," Wolf said. "But he is a hell of a lot better than Daryl Lamonica [the Oakland Raiders' quarterback in the late 1960s and 1970s]."

The Bucs liked Spurrier's competitiveness, too.

"I saw him get knocked down last year," Wolf said. "He couldn't get up. The crowd cheered. He got up, waved the trainer away and returned to the game.

"He has played at the championship level and won at that level. We now feel quite comfortable with our quarterback situation. This ends our search for an experienced quarterback."

Compliments aside, Rauch offered a disclaimer for Spurrier in the Bucs' fast-approaching first season.

"Having played quarterback and coached them, I know that the quarterback is at the mercy of the people surrounding him," Rauch said. "No matter how great he may perform, if the people with him do not perform, he is in for a difficult time. If they perform above him, then his job is made much easier.

"Too many times, I think, the quarterback is given too much of the credit for the success of a club and on the other hand, the quarterback can receive too much abuse for a team's failure."

Judging from comments Spurrier made to the *Tampa Tribune*, McKay's philosophy seemed to fit Spurrier at the outset.

"Coach McKay is offensive-minded," Spurrier said. "You hear most of the National Football League coaches say, 'If you don't let them score, you won't get beat.' That's the defensive approach. But Coach McKay, he says, 'If we have the ball, they can't score.' I like that.

"Also he's pass oriented. He wants to pass to establish the run. And what we will do different from most NFL teams is we will pass a lot out of the I-formation. It should work."

Spurrier had other compliments for the Bucs prior to the organization's first game, like the schedule Bucs coaches followed.

"At San Francisco, we had a meeting at night scheduled from 7:30 to 9 P.M.," he said. "If we finished our work at 8:30, we still stayed around to 9. Not with the Bucs. You have meetings. When the work is done, you leave."

He liked the practice facilities and treatment of players, too.

"We probably eat as good as any NFL team," Spurrier said. "Many of them train at colleges so they eat college cafeteria food. Not us. We eat the good motel restaurant food prepared for us.

"And we have our quarters about 50 yards from the practice field, 50 yards from the dining room, and within sight of the stadium and airport. And, best of all, the stadium has real grass, not artificial turf. Am I still glad for the move? You bet."

Finally, Spurrier threw compliments toward the offensive line.

"Coach McKay and Ron Wolf got themselves some fine offensive linemen," he said. "That's the first thing I looked at when I saw the allocation draft."

Spurrier's compliments toward his line, had they been reconsidered, would have been classified as a form of exaggeration.

The Bucs had the first selection in the NFL draft prior to the 1976 season, and clearly their goal was to build a solid defense, evidenced by their using the top pick to select future Hall of Fame defensive end Lee Roy Selmon from Oklahoma. In the second round the Bucs selected Oklahoma linebacker Dewey Selmon, Lee Roy's brother.

Receiver Lee McGriff, who had been an All-SEC receiver at Florida and had attended high school at Tampa Plant, was a starter on the inaugural Bucs team. He had a history with Spurrier and looked forward to playing in his hometown and catching passes thrown by his hero.

"I grew up going to Florida football games, was very closely connected to Florida, so obviously, Steve had been one of my heroes," McGriff said. "I was born in Gainesville and lived [in Gainesville] until I was 9 years old. My parents divorced and my dad stayed [in Gainesville]. So every summer I would come back and spend the summers with my dad.

"When I got old enough I worked in the maintenance department at the [University of Florida] athletic department every summer, working on the grounds, doing different jobs. At lunch time we'd all come back into the shop, which was in the stadium. I'd get my lunch and sit in the stadium and eat. I mean, everybody there was older than me."

McGriff's lunches turned into wonderful chance encounters with Spurrier, who lived in Gainesville and was a member of the 49ers at the time.

"Steve would come in alone and bring a few footballs," McGriff said. "He'd punt 'em, not that he was killing himself working hard. So when I was about 14 or 15 years old, I'd go down there and say 'do you need anybody to catch?'"

"Of course, I had met him and I think he sort of knew who I was because I grew up going to every Ray Graves sports camp. They used to let the players get involved, and Steve was one of those, so he kind of knew who I was. I would go down there, sometimes shag a few punts, run a few routes. That would be my lunchtime. He just kind of threw it around. He was bigger than life to me. I was in junior high, and young, and Steve Spurrier was the star, winning the Heisman Trophy, all that kind of stuff. He'd throw it to me and kick it to me."

Even though McGriff viewed Spurrier through a youngster's eyes, he recalled being able to recognize something special about him.

"I will tell you he does have some gift," McGriff said. "It's unique the way he goes about it. Like when I was in the stadium and when he'd throw and he'd say 'run a curl, run an out,' whatever, and his sense of timing with me was like most people who had been spending hours working together. He has a sense of timing. A feeling for things. That's unique."

Joining Spurrier in the Bucs' huddle made McGriff's return to Tampa special.

"Even though I'd been around Steve, it was still a thrill to me, to be in the huddle around Steve," McGriff said. "And, of course, I always felt like he had some magic in his pocket. You always felt like this guy sees things, feels things differently, and he's going to find a way to do a little magic. That was a thrill."

But almost from the start, Spurrier rubbed McKay the wrong way.

"Oh, ho-ho," McGriff answered when asked if there was a rift between Spurrier and McKay. "That progressed as the season went along. There was great tension. John McKay had no appreciation for Steve Spurrier. Steve's a different guy the way he goes about doing things. And his vision of what football is, it's clear to understand now that [Spurrier] has been coaching this long, his vision of how football is supposed to be played, meaning Steve Spurrier versus John McKay were two different things."

McKay and Spurrier had drastic differences when it came to offensive philosophies.

"John McKay was a runner and then you tried to use the passing game to make a big play," McGriff said. "Steve, you know what Steve was. What you see in his coaching, that's been in his brain since the first day he played, really. Trying to fool people, keeping them off balance, throw the ball around, being daring. That's just who he is. He didn't have to learn that."

McKay had coached at USC, where his team usually had better talent than any team he played; McGriff believes this contributed to McKay's coaching philosophies.

"Obviously at Southern Cal, they were just better than anyone, they could just line up and whip you," McGriff said. "I certainly think Steve, and what he thought he could do with the passing game, was much more visionary than John McKay. To me, John McKay, and again, we're talking about one of the all-time great coaches, and Spurrier, they just weren't a fit.

"John McKay wanted to line up in that I [formation] and pound it, then catch you off guard and hit a pass play every once in a while. And Steve wanted to put people all over the field, even then, spread it out and catch you off balance. I certainly think there were times when Steve would have checked off and thrown a pass trying to catch them off guard, and John McKay would not have wanted that, would not have allowed that. There were times, without getting too personal, when John McKay specifically wanted the ball to go to a certain person, his son [J.K. McKay, who played receiver for the Bucs]."

McGriff pointed to several things Spurrier did during his early going with the Bucs that likely escalated the tensions between Spurrier and McKay.

"There were some things that were so Spurrier-like," McGriff said. "I remember the first minicamp we had. (McGriff chuckled.) We're out there. All it was going to be was helmets and T-shirts. And Steve showed up with no socks and no shirt on. Now he put his shirt on, but he still didn't have any socks. That blew my mind. That somebody would show up like that. I think it blew Coach McKay's mind."

McKay held brutal two-a-day sessions prior at the opening of training camp.

"They lasted an unbelievably long amount of time," McGriff said. "Especially for those of us who ran and ran. So it was exhausting. But Steve, sometimes in between practices, would go to hit golf balls. I promise you. I thought, 'This is unbelievable. We're all dying; we've been doing this forever, and this guy's out here hitting golf balls.' And that drove Coach McKay insane."

Spurrier didn't do much to endear himself to McKay during team meetings, either.

"Sometimes Steve would be sitting in those meetings, he hears everything, but he doesn't give you that focus," McGriff said. "Visually, you don't see that he's hearing you. His mannerisms are different and pretty unique, and Steve would act disinterested and bored. And he was. And that irritated the fire out of McKay."

Finally, Ray Graves pointed to something Spurrier had told him.

"Steve told me why he and McKay didn't get along," Graves said. "He said 'I don't know. It might have been when at practice he asked me 'Why aren't you throwing to my son?' And Steve told him, 'Well, he's the worst receiver on the squad, Coach.' He said, 'I don't think [McKay] liked that.'"

The Bucs played their first game July 31, 1976, an exhibition contest against the Rams in Los Angeles, which they lost 26-3. And the relationship between McKay and Spurrier grew more strained.

"In the very first game [the Bucs] ever played, I think Steve was late for a meeting or something," McEwen said. "I remember walking in [to McKay's office] and McKay said, 'Your quarterback is late.' I said, 'My quarterback?' And McKay said, 'He kept somebody out with him, too.'"

The Bucs won 17-3 two weeks later against the Atlanta Falcons, giving Bucs fans hope for the coming season. Those hopes took an immediate hit in the Bucs' first-ever regular-season game, a 20-0 loss to the Houston Oilers September 12, 1976, in Houston.

Spurrier started and completed eight of 21 passes for 90 yards and two interceptions. The less than awe-inspiring performance prompted McKay to hint he was not happy with Spurrier.

During a Monday press conference following the Houston game, McKay was disussing the team's offensive problems when he was asked if he had considered changing quarterbacks. His answer, delivered without a great deal of conviction: "Not right now, no."

"But I imagine that 14 coaches in the National Football League might be thinking about that, too," McKay said. "We gave him some rollout plays last week. He just didn't seem to be comfortable in the pocket."

The Oilers sacked Spurrier three times, but McKay said the films showed the offensive line "protected better than we thought we did."

McKay called most of the plays, but Spurrier had the option to audible. While calling an audible, Spurrier made an error in McKay's judgment. He said Spurrier changed the passing route of running back Essex Johnson but had not bothered alerting McGriff about the change. Johnson and McGriff nearly collided on the play and C.L. Whittington intercepted Spurrier's pass, returning it 50 yards.

"If [Spurrier] changes one guy, then he had better tell the other," McKay said.

Spurrier couldn't be faulted for all of the team's offensive woes as the team had only 108 net yards on offense, averaging 1.5 yards per carry rushing.

"I'm worried about our lack of offense," McKay said. "I don't know whether it has been a matter of the last three teams we have played [during the exhibition season] being better or whether they were not."

McGriff said the offensive problems were obvious: "We didn't have the talent to take the ball and stuff it down their throat."

At the home opener a week later, the Chargers defeated the Bucs 23-0. The Bucs failed to score a touchdown in their first three games.

Spurrier never had an open disagreement with McKay.

"Steve certainly was not a disrespectful, loudmouth kind of player," McGriff said. "But, I promise you John McKay chastised him openly. And Steve, now I wasn't with him with the 49ers, but you know he was the golden boy at Florida and Ray Graves loved him like a son. Steve wasn't used to being talked to that way. And it was hard on him.

"I remember the Cincinnati game, McKay pulled Spurrier out on third down. Which I had never seen any time in my life and never saw again, except when Steve was a head coach, which is an odd twist of fate, when McKay pulled [Spurrier] off the field on third down and sent Parnell Dickenson in and said 'the fucking honeymoon is over Spurrier' in front of the whole team. What humiliation for a quarterback."

Still, Spurrier displayed leadership skills.

"Spurrier relaxed you in the huddle," McGriff said. "He always made you realize you were playing a game. Nothing rattled him. Which was something that [would become] part of his demeanor and style at Florida, calm, poised, no matter what. So his wild behavior and intensity as a coach was totally out of character for him."

Spurrier's flair for the unlikely continued, even under dire circumstances.

"One of my most memorable plays that colored Steve in the light I'd grown up seeing him play, I think it was against the Bears," McGriff said. "It was a pass, Steve dropped back. He got in trouble and headed for the ground to be sacked. And right before he went to the ground he threw an underhanded pass for a touchdown. That was just him. He could ad lib.

"He had tremendous hand-eye coordination. He was never a mechanical kind of player. Steve could run and had quickness better than most people want to remember. But obviously his feet were not his greatest asset. But you could get into any game with him where it's hands and eyes and you're in trouble. Ping-pong, pool, shoot baskets, golf, whatever, he's deadly."

During a 13-10 loss to the Seahawks on October 17, Spurrier got kicked in the left knee and did not start the Bucs' October 24 game against the Dolphins.

Dickinson led the Bucs to a 7-3 lead against the Dolphins in front of a Tampa Stadium crowd of 61,427; Dickinson then went down with an ankle injury. Terry Hanratty relieved Dickinson briefly before McKay called on Spurrier.

The offensive line protected Spurrier well, which allowed him to throw for 143 yards and two touchdowns. Both touchdowns went to Morris Owens, who caught three for the game.

The Bucs came up short, losing 23-20.

"It was close, but not quite good enough," Spurrier said.

The Miami loss was the closest to victory the Bucs came during their initial campaign en route to their 0-14 mark, giving the team the dubious distinction of being the first NFL team to go winless since the 1960 Dallas Cowboys.

Spurrier started 12 of the team's 14 regular-season games, completing 156 of 311 passes for 1,628 yards and seven touchdowns; he also threw seven interceptions.

"We need to regroup and see what happens," Spurrier said after the season's final game, a loss to the New England Patriots.

The Bucs did regroup, and waiving Spurrier became part of the team's regrouping effort.

The Bucs waived Spurrier on April 13, 1977, after the team signed ex-Chicago Bears quarterback Gary Huff to a three-year contract.

McKay notified Spurrier with a telephone call at 5:15 in the afternoon, noting the move was "in [Spurrier's] best interest."

Because of a new collective bargaining rule, players with four years experience could pick the team they wanted to play for, if a new team showed interest. Once a player falling into that category passed waivers, he could turn down offers and strike his own deal.

"It was our sole purpose of doing it this way so he can go where he wants to go," Wolf said.

"This gives Steve a chance to develop his own deal with whichever team he prefers of those who he finds interested in him," McKay said.

McKay complimented Spurrier's effort during the expansion team's first season.

"He took his lumps," McKay said. "He had a difficult job with us as a first-year team. He did a good job for us. We wish him well."

Spurrier did not take the news well, leaving his Gainesville home to go play cards immediately after the call from McKay.

Jerri spoke for her husband when reporters called.

"Well, yes, I guess news like this always hurts," Jerri told the *Tampa Tribune*. "But things will turn out all right. It was good being with Tampa Bay for a year."

When she was asked if Steve could be reached, Jerri responded: "No, he said, 'It's a good thing I'm playing cards tonight.'"

Spurrier talked to the media the next day and admitted being blindsided by the move.

"What was the reason?" Spurrier said. "I talked with Coach McKay and he didn't give me much of a reason.

"It was a surprise after being [in Tampa] two weeks ago and working with them in the minicamps. But I'm not going to worry. I still think there are a lot of teams I can play for. I'm not going to say that I'm happy. Nobody likes to see his name on a waiver list. But, there is a chance that I may get to play on a winner. You don't have to feel sorry for Stephen Orr. I've had more thrills out of football than 99 percent of the guys who have played it. I've been one of the most fortunate who ever played the game of football."

Spurrier would not criticize the Bucs, but it was widely known he didn't like not calling the plays and he said McKay wanted him to throw to his son, J. K. McKay "sometimes when I didn't think I could."

McGriff was not surprised by the Bucs' move.

"No, I wasn't surprised, but it wasn't because I didn't think Steve was a good player," McGriff said. "The relationship with him and Coach McKay just wasn't very good."

Even today Spurrier acknowledges there was a problem playing for McKay.

"I just think it was difficult for Coach McKay and myself," Spurrier said. "His son being the wide receiver. I don't know, it was just difficult."

Spurrier worked out a deal with the Denver Broncos but was waived in late August when he couldn't win the No. 3 quarterback spot, leading to speculation he might return to the Bucs after Huff hurt his left knee. The Bucs never bit.

Spurrier signed with the Dolphins September 5, 1977.

"I'm healthy and I feel like I can still play football," Spurrier said. "Basically, the systems of all teams are the same, so I should fit right in."

Spurrier's signing came as a result of a strange climate in Miami.

Starting quarterback Bob Griese was having a difficult time adjusting to playing with contact lenses; he later would play with glasses. Backup Don Strock had several physical problems, and third-string quarterback Gary Valbuena had not been impressive leading the team.

"Our uncertainty at the position caused a change in attitude about our third quarterback," Miami coach Don Shula said. "Originally, we had thought of the No. 3 spot as developmental, but with Griese having trouble with the glasses and Strock having a sore thumb, we had to change our thinking."

On September 12, 1977, the Dolphins waived Spurrier to get down to the 43-man roster limit, dealing Spurrier the final blow to his playing career.

"I was cut, released," Spurrier said. "That's the way most people get out of the game. You go 10 years having to make a new life every six months, and finally it ends."

Spurrier's final NFL statistics: 597 completions in 1,151 attempts for 6,878 yards and 40 touchdowns.

Asked to reflect upon his pro career today, Spurrier says, "I probably didn't have the best attitude in the world, the best commitment, I didn't have the best ambition.

"At times I could get excited about playing and at other times maybe I settled into being a backup quarterback," he said. "But anyway, that's the way it worked out. Looking back now, somehow or another I did get 10 years in the league. I only really played about two of the 10, so I didn't get beat up.

"I see a lot of my former teammates with a lot more aches and pains than I have. So, looking back, you've got to look at all your experiences as a positive, and that's the only way I look at it now. I didn't get beat up too bad being the backup quarterback. So it may help me now and later in life."

11

COACHING BECKONS

Steve Spurrier returned to Gainesville in the fall of 1977 left to ponder what he would do for his next career.

Spurrier's schedule became fairly predictable during this period. He'd jog on the University of Florida track in the morning then find his way to the Gainesville Country Club in the afternoon. Family, card games and mulling over different business ventures occupied the rest of his time.

"I talked to him all that time during the year he didn't work," Tom McEwen said. "He went to the [Gators] games in Gainesville [that year]. He sat in the stands an entire year in Gainesville. Not a lot of people know that. He wasn't worried for himself [about what he was going to do]. His friends were."

Meanwhile, the University of Florida football program took a turn for the worse under Doug Dickey, the man who succeeded Graves as the Gators' head coach in 1970. In 1977, the Gators dropped from 8-4 the previous season to 6-4-1 and Gator alumni demanded change.

"Through 1975, Coach Dickey's career was on the rise," Lee McGriff said. "[Florida] went to four straight bowls, things were going good. My senior year [1974] and the year that followed, we had a chance to win the conference and didn't do it. The program was headed that way, then it started sinking. And, of course, being in the wishbone, fans started to grumble. Teams were coming out of the option and Florida lingered in it.

"The rumbles were to fire Coach Dickey. He was given a reprieve if he would change the offense and hire new offensive coaches. Steve and I were the answers."

Spurrier and McGriff were hired prior to the 1978 season.

"I had only been out of football three or four months," Spurrier said. "But when the opportunity came, I was ready to jump back in there."

Graham Spurrier wasn't surprised about his brother's decision to become a coach.

Spurrier became the Gators' offensive backfield coach for a 4-7 Gators team. Dickey lost his job following the season and new coach Charley Pell elected not to retain Spurrier.

Joe Biddle pointed to Spurrier's recruiting work as a contributing factor to his not being retained.

Charley Pell "brought Steve in for the interview and there was a running back named John L. Williams up at Jacksonville the Gators were trying to recruit," Biddle said. "All-America, everybody in the country wanted him. So Pell asked [Spurrier], 'How do we stand with John L. Williams?' Steve said, 'I think we're OK, I think we're pretty high on his list.'

"Pell said, 'What do his parents have to say? What does his mom say? She's usually the one who makes the decision.' He says, 'Well, I don't know.' Pell says 'You haven't been to their house?' He said, 'No, I watched him play one game.' And that was just Steve. He wasn't going to anybody's house to try and get him to go there. And so, Pell didn't retain him."

Spurrier didn't make a fuss about Pell's decision.

"I didn't go into Charley's office with hat in hand asking for a job," Spurrier told the *Tampa Times*. "If he had asked me to stay on, I probably would have. But there comes a time when you've got to leave your home school if you're hoping to advance. You've got to go out and do something where you don't have so many roots."

Spurrier turned to old friend Pepper Rodgers for his next coaching assignment.

Rodgers had returned to Georgia Tech, his alma mater, five years earlier to try and lead the Yellow Jackets back to respectability. Though he enjoyed moderate success, with an upset here or there, he wasn't exactly on solid footing when Spurrier came aboard as the quarterback coach.

Georgia Tech signaled an uncharacteristic seriousness in Spurrier, who knew he needed to establish himself if he was going to advance in the coaching profession. He even put his golf clubs aside to a certain degree.

"I don't get the bug as much anymore," Spurrier said during the 1979 season. "I don't belong to a country club here and the courses aren't as easily accessible as they are in Gainesville. When I want a game, I almost have to go out and hunt for one."

Spurrier did the Yellow Jackets' play calling from the press box and tried to do his homework.

"I never had to sit and study in the pros," Spurrier said. "This is all new."

Spurrier seemed to embrace his new livelihood for the first time.

"Being in sports so long, I need competition," he said. "This is a release . . . I can't imagine doing anything else. It's my thing.

"I hadn't really thought about coaching until I got out, but I really enjoy everything there is about it. Some guys say when they get out of football they don't even want to watch it anymore. That wasn't for me. I didn't expect to play forever, and 10 years was a good time. On Saturdays I was still a good spectator. I was just grooved to be at football games on the weekends."

Though Spurrier had been humbled by Pell's decision not to retain him, he didn't waiver in his confidence about what he could do in the coaching profession.

"I'm a good coach," Spurrier said. "I have been able to teach the things that are important in the game. I'll tell you, I'm teaching things I wish I had been taught, things I wish I had been made to learn when I was in the NFL."

Spurrier even showed a rare reflective side in a 1979 story appearing in the *Tampa Times*.

"Sitting and watching [football games as he did in 1977], I realized the magnitude of the game in people's lives," Spurrier said. "When I was an active pro, I didn't understand how important it was to all of them, but their team is really a part of them. I didn't know how much interest they really have, but this is sort of how they live and die."

Spurrier got results during the 1979 season working with Georgia Tech quarterback Mike Kelly, who became the first quarterback in the school's history to throw for 2,000 yards in a season.

"I saw a real rapport between the two," Rodgers said. "Steve's a great quarterback coach. Mike Kelly was a guy who developed under Steve. I don't think anybody could have done a better job of coaching him than Steve."

Rodgers believes Spurrier's experience at Tech was critical to his development.

"Steve is like anybody," Rodgers said. "He was a great player and great players do just about everything naturally. But being a football coach is a lot more than being a natural. It involves a lot of things. I think the Tech experience was a good learning experience for Steve because, one, to get away from Florida, where he's been all his life. I thought at Georgia Tech he became a real football coach. You don't have to win 11 games to be a real football coach. And Steve, to me, really realized that he wanted to be a football coach at that time and I think, to me, he's one of the greatest."

Later as a head coach, Spurrier would recount Rodgers' words to his coaches.

"Steve always said, 'You know what I always tell my coaches, Coach Pepper?'" Rodgers said. "He said, 'I always tell them what you used to tell me.' And I said, 'Steve, I've said so many things I can't remember what I've said. What did I say?' He said, 'You said when you get to be a head coach you can do anything you want to. But until you get to be the head coach, I can do anything I want to.' That's what he always tells his coaches. I like him saying that he remembers that."

The 1979 season did not have a happy ending.

Rogers got fired shortly after the Yellow Jackets lost to Georgia 16-3 in the final game of the season, capping a 4-6-1 mark. Subsequently, Georgia Tech hired Bill Curry, who did not offer Spurrier the chance to join his staff.

"Curry interviewed [Spurrier] and didn't think he'd work hard enough," Biddle said.

Spurrier didn't take the news well. He thought he was in line to be Tech's offensive coordinator. He had just purchased a home in Marietta, just outside Atlanta, where Jerri and he were raising their three young children.

Rodgers' firing and the snub from Curry were significant events to Spurrier, who is extremely loyal and likes to prove people wrong. In future seasons, Spurrier would never lose to a Bill Curry–coached team, and he ran up the score every chance he had.

"You go back and look at the times Spurrier's teams have played Curry's," Biddle said. "Steve ran up the score. He's got a mind like an elephant when it comes to stuff like that."

Spurrier exacted revenge on Georgia, too. As the Florida head coach, Spurrier's Gators lost just once to the Bulldogs in 12 games. In one of those games, Spurrier instructed his quarterback to throw long for a touchdown with 2:23 left in the game in a 47-7 Gators rout.

Rodgers had been Spurrier's guest at the game and afterward he presented his old coach and friend the game ball, noting, "He dislikes [Georgia], just like all of us Gators."

In Spurrier's mind, Georgia had beaten Rodgers in Rodgers' final college game, which was more than ample fodder for running up the score.

Rodgers said of the experience, "I don't hate anyone. In fact, I called up Vince Dooley [Georgia athletic director and former head football coach] and said, 'Vince, I never said I hated Georgia.'"

However, Spurrier's treatment made Rodgers feel special.

"I loved it," Rodgers said. "How could I not love it? He calls me 'Coach Pepper' and I call him 'Coach Steve,' and certainly that makes me feel fantastic. But Steve and I have been friends since he played. I couldn't be more thrilled than when he gave me that ball."

Not being retained by Curry gave Spurrier the experience of being let go five times in four years, as a player then a coach. But good news waited just around the corner.

Duke coach Red Wilson hired Spurrier in January 1980 to be the Blue Devils' offensive coordinator prior to the 1980 season.

"Steve's turning point was Red Wilson at Duke, who turned the whole offense over to him," Biddle said.

Spurrier called Eddie Williamson, the Duke offensive line coach, to ask about the situation at Duke.

"Yes, I made the initial contact and Coach Wilson asked me to come up and talk about it," Spurrier said. "It's a better job for me here, a little more money, and Coach Wilson is giving me the freedom to work with the offense.

"I didn't have all this at Tech. In fact, in the Duke game—we were 1-5-1 going in—I went to Pepper and said, 'Look, let me help you,' and he let me call the plays but that was the first game all year I did it. At Duke, I'll have more freedom."

Wilson wanted to hire a name, but he wanted more.

"You also want a coach," Wilson said. "It will be an identity for us. People can identify with Steve Spurrier. Also, his identity with what we're doing will be quite synonymous."

Spurrier admitted to Blue Devils fans he still was learning how to be a coach.

"When I got into college coaching, I thought I knew what I wanted to coach," Spurrier said. "But the college game is much more involved than the pro game."

He elaborated by pointing out the college game's wider hash marks, option offenses and varied defenses, all of which give the college game more variety than the pro game. He vowed to use a pass-oriented offense, without the option.

"We're going to be doing a lot of things that we haven't been doing in the past," Spurrier said. "We will have a lot of different ways of throwing the ball. But it won't be that complicated, and I don't anticipate any trouble learning it because it's a fun thing to learn."

Eliminating choices for the quarterback became the key to Spurrier's offensive thinking.

"Instead of dropping back with five choices, [the quarterback] will have just two," Spurrier said. "We'll have five receivers but only two choices. If he's going to be dropping back with the ball, he's going to have to make good choices."

Spurrier signed a one-year deal with the Blue Devils and understood the bottom line.

"Right away, Red and I liked each other," Spurrier said. "But I'll be judged by what our offense does. I want an exciting offense and I want it to be fun for the players. It's no fun losing every week. But I want practice fun, too. . . ."

"I chose coaching because I wanted to be around the action and I felt I knew how to coach. I'd been around good coaches and bad ones as a player. I want to give it a shot for at least about five or six years. If things work out, fine."

Today Spurrier says, "Whatever kind of coach I became, or am, happened basically when I got to Duke University in 1980."

Red Wilson "was the coach who handed out a lot of motivational sheets," Spurrier said. "He handed out a sheet called winners and losers that talked about how winners act and the way losers act, and talk also. It's about 30 of those and working under Coach Wilson and how to be a good coach, trying to learn how to become a winner."

The motivational sheets pushed Spurrier's hot buttons.

"I read all that stuff and said, 'You know what, that all makes sense,'" Spurrier said. "Most people, most coaches, they get into coaching and they don't have a plan. And every team I coach, we go over the winners and losers. I've got sort of a game plan for all of our coaches. Guidelines for how to be a good coach. Stuff like if you criticize, criticize to a player's face; don't criticize behind his back. There's about 35 of those things."

Spurrier worked with quarterback Ben Bennett for the first three of Bennett's four years at Duke and Bennett thrived, setting Atlantic Coast Conference and NCAA records with 9,614 passing yards and 55 touchdown passes. He had nine 300-yard games and his passing total was the NCAA Division I record when he completed his career.

Bennett already had signed a national letter of intent to attend Duke when Spurrier decided during a spring visit to California to visit the rising quarterback at his high school in Sunnyvale, approximately 40 miles south of San Francisco. Bennett called the visit "a precursor to what I was to be involved with in my three years with Steve."

"Turns out I had a racquetball class I had the second half of my senior year and that's where I was when Steve showed up," Bennett said with a chuckle. "And Steve said he wanted to get in and play, because he's obviously a pretty good athlete and quite a competitor. I got in there and beat Steve pretty bad in racquetball. I've never heard such complaining and 'that doesn't count.' I thought to myself, 'this guy is a crappy loser.' And in reality, he is. Steve will try to beat you to death in anything he can. As I look back on it that should have told me what type of guy I was going to play football for."

When asked about the racquetball encounter with Bennett 22 years earlier, Spurrier responded: "We tied." Then followed with: "Did he say he won one and I won one? He was screwing around and I won the first game in racquetball. He won the next one and said, 'All right Coach, this one will be to see who the winner is.' I said, 'Ben, I'll tell you what, we're going to call this a tie. I've got one, you've got one, let's go.'"

Bennett marvels at the competitiveness and unique talents he would come to know in Spurrier.

"The things Steve can do on a football field," Bennett said. "He never had that strong of an arm, but he had an accurate arm. But something else Steve can do, Steve can take a football and he can punt it and turn that thing over and drop it anywhere. I don't care where you are on the field, if you're within about 35 yards he can just pick it up, not even stretch, and just punt it, turn it over and drop it right into your hands. That's just one of the little things he can do. You play him in tennis and he'll dink you and lob you and run you to death until you want to kill yourself, kill him. He'll get you on the golf course, he'll rattle his keys and talk to you, whatever he needs to do to win. And that's not a contrived thing. It's just Steve Spurrier. That's who he is."

Spurrier clearly has a warm spot for Bennett, chuckling before recalling the days when he coached him.

"When I was coaching old Ben at Duke, gosh, I was only 34 or 35, and I'd been coaching quarterbacks, and I could fundamentally demonstrate pretty well back then," Spurrier said. "In fact I was a better passer than I ever was in college or the NFL because I'd sort of learned. Nobody had ever really taught me the exact fundamentals and footwork. And I used to go out there with Ben and ask the receivers, "Let's see who can make the best throws.' And Ben would get nervous, he'd throw grounders and everything."

According to lore, Spurrier had such a creative offensive mind that he tapped Bennett on the shoulder during a pregame breakfast and "right there in the oatmeal!" scribbled out a new play to use in the game.

Bennett said the story got taken literally when he had just said, "right there in the oatmeal!" to illustrate when Spurrier told him about a play that had come to him.

"It's funny, Steve gets inspiration at all hours of the day or night," Bennett said. "And people don't give him enough credit for the amount of work and the time and effort he puts into it. Because he's not going to tell you how much work he does. But he goes home and watches tape at night, the whole bit.

"He comes in one morning before the Wake Forrest Game at the pregame meal and says, 'I've watched a little more of this tape and I think if we run this toss against this coverage and this defense, the free safety is going to come up and the strong safety is not going to be able to get back and I think old Gray Dog can whiz one in there.' That was our halfback, Mike Grayson, [Spurrier] thought he could throw it down the field 50 yards to Chris Castor. Sure enough, he came over. We ran a little deal. The safety did exactly what Spurrier said he was going to do and the strong safety did what Spurrier said he was going to do and Grayson threw a dart and hit Chris Castor right in stride for about a 60-yard touchdown pass. Saying he drew that up in my oatmeal, I didn't mean that literally. It's when he's at his best, when he gets that inspiration, gets a hunch, he's usually pretty good about what he does."

According to Bennett, Spurrier formulates a game plan that utilizes everybody's strengths and hides everybody's weaknesses.

"If it weren't for him, I wouldn't have come close to doing what I did," Bennett said. "He can be classified in the Bill Walsh category of offensive geniuses."

Bennett started as a freshman at Duke, Spurrier's first season as a college offensive coordinator.

"So he was learning as much how to teach his offense as I was learning to run his offense," Bennett said. "And I think the thing is we both got better at, I got better at running it over the years. He got better at teaching it over the years. Now you can take about anybody and put him in Steve's offense and if they work hard they're going to figure out what's going on."

But there were growing pains. Bennett called his first training camp with Spurrier "enlightening and frustrating all in the same boat." Bennett had been allowed to call his own plays in high school and thought he knew everything.

"When I came in when I was 18, and here's the best way to sum up [the situation]," Bennett said, "I thought that I knew everything when I came into college when in reality Steve did know everything. And it just took me awhile to realize that."

By Bennett's junior season in 1983, Duke's offense was one of the best in the country. In part this was due to a nice chemistry among the players, but Bennett credits Spurrier.

"Look at what we had that season," Bennett said. "I had a weak-side wide receiver, who was a 4.65 guy [in the 40]. I had a 5-foot-10, 175-pound sprinter, both kids were white at wide receiver. I had a tight end who was 6-1, 220, starting in the ACC. I had a fullback who was 5-9, 195 pounds, a tailback who was 5-7, 185 pounds. And those were our offensive weapons. A lot of those guys were undersized and lacked the speed of the players of that time. But we were armed with one of the best systems in the country."

Bennett described playing in Spurrier's offense as a wonderful adventure.

"If you go out there and do what he thinks you can do," Bennett said, "if you do it on every play, it's one of the most enjoyable experiences a football player can have. Because no matter whom you are on offense, you may very well get the ball on any given play. It's not an offense where you say, 'we're going to feature

Steve Spurrier, Heisman trophy-winning quarterback of the University of Florida. *The Tampa Tribune*

Spurrier took his lumps while playing quarterback for the expansion Tampa Bay
Buccaneers. *The Tampa Tribune*

Spurrier addresses the media as head coach of the USFL's Tampa Bay Bandits. *The Tampa Tribune*

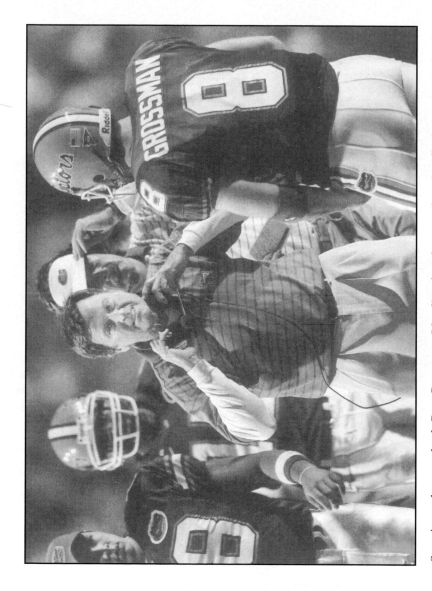

Spurrier and quarterback Rex Grossman (No. 8) enjoyed a record-setting final season together in 2001. *The Tampa Tribune*

this guy, this, that and the other.' The offense really isn't designed to focus on one guy. I knew I was going to get the chance to throw the ball. I didn't realize I was going to have the opportunity to catch it and run with it a little bit. Same way with our receivers. . . .

"You get a chance to throw it some, run it some, now you're pretty excited, because on any given play, one guy can be the focus. And then the play evolves and the next guy gets to be the focus and you never know who's going to do what on any given play. So you try to play hard on every snap because you never know who's going to get it."

During Spurrier's tenure as the Blue Devils' offensive coordinator the offense went from 127th in the nation, their ranking before Spurrier arrived, to third. In 1982, Duke's offense averaged 453 yards a game, an ACC record at the time. Unfortunately for Duke, the defense could not match the offense and the best the Blue Devils could do was back-to-back 6-5 seasons in 1981 and 1982.

"I was very lucky," Spurrier said about his Duke experience. "[Wilson] gave me free reign with the offense. I asked him if there were certain things he wanted me to carry over. He said, 'No. What we've done in the past hasn't been real good. But I do like little trick plays now and then.' I said I liked 'em, too.

"So I was able to really to put together a complete offense taking a little of this and that I learned along the way."

Spurrier and Williamson tried to put together an offense that would be easy to learn, but would be hard to stop.

"We experimented a lot, went through a lot of trial and error to see if it would work," Spurrier said.

Spurrier's coaching personality hasn't changed much from his days at Duke.

"But what I think he learned was the extent that he could push people," Bennett said. "Right out of the box you can't expect a bunch of 18 and 19 year olds first learning the offense to execute everything perfectly. That's just not going to happen. So I think a lot of Steve's frustration was as much with his inability to get us to do what he wanted us to do as it was with our inability to get it done. . . .

"Instead of trying to say, 'here's my offensive philosophy, you guys better learn it or we're all going down,' he learned to take his offensive philosophy, gear it to not only best utilize our individual strengths, but he also took it a step further to use his offensive philosophy and our strengths to attack certain weaknesses both scheme-wise and personnel-wise when we played other teams. Steve really learned not only how to teach [his offense] but to adapt what we did as an offense based on our strengths and weaknesses, in attacking the other team's scheme and their individual strengths and weaknesses."

A 34-17 Duke victory at Clemson in 1980 told the Duke players they were in the presence of an offensive genius.

"We were 0-5 at the time and it just seemed like everything we did, whatever [Spurrier] called, turned out successfully," Bennett said. "We had one pass dropped in the end zone and another called back. If we had those things go our way, we would have blown Clemson out, which is very hard to do. Especially when you consider that same group won the national championship the next season. That game was kind of the tip of the iceberg for us. We began to see the light there, like, 'Whack, look what this thing can really do.'"

Bennett said Spurrier had an ability to vent at his players without holding a grudge.

"He'll get on you for mental mistakes," Bennett said. "It's when he thinks you're letting down as far as your focus. That's when he gets irate, gets mad about something. Things he thinks you can control. If you don't know the system. If you don't know the reads. If you don't do the things that you've practiced. When you don't do those things. When you make silly mistakes. That's when Steve gets on you."

A quarterback in Spurrier's offense will know most times where he's going to go with the ball before taking the snap.

"Things change as the play unfolds and you have to get a progression of reads, but really, the big key in Steve's offense, if he gives you a play, that's his best guess about what he thinks the defense is going to be," Bennett said. "And he's not always right. But what he teaches you is, if he calls a bad one don't run it and say, 'Well, that's what you called.' Get yourself to a better one. Get yourself to a good play. You should have thought through it enough in the summer leading up to the season. You should know those things by the time you get to the line. Get yourself to a better play."

Spurrier's recruiting skills, though improved, remained somewhat off the traditional track. McGriff recalled a story when he'd gone to Sarasota, Florida, to recruit a player from Cardinal Mooney High School and ran into Spurrier, who was at Duke and trying to recruit another player from the same school.

"Two kids a lot of schools were recruiting," McGriff said. "A fullback we were really after, who was a high-profile guy, and another guy, who was marginal, who Steve was interested in. So I went down there, and of course, that's a private school. I know the nature of the school, so I've got a tie on."

McGriff went to a weight-lifting competition held at the school where he encountered Spurrier.

"Steve didn't like weight-lifting at all," McGriff said. "I didn't know he was going to be there. We show up at the same time. I see him in his casual way.

[McGriff begins to imitate Spurrier's high-pitched drawl as he gave his account of their conversation]."

Spurrier: "Hey, how you been, whatcha gonna do? You gonna watch this weight-lifting stuff? You like that?"

McGriff: "No, I don't really, I like to work out and all that, but I don't know that I want to watch this competition. But I'm going to do it, because that's what the guy's doing and he's going to see me."

Spurrier: "Then whatcha gonna do?"

McGriff: "Well, hopefully, I'll see him, then I'll be back at the school to-morrow."

Spurrier: "Well, I really don't like this stuff. Whatcha wearing a tie for?"

McGriff: "Well, I don't wear this to every high school. If I'm in Pahokee, I don't have this on. Or if I go to [Tampa] Plant High School, I don't have this on. But I'm here at Cardinal Mooney."

Spurrier: "I don't like to wear ties. I don't know, I don't think I'm going to watch this stuff. I'll see you in a little while."

Spurrier retrieved his workout clothes from his car and changed in the Cardinal Mooney locker room.

"He goes out there with the Cardinal Mooney baseball team and starts shag-ging flies," McGriff said. "He doesn't see shit for the weight-lifting thing. So the great part of the story is, somehow he's got his car keys, but he stayed out shag-ging flies for so long that he gets locked out from his clothes. He can't get them out. Well, he had a home visit that night. He goes to this boy's home. Shows up, he'd been sweating, because it's May, it's hot. He doesn't have a shirt on. This boy comes home and there's Steve Spurrier sitting on his couch, on a towel, no shirt on, drinking a beer with the guy's dad. And of course, I know Steve, and I'm laughing my brains out the next day when Steve is telling me this story. Then I see somebody else who confirmed the story. Well, I'm working my butt off to sign my guy. I don't sign him. You think Steve signed his guy? He did."

Spurrier's final game as Duke's offensive coordinator was a 23-17 victory over North Carolina that was a work of offensive art.

"[North Carolina] was the No. 1 or 2 defense in the country," Bennett said. "And we blistered them. The things we did offensively were unbelievable. I think Grayson ran for over 100 yards. [Running back Greg] Boone was close by. I think we had over 500 yards total offense, something ridiculous like that. We were 18 of 25 on third down conversions. The things we did in that game." Ben-nett's voice turned wistful. "If Steve would have hung around for my senior year, I may have thrown for over 4,000 yards in one season. I mean that's just the way it was."

12

BANDIT BALL

The United States Football League announced its formation on May 11, 1982, at the 21 Club in New York City. By design, the league would provide a fan-friendly alternative to the NFL that would begin play in the first week of March and conclude with the USFL Championship game in late July.

Franchises were awarded to 12 major markets: New York (New Jersey), Los Angeles, Chicago, Detroit, Boston, Tampa, Oakland, Denver, Washington, Philadelphia, Birmingham and San Diego.

Among the more high-profile owners was John Bassett, who owned the Tampa Bay Bandits and strongly believed spring football could succeed.

"Bassett came to Tampa and said he was bringing in a football team," Tom McEwen said. "And we said 'sure, we'll help you any way we can.' They don't like that kind of thing now, down at [the newspaper]. He came back and said, 'I've got to have a coach. You got anybody you'd recommend?' I said, 'Go check the offensive coordinator at Duke. He said, 'What's his name?' I said, 'His name is Steve Spurrier, just go talk to him.' So Bassett flew up there, talked to him and hired him on the spot."

Jim McVay, who now holds the position of executive director of the Outback Bowl, was the Bandits' director of marketing and remembered Bassett looking for the perfect head coach.

"I really didn't have any input other than John told me one day he was going up to visit with Steve Spurrier at Duke and he asked me, 'What do you know about him?'" McVay said. "I said, 'I know he won the Heisman Trophy. I know he's a very popular guy in Florida. I know he's done amazing things as an assistant from an offensive standpoint. He's young, kind of a charismatic guy.' And

Steve's one of those engaging guys, and of course there were some strong
Florida voices that were encouraging John to consider and look at Steve. Anybody we'd ever talked to spoke highly of his coaching skills. John Bassett didn't
check with me when he made that decision. If he would have asked I would have
said, 'What a great choice.'"

Bassett had a "great feel for people" according to McVay.

"John was one of those guys, and this was truly amazing, he was one of those
guys who could immediately size people up," McVay said. "He was a very bright
guy, very intuitive. He could meet you and talk to you for five minutes and he had
a feel for you. He was a quick study. And he was very selective about who he
would surround himself with. And especially for the key, high-profile position of
the organization, that being the head coach.

"A lot of our teams in the USFL were head-coach driven as opposed to star-
player driven. George Allen, Lee Corso and Mouse Davis all coached teams. A
lot of the guys were big, high-profile guys. John was very selective when looking
for a coach. He took his time. But he got around Spurrier and was just drawn to
him. He was right. That was the absolute perfect decision for our Bandits at that
time. [Spurrier] was a dream for a marketing director. Steve was one of those
unique guys. Not only was he a great football mind, but he also was a huge, high-
profile sports celebrity with a lot of charisma. One of those larger-than-life
figures to a lot of the fans. He brought a real marketing pizzazz around him,
along with great football instincts and skills. Now we had something to sell because we weren't getting all the top players. We had a handful of really good
high-profile players that were going to be beneficial. But the best players were in
the National Football League."

When Bassett announced the hiring of Spurrier to the media, he elaborated
on why he chose him.

"It was close," Bassett said. "Until I found out he has a dog named Bandit.
Of course it helped that he is young [Spurrier was 37]. It helped that he is not
someone who will come here and try to take over the whole franchise as some of
the ex-National Football League coaches are trying to do. It helped that he is
offensively oriented, so we will have an exciting product on the field. It helped
that he has a lasting relationship in this state and in this Tampa area, someone
who would not be a major education project. I knew those things, met him, liked
him even more than I thought I would, and then I found out about his dog, Bandit. Perfect, I said, and so here he is and yet, we have not even signed a contract."

Spurrier resigned his position at Duke on November 21, 1982, and accompanied Bassett to a press conference the next day; ironically, Red Wilson and all
the other Duke assistants were fired on November 22.

"If I could have picked a head job in the United States Football League, it would be the one Mr. Bassett has hired me to do," Spurrier told the *Tampa Tribune*. "You know all the reasons. And practically, just think that we will train and perform here, live here, won't have to train in Florida and return to the franchise city, as will so many teams. And, you know about all the friends we have here."

Spurrier's offense had done a remarkable job at Duke, which prompted the question of why he opted to take his coaching skills to the professional level.

"This was my third season at Duke as an assistant coach," Spurrier said. "You try to do a good job where you are. I didn't intend to make Duke a career. I am proud of what we did.

"[But] I am 37 and felt the need to advance. Jerri and I have always been close to Tampa when we were at Florida, then with the Bucs. The Buc year was tougher on Jerri and the kids than me. The bad thing was we didn't win any games. Had we won two or three it would have been different. We did win one exhibition game and I got my picture on the cover of *Sports Illustrated*. The people treated me decently here. Boos are part of football. If you can't take a little heat and criticism, you ought to be in a different profession. Well, the chance came and I'm grabbing it."

Spurrier had to answer the same question that plagued him throughout his playing and coaching careers: Would he work hard enough to succeed?

"Football is football," Spurrier said. "Only thing I have coached is the offense and my record as an offensive coach is good enough, I think. I will have a defensive coordinator and he will run that side of things. I am aware that there have been times in my career, as a pro player, I had trouble motivating myself, such as when games did not seem to count. Hopefully, I have matured. The important thing here is that I have chosen coaching as my profession. That is it. Life is doing what you want to do and doing it the best you can. I won't get lazy and let an opportunity like this slip away."

Lee McGriff was the first to tell Spurrier about the job, then Bandits player personnel chief, Bugsy Englebert, whom Spurrier had a relationship with from Florida, called Spurrier to feel him out. Englebert first asked Spurrier if he wanted to be the offensive coordinator, next came the question about whether he would be interested in becoming the head coach. Spurrier expressed interest in the job, prompting a visit to Durham from Bassett and Englebert, who brought along partners Don Disney and Maston O'Neal,

"I remember, Mr. Bassett said, 'Hey Steve, we want you,'" Spurrier said. "And I said, 'Hey, I want to come, but can't until the season's over.' He said, 'OK, looks like we have a deal.'

"So I am coming back to Florida and to Tampa in still another role. I am aware I have to prove that I can be a head coach. Fine. One great one, Vince Lombardi, was never a head coach until he went to Green Bay. I have a lot to prove. And I can't do it without an opportunity. I don't need early praise. Mr. Bassett is saying, 'Hey, he has done enough to qualify for this shot.' He's given it to me. Now we'll find out if he was right and if I am right when I say I think I can do it."

Tampa, of course, still had the NFL's Bucs, but they were growing unpopular with the fans.

"The Buccaneers were struggling," McVay said. "There was a strike. The fans were down on the players. Down on the National Football League and here comes this new spring football league where guys were making twenty-five, thirty thousand dollars a year and just wanted to play football. Plus, we did something that was pretty clever, we had a territorial draft.

"We allocated schools close to your franchise so you could get some kids with some name recognition. We had the rights to the kids from Florida, Florida State, Miami, Bethune Cookman, Florida A&M, you know, so we had the rights to all the guys who had a little bit of a name in Florida anyway."

Among those names were former Florida and FSU quarterbacks John Reaves and Jimmy Jordan.

Reaves grew up in Tampa and had always admired Spurrier.

"He and Larry Smith were my heroes," Reaves said. "Larry grew up the next street over from me [in Tampa]. I became a huge Gators fan early on; I don't know why. I'd listen to Gator games on the radio. Otis Boggs [doing the announcing] and I guess reading those Tom McEwen articles. Then Larry went there and I always wanted to go there. And I got the opportunity to go there and play."

Reaves flourished under the tutelage of offensive coordinator Fred Pancoast and the Gators' offense thrived.

"As a sophomore there, we led the nation in passing and set the SEC record in total yards per game," Reaves said. "We set up the run with the pass and all our runs were set up with I-formation movement. It looked like the run to begin with."

Reaves first met Spurrier during a summer when Spurrier was home in Gainesville.

"He was very nice," Reaves said of his first impression. "I had always admired him. And then when he came back [to Florida after the 49ers] he was extremely nice. Then I remember one time during my sophomore year, we broke his passing record for a single season, like in six games. And Steve was quoted as saying in the paper something like 'I knew he was pretty good, but I didn't want him to break my record in six games' or something like that." Reaves laughed. "But it was a nice compliment coming all the way from Frisco."

Reaves graduated in 1971 as a first-team All-America selection, completing his three-year career (freshmen were not eligible to play varsity sports at the time) as Florida's, the SEC's, and the NCAA's all-time leading passer with 7,581 yards. He also established an SEC standard for touchdown passes with 56.

Reaves played in the East-West Shrine Game in San Francisco following his senior year, which led to another meeting with Spurrier.

"The Niners were in the playoffs," Reaves said. "And [Spurrier] got us tickets. My roommate was Ed Marinaro, and he got Ed and me tickets. We went out to dinner one night with Steve and he's always been a cutup. And we're sitting there at dinner with him, and one of the scouts from the Niners was there, who I don't think knew who I was or Marinaro was. And Steve made a comment, 'Yeah, I hear that John Reaves isn't very good.' The scout, sitting right there, said, 'He's looking pretty good to me,' which was good to hear. Even then he liked to have some fun and stir it up a little bit."

Reaves was selected by the Philadelphia Eagles in the first round of the 1972 NFL Draft and played for the Cincinnati Bengals, Minnesota Vikings, and Houston Oilers before signing with the Bandits.

"I had played for the Oilers in '81," Reaves said. "I'd done well. We won the two games I started. I was a free agent after that year and ended up signing with the Bandits. So I guess I was scrambling for a job a little bit. I'd fallen into that backup quarterback syndrome, like a lot of guys who start to bounce around. But I was fortunate to get an offer from the Bandits."

Reaves signed his contract with the Bandits in the summer of 1982, prior to the team's hiring of a coach.

"So when they were going through the process of hiring a coach, they talked about [Spurrier] and Lindy [Infante], who was my freshman coach at Florida and later the running backs coach there," Reaves said.

"I'd watched Steve's career and seen all the numbers he'd put up at Duke. Ben Bennett set the career passing record. They were putting up great numbers there. I thought it was an exciting opportunity. It was a good league. It gave a lot of coaches an opportunity to coach; gave a lot of players a chance to play. And I know that it's often maligned by the old pros, but one thing I heard, 27 of the 44 starters in the Pro Bowl the year after the USFL folded were former USFL players."

Reaves called signing with the Bandits a "chance to come home."

"Tom McEwen had called me about something and said they were going to start a team here for the new league and 'I've been talking to the owner of the team that's going to be here, John Bassett, would you be interested?'" Reaves said. "I said, 'Let them know I would be.' Then I got a call from Bugsy Englebert and I ended up signing with them."

Reaves remembers being idle in the fall of 1982.

"We had a press conference here in the fall, and I remember [actor] Burt Reynolds [a minority owner of the team] was here and Bassett, but Steve hadn't been hired yet," Reaves said. "Then Steve came down right after the [Duke] season. He was great. We had about seven quarterbacks at that time. Myself, Jimmy Jordan, Bob Hewko, Terry Bradshaw's little brother, I forgot his name, there were a bunch of quarterbacks when we started out."

Reaves' friendship with Spurrier didn't get in the way when playing for him.

"Not really, because he was in a position of authority," Reaves said. "And I treated him in that regard. As a matter of fact, I'd say yes sir and no sir to him then. And he'd say, 'What are you doing?' And I'd say, 'You're the head coach now.' I never called him Steve or anything, just 'Coach,' where I had called him 'Steve' before."

The Bandits held three minicamps and it quickly became clear that football under Spurrier would be different.

"You just knew it would be because of the way he installed the offense and the way we were pitching it around," Reaves said.

Nick Pugliese was informed in the winter of 1983 that he would be covering the Bandits for the *Tampa Tribune*.

"They started training right after the Super Bowl," Pugliese said. "I was driving to a Gators basketball game with Richard Lord [the *Tribune's* executive sports editor] and Mick Elliott [another *Tribune* staff writer]. I was the prep editor at the time; I was covering high schools. Tom Ford was going to be the beat writer, but he also was doing motor sports. In the springtime, between Daytona, Sebring and Gator Nationals, [Ford] was going to be busy. So how was he going to cover the Bandits and motor sports? They made it a two-person beat, a cobeat. I was going to the Gators' basketball game and I'll never forget it, I was sitting in the back seat and Richard turned around and asked, 'Would you like to cover the Bandits?' I said yes."

Because Ford was covering motor sports most of the time, Pugliese covered the team by himself much of the time, which meant getting to know Spurrier.

"I'd gone to [college at] Florida," Pugliese said. "I knew he'd won the Heisman and all about his pro career. But I'd never met him. I remember the first time I introduced myself, you could tell he was different. Most coaches have a certain persona. Almost like a Bear Bryant persona; he was like your next door neighbor type of guy.

"I introduced myself at the first Bandits practice and said I'd be covering the team. He loved the *Tribune*, because he loved Tom [McEwen]. And we were really the only paper covering the Bandits. You knew he was going to read everything in the paper."

Spurrier's relationship with the media was looser in those days.

"At practice he let the beat writers catch punts—the beat writers," Pugliese said. "We were standing out there and he says, 'Go on out there and take a few punts.' Three or four of us went out there and started shagging punts. Players were laughing at us.

"During practice he'd let us stand on the sideline and you could talk to players. With the Bucs, you're standing 10 miles away, and rightly so. The Bandits, you'd be talking to coaches and players during practice. It was very loose, very informal, which was kind of fun. You could just tell Spurrier was different. But his coaching? One of the first times I wanted to pick his brain about his offensive philosophy, he made a point that if his system was working right, the play was in place, the quarterback calls the right play, he switches up and calls the right play, everyone does the right thing, the receivers and the line, there should be somebody open and every play should be successful. And I'm thinking, OK, but what about the defense? But in his mind he thinks every play should be successful. That's why he gets frustrated."

Pugliese said the Bandits provided a popular contrast to the Bucs.

"Remember, the Bucs had been good until then," Pugliese said. "They made the playoffs in '81 and '82. The 1983 season [their first season after the Bandits began playing] was the beginning of their end. Jack Thompson became the Bucs' quarterback in 1983 and the team would start going downhill. At the same time, you've got the Bandits with John Bassett and Jim McVay, and they knew the Bucs were ripe for the picking because [the Bucs] treated their fans like crap. [The Bandits] had this attitude that they were going to come in and be people friendly, do all these promotions and giveaways and cheaper tickets. Sometimes free tickets. The NFL wasn't fun. And [the Bandits] did a great job doing that. The real key was hiring Spurrier."

Not only did the Bandits have good marketing and players with name recognition in the area, they got off to a 4-0 start.

"They got the best start of any team," Pugliese said. "And when they started winning early and they were exciting, throwing the ball all over the place, 'Banditball,' all of a sudden they were getting 30, 40,000 people at these games and getting televised nationally. They became the quick story of the USFL."

After posting a 3-0 preseason record, the Bandits and their catchy slogan, "Bandit ball, all the fun the law allows," attracted 42,437 fans to their inaugural regular-season game against the Boston Breakers, March 6, 1983. Spurrier opened up with a no-huddle offense.

"He invented that and I don't care what anybody says, nobody ever opened up the game or ran no-huddle offense in the first half anywhere I had ever seen at that point," Reaves said. "All I can say, in my knowledge, my recollection, I'd never seen anybody open games or run the no-huddle offense in the first half, other than at the two-minute mark. Defenses didn't know how to react [to the no-huddle] because they couldn't make their calls. They had to stay in a base front, a base defense. We'd be shuffling personnel in and out, too, and a lot of those coordinators want to see who is in the game before they make their call.

"Anyway, we opened the season with the no-huddle and marched down the field. Actually I missed a pass on third and short when I should have gotten it and we had to settle for a field goal. The fans went nuts, they'd never seen this. They went absolutely bananas."

Reaves threw 39 times in a 21-17 Bandits win. The lead changed five times before Reaves hit Willie Gillespie for a 33-yard touchdown that put the game away. He also connected on touchdown passes to Ricky Williams and Eric Truvillion.

"If you can show me a team with better passers and catchers than we showed there today, tell me so I can buy a ticket and go see them," Spurrier told the *Tampa Tribune*.

Boston coach Dick Coury knew he'd seen something special.

"Give John Reaves a lot of credit and give Spurrier and John Bassett a lot of credit for giving Reaves the chance to show what he can do," Coury said. "I admire them for what they did and I admire John Reaves. We lost the game, but it was a good one. This league is going to play great football. Maybe Dick Steinberg should see the game films. He might want to recruit some of the players out there today."

Steinberg, who was the personnel chief for the New England Patriots, had looked down his nose at the new league and declared that the new league was subpar and the Bandits resembled a semipro team.

Ever the marketing genius, Bassett countered Steinberg's remarks by challenging the Patriots to a $1 million charity game with the Bandits. Half of the proceeds would be earmarked for charity and the other half would go to the winner.

"I mean it," Bassett told the *Tampa Tribune*.

In addition to the fun atmosphere that included the team mascot, a Bandit who rode a black stallion inside Tampa Stadium, a Hollywood element existed at Bandits games thanks to Reynolds' involvement. Reynolds could not make the opener so he sent Jim Nabors in his place and TV's Gomer Pyle sang the national anthem. Then the game began and the crowd went electric after the Bandits' first drive.

"After that first drive when we had to settle for a fielder, they started that Bandit-Ball cheer where one side of the stadium would yell "Bandits" and the other side would answer with "ball" and it would go back and forth like that,"

Reaves said. "We're throwing the ball all over the field and then we get down, we're marching to put the game away. We've got the ball on their one and [Spurrier] calls a slant. I throw it and it gets batted and a guy picks it off in the end zone and runs 95 yards the other way. Eric Truvillion caught him on the five. So instead of us icing the game, now they're back in it. Then we drove down and I checked to a pattern and hit Willie Gillespie for a winning touchdown. But it was [Spurrier] coaching me up on getting that pre-snap read of coverages and seeing they were in the blitz."

Spurrier, who had gone 0-14 while quarterback for the Bucs, ran toward the locker room a winner for the first time at Tampa Stadium.

"This is the best kind of win," said Spurrier of his team's work. "Boston was better than we thought they would be, and yet, we came from behind to win."

Pugliese called the first game "the most fun I'd ever had at a pro football game."

"You're covering the game, but you see the horse running up and down, there's all these giveaways and promotions and you've got Spurrier throwing the ball all over the place," Pugliese said. "You saw all these things you've never seen before and you're like, 'whoa, this is different.' And, again, this coincided with the Bucs going down, especially in '84 and '85 when the Bucs were really awful. [The Bucs] were one of the worst teams in the league and you had the Bandits throwing the ball all over the place. They got a lot of frustrated Buc fans to come over. They were smart to do it that way. They had the right timing. The 4-0 start was almost like a Camelot. You have this new team, it's 4-0, Burt Reynolds. Nowadays, it's pretty common to see the no huddle, stuff like that. Back then it was something new. You didn't see it."

McVay, who is the son of longtime NFL coach and executive John McVay, was an option quarterback at Dayton University and understands football. Asked to describe the difference between what the Bandits were doing at the time and what the Bucs were doing prompted him to laugh.

"I mean it was totally different," McVay said. "I mean this was a whole different situation. Here we had a wide-open, wild passing attack where Spurrier would start games with onside kicks. Steve was just a very creative guy. He was just ahead of everybody.

"This was a guy who knew how to attack the weaknesses by trading offensive schemes and shifts and flooding zones. A lot of people used to run, run, run, then throw. He'd pass, pass, pass and keep you off balance with a run. He was great at working zones and teaching quarterbacks to throw to spots and back safeties off. He was just ahead of everybody. He knew how to scheme. He was thinking. He'd sit down at his desk and come up with plays then find the right players to make them work. The guy really is exceptionally skilled."

Reaves marveled at how Spurrier's offense developed during his years coaching the Bandits.

"He'd known the San Francisco offense when he came in, which was a good one," Reaves said. "It was the old two-back, tight end, two-wideout set, with a split back passing game, etc. About the biggest thing they'd do was flex the tight end. And he had an excellent play-action system out of the I. Better than anyone I'd ever been involved with. Then, as we went through with the Bandits, he started developing the three and four wideout stuff."

Spurrier interchanged Reaves and Jordan.

"It's funny, Reaves was his starter, but Jordan played a lot, too," Pugliese said. "Spurrier was jacking around quarterbacks even back then. But his offense was the same. He threw the ball all over the place. Although the one thing different back then was he used the tight end a lot more than he does today. The last couple of years coaching the Gators he used the tight end more for blocking than as a pass receiver. But I think he's been using more of the multiple receiver sets than he did with the Bandits. Back then he'd use two or three receivers, he rarely used four."

Spurrier managed to remain loose, which rubbed off on his team.

"He always had his team prepared," Pugliese said. "But they were never up tight. They never went into the game nervous.

"If somebody screwed up, he would criticize them, whether it was Reaves or Jimmy Jordan. He probably was a little easier going back then. He used to have nicknames for all the players. Greg Boone, he was 'Boonie'; Truvillion was 'E.T.'; Jim Fitzpatrick, the wide receiver, was 'Fitzy.' I was 'Nicky.' Everyone had a nickname. I don't think he was quite as critical, but I think he knew his talent was somewhat limited there in the USFL. How many good players did he really have? Most of them didn't make the jump to the NFL."

Spurrier's USFL experience afforded him the much-needed opportunity to emerge as a head coach.

"He determined he needed a quarterback and a running back and a receiver and forget about everybody else," McEwen said. "And he got them. He got Reaves. Gary Anderson. And before Anderson, Carl Franks. And he was smart enough to stay on the offensive side. Anyway, to me, that was the proving ground. He got to be a head coach. And he ran that loose." McEwen laughed. "Shoot, he'd let me go into his coaching meetings. He'd let us go into the locker room before the game. Listen to him. He's the only one I've ever seen let anyone in there before a game. I got enough brains to know when to leave. Anyway, everything was fun, the horse, Reynolds, Spurrier. The whole thing was exciting."

McEwen and Pugliese recounted anecdotes personifying Spurrier's relaxed manner during his USFL days.

The Bandits "were playing a game in London," McEwen said. "And, of course, the *Tribune* isn't going to send me, but I went on the team plane. Bassett took my ass on the plane, Linda [McEwen's wife], too. We all went.

"They were playing the British Open at the same time we were there. So once we got there I flew up to St. Andrews, got me a cab driver who drove me to St. Andrews. I got him a ticket [to the tournament] and he waited on me. On the Saturday, it was the finals, I don't remember when [the Bandits] game was, but Spurrier heard I was going to the Open and said he wanted to go. So Spurrier, Linda, me, and Jimmy Dunn, who was coaching for the Bandits, got on an airplane and flew to Edenborough, called my cab driver, he was off that day, so he was waiting for us. We crowded into one of those little black cabs and drove our ass all the way to St. Andrews. I think it was the first time [Spurrier] had seen St. Andrews. For me, it was just something else to write. It was kind of funny. Spurrier loved it. That was fun. Relaxed. That's Steve."

Pugliese remembered a game the Bandits played against the New Jersey Generals at the Meadowlands.

"My family was from New Jersey," Pugliese said. "Right before the game they came to the hotel to see me, my uncle, my cousin, must have been about ten of them. All of a sudden, these players are in the lobby and [my family] starts getting autographs. [The players] all know me, so they're giving them their autographs. Then Spurrier walks through. My aunt goes, 'You think Steve would sign an autograph?' Right before a game, he's the head coach. I said, 'What the hell.' I pulled him over; he meets everyone, signs autographs, poses for pictures. Shooting the breeze." Pugliese laughed. "It was just very refreshing."

Pugliese attended a party the Spurriers hosted at their house in the Carrollwood section of Tampa.

"He invited all the media over and I'll never forget walking into the door and seeing the Heisman Trophy," Pugliese said. "That was a copy, because he gave his to the University of Florida. But I remember walking over to it and looking at it, and I said to [Spurrier], 'This is very impressive. Not many people have a Heisman Trophy in their foyer.' And he was like, 'Ah, that's a little ole trophy, Jerri made me put it out.'

"The party was very casual. He's almost like nervous. He'll be friendly. But he doesn't really like to shoot the breeze. But Jerri, she's the real social butterfly. I think she makes him more sociable."

Pugliese liked Spurrier but said covering him had its pitfalls.

"I wasn't really that prepared for [Spurrier's] personality back then," Pugliese said. "I didn't know that much about him and it was my first major beat. But I found out real fast that he doesn't like criticism at all. He would actually take on writers at press conferences. If you wrote something in the paper he didn't like, he'd actually single you out. Like 'Ole Nicky there wrote in the *Tribune* today, and I'm not sure I'd agree with that.' Almost embarrass you."

Pugliese and other reporters learned to quote Spurrier accurately, to the word.

"If you wrote that he said 'we hardly threw the ball today' he'd read it and say, 'That's not what I said, I said we barely threw the ball today,'" Pugliese said. "So I started using a recorder, so that the next time he challenged me at a press conference, I could say, 'here you go.'"

"I learned that when a coach attacks, it's not necessarily an attack on me. It's his way of defending his program or doing it for the team. [Former Bucs coach Tony] Dungy would do it a little more subtle. Every coach does it. [Former Bucs coach] Sam Wyche would wait until after the press conference and he'd start screaming at you. Every coach is different."

Spurrier likes to "clear things off his chest" according to Pugliese.

"He probably doesn't remember half the things I'm telling you," Pugliese said. "If I saw him today, he'd shake my hand. I think he's a terrific coach. I don't think there's a better offensive coach in the country. But he does have thin skin. And he does rub people the wrong way because he's brutally honest. But you know what, he wins, that's the bottom line."

The Bandits appeared headed for the playoffs in 1983, but they lost four of their last six games and came up short by one game with an 11-7 record. They topped the league with 4,580 yards passing, but Reaves and Jordan combined to throw 36 interceptions, which took some of the luster from their 26 touchdown passes.

Wideout Danny Buggs finished second among league receivers with 76 catches for 1,146 yards, and Truvillion hauled in 66 for 1,080 yards.

Gary Anderson joined the Bandits in 1984 and was one of the most talented players in the league, rushing for 1,008 yards, scoring 19 touchdowns and catching 66 passes for 682 yards. Reaves had a masterful season, throwing for 4,092 yards and 28 touchdowns. And tight end Marvin Harvey caught 70 passes for 938 yards and provided some added entertainment for the fans.

After making a touchdown catch, Harvey introduced his full-body flip as he ran off the field. Subsequent touchdown catches would see the fans, and Spurrier, pleading for another flip. Harvey always complied.

The Bandits finished the 1984 season at 14-4, which was good enough to reach the playoffs where they lost 36-17 to the Birmingham Stallions. The Bandits had five turnovers in the game.

"We used to draw huge crowds," McVay said. "There were so many big games and fun games that we had, it's tough to remember. We didn't win a championship, but we were always there. Our players used to say we had the 'cream of the crap.' And what that tells you, we weren't spending money."

Reaves called the '84 season the Bandits' high-water mark. The team beat Jim Kelly and the Houston Gamblers in the opener en route to a 3-0 start.

"But even after we were 3-0, my quarterback rating wasn't so high because it was a thing where we'd pass the ball down close a lot, but we'd run it in," Reaves said. "I didn't have a lot of touchdowns to offset some interceptions, so that can kill you on your quarterback rating.

"The press is saying 'Reaves' quarterback rating isn't too high.' Then we go out and play the Denver Gold. And it snowed and they beat us in overtime. We lost 36-30 and I throw an interception they return for a touchdown to beat us. And I made a couple of other flub ups. In the meantime, [the Bandits] signed Wayne Peace to a big, fat contract prior to that season. Jimmy Jordan was still there, too."

Reaves figured a move was going to happen and figured correctly.

"They signed Wayne to that big contract and Steve liked him, so sure enough, I come in on Monday or Tuesday and Steve says, 'We're going to give Wayne a chance,'" Reaves said. "I said 'OK.' I kept my mouth shut, kept working, tried to be supportive. And we played the Birmingham Stallions, who were a very good team with Cliff Stoudt at quarterback and Joe Cribbs at running back.

"Wayne started, but he didn't do too well, and we kind of got drubbed. The next week we went to play the Philadelphia Stars and we're behind in the first quarter 21-0. So Coach Spurrier turns around and says, 'John, get back in there.' I go in and we get hot as a firecracker. And we ended up losing that game 38-31. We're on their one when the game's over. I threw for like 300 yards, completed 28-of-31, something like that. Then we go on a roll and win nine games in a row. And that's the best I've ever played in my life, and it was because of [Spurrier] and maybe getting a little more focused at the opportunity at hand. That's why I think [Florida quarterback Rex] Grossman played so well at the [2002] Orange Bowl after [Spurrier] benched him for that curfew violation. When [Grossman] came in he was on target. When you get benched for whatever, you're sitting there going, 'Hey man, what an opportunity I've blown.' When you get back in there you're going to be different."

Reaves managed to fend off Jordan, as he did Peace, for playing time.

"Jimmy was an outstanding quarterback, threw a beautiful ball," Reaves said. "Thank goodness for me he threw more interceptions than I did. I remember one time we were playing Houston and we were behind like 28-21 to them. Steve was mad, especially at me. And he puts Jimmy in there. Jimmy threw an interception on one play, and the guy returns it and gets hit and fumbles. We get the ball back. Steve calls a pass on the next play and [Jordan] throws another interception. On the Monday meeting he said, [Reaves goes to his Spurrier voice] 'I don't know if I've ever seen a guy throw interceptions on back-to-back plays. That might be a record breaker in history.'"

Jordan was Reaves' road roommate.

"Jimmy J, the 'Pride of the Bay,'" Reaves said with a smile. "He was like Oapie. He'd never had a car, believe it or not, until he came to the Bandits. So he bought this big old gigantic Ford Bronco, one of those big fat ones. So we're having a team barbecue out there with the wives and children, it was during the season, Steve would have them once in a while. Around the old Banditball House on the [Hillsborough Community College] campus. And they had this retention pond out there. Some of us had SUVs. I had one of those little Jeep Cherokees, four-wheel drive. So someone says, 'All right, let's see who can go through the retention pond.'

"James Ramey had like a Jeep Cherokee. We all line up [with their vehicles]. I go through first and I go *vroom* through this retention pond and out on the other side. Then James Ramey goes through with his Cherokee, *vroom*, out on the other side. Then comes Jimmy with his brand new Bronco. Four-wheel drive and he goes in there and gets stuck and I've never seen Spurrier laugh so hard. Fred Nordgren had this big old Jeep thing that had a hook on it and they had to tow [Jordan] out of there. It was hilarious. I don't think I've seen Spurrier laugh so hard."

The 1984 season saw the USFL add the Houston Gamblers, Memphis Showboats, Pittsburgh Maulers, San Antonio Gunslingers, Oklahoma Outlaws and Jacksonville Bulls.

Pepper Rodgers coached the Showboats, which allowed Spurrier to go up against his mentor. Rodgers laughed recalling those games.

"When we played Tampa the first time when I was at Memphis, I told my players on Monday before the game that if we scored first in this game, we'd go for an onside kick," Rodgers said. "I knew Steve wouldn't be able to stand being behind so they'd fly back so fast that we could kick the ball and do an onside kick. So we scored first and did an onside kick. We'd practiced the thing all week. We recover it and we go on and score, win the ball game. I think we were slight underdogs. They'd been in the league a year and we were an expansion team.

"Then we go down to Tampa to play there. On the opening kickoff I'm sitting there getting ready for the Bandits to kickoff and one of my coaches is standing down there and young Stevie Spurrier [Spurrier's son] says, 'My daddy's got a real surprise for Coach Rodgers.' And he runs up to me and says they're going to try an onside kick. So I start yelling to my players, 'Onside kick! Onside kick!' And goddamn, it bounces up in the air, about 10 bodies flying, and they get it and they score. Then they lined up to kickoff and the little boy comes back and says they're going to try it again. And Steve, he had to one up me, he had to do two of them. No way was he going to let me top him."

Rodgers clearly enjoyed competing against Spurrier.

"Steve is dangerous, but I always considered myself dangerous, too," Rodgers said. "I have great respect for Steve as a coach because he's smart as a whip in football and he's not afraid to take a chance. His players are well schooled and they play hard. And he does things on offense that a lot of people try to do, but can't do."

Spurrier had grown confident enough in his coaching abilities to know when he'd finished his work, too.

"Several times I would cover the [Bandits] practice, went back [to the press work area] and did some notes, or whatever I'd do," Pugliese said. "Then I'd be in my car driving home and all of a sudden a car whizzed by me and it was Spurrier."

Added McEwen: "Steve has the right perspective. Unlike, say, John McKay, if he doesn't have anything else to do, Steve goes home. John would just sit there and everybody was scared to leave. I think [Spurrier] kind of revolutionized all that. You do your work, then you go home, play golf or whatever."

Along with the new teams in the USFL came new owners, such as real estate tycoon Donald Trump, who became the new owner of the New Jersey Generals, and a feeling that the league might actually be able to go toe-to-toe with the NFL. The league's emphasis on keeping player salaries down, which allowed teams to be more fan friendly, went the opposite direction of those who believed the league could succeed in competing with the NFL. Marquee players began to get signed, changing the competitive balance of the league as well as challenging some teams to be able to keep their finances in order.

The Bandits' final campaign in 1985 was tinged with sadness. Bassett fought a battle with cancer and, prior to the start of the season, the USFL announced plans to switch to a fall schedule in 1986 and to file an antitrust lawsuit for approximately $1.32 billion against the NFL. In anticipation of the league's coming fall schedule, several teams relocated to avoid direct competition with NFL teams in their cities. After winning the 1984 USFL Championship, the Philadelphia Stars moved to Baltimore, which did not have an NFL team; the Colts had moved to Indianapolis by then. The Michigan Panthers merged with the Oakland Invaders, the Pittsburgh Maulers folded, the New Orleans Breakers moved to Portland, Oregon (the team's third city in three years of existence), the Chicago Blitz folded, the Oklahoma Outlaws and Arizona Wranglers merged to form the Arizona Outlaws and the Washington Federals moved to Orlando where they became the Renegades.

The 1985 season "was the low point for the Bandits," Reaves said. "John Bassett got sick and you saw a man of 47 years old go from a handsome, vibrant, powerful marketing genius to losing his hair and his head swelling up, then the league folding. And two or three weeks we didn't get paid. That was the low point."

The Bandits finished with a 10-8 mark, which got them into the playoffs where they lost to the Oakland Invaders 30-27.

"We beat all the champs, we just couldn't hang with them toward the end because of injuries and we didn't have the depth," Reaves said. "Spurrier never made an excuse or anything. 'Let's coach 'em up and go play ball.'"

Pugliese agreed.

"The Bandits stayed within their budget," Pugliese said. "Other teams were going wild. Outside of Gary Anderson, who was a heckuva player, they didn't spend much money. I mean, Bassett wasn't Donald Trump. I don't think [Spurrier] really worried about it. He was like, 'Give me the players and we'll win with these players.' But I think the reality was he didn't have as much talent. You could buy better players."

Bassett remained true to the league's initial mission statement.

"John Bassett was adamant about staying within the financial parameters when some of these other owners were spending money like crazy," McVay said. "Steve did more with the talent that we had than anyone else. And we operated under much tighter financial parameters than all these other guys that were in the league, which ultimately was the end of the league. They outspent their income. You can only do that so long before guys say, 'Why are we doing this?'"

Pugliese believes Spurrier did feel some pressure during the Bandits' final season, which led to a memorable confrontation between the two.

"That last year, when things were kind of falling apart, Bassett had cancer, the future of the league was shaky, there was a lot of pressure anyway," Pugliese said. "Eric Truvillion was thinking about jumping to the NFL, like a lot of the other players, because the league was going to die. So he got hurt, it wasn't that serious of an injury, but he was afraid of really getting hurt worse so he couldn't go to the NFL. So he kind of dogged it.

"He could play, but he wasn't playing. So the Bandits kept saying, 'Oh, no, he's really hurt, he's on the injured list, not playing this week.' Finally somebody said, 'He's not really hurt, he's just dogging it.' So I wrote a story about it. I talked to Truvillion. He told me everything. He said, 'I'm mad at Spurrier, this league is going nowhere' and that he pretty much wanted out of Tampa. [Truvillion] was my source and I wrote it. I made one big mistake, I never got ahold of Spurrier. It was pretty late at night and I didn't call Spurrier."

Spurrier wasn't pleased when the story came out the next morning in the *Tampa Tribune.*

"The next day, Spurrier basically calls a press conference to say this story's wrong and basically the *Tribune's* lying," Pugliese said. "I was pretty embarrassed. I should have called him and said, 'Look, we're going to run this story tomorrow on Truvillion and get his side of it.' And I didn't do it. We were both learning at the time. Think about it. He'd never been a head coach anywhere before and he always got pretty good publicity."

A documentary on the Bandits' final season eventually vindicated Pugliese.

"Turns out, that movie, it shows a great scene in which Truvillion is in the training room and one of the players, Chuck Pitcock, says, 'E.T., what's the matter? You're dogging it. We know you can play.' I mean, basically, that was going on," Pugliese said. "So my story was right. Spurrier got mad because, A, he was embarrassed in print. And, B, I should have gone through him. I should have."

In addition to proving he could be a terrific head coach while with the Bandits, Spurrier had shown maturity, effectively putting to rest the idea he was a cutup incapable of the necessary seriousness to coach.

"I was pleased to see it," Reaves said. "He made playing so much fun. Another thing he does is take the pressure off. There's enough pressure already, but when he alleviates the pressure by making you feel comfortable and confident, to me that can make a world of difference. And a guy can play better and his natural talents can come out. But Steve likes to cut up, and I like to cut up, too. Now some guys couldn't take it. But he'd crack something on me and I'd just laugh. It was funny.

"I remember one time we were playing the Orlando Renegades and I couldn't hit the broad side of a barn in this game. And Steve, as he likes to do sometimes, was calling a pass on every down. So I miss another one and I come off on third down and he starts that stare at me. And he says, 'You looked so dog gone good in practice and you can't hit a thing in the game.' So I told him, 'Well, why don't you call a running play now and then and maybe I would.' And he said, 'Well, if you don't like it, I'll put someone else in there.' And I'm like, 'Let's go.' But we would go like that back and forth. Sometimes if I had a bad play, I'd know he was over there steaming ready to get me and I'd go down there to the other end of the bench when I came off the field where there were about 90 guys in between us so he couldn't get to me. By the time he got to me he was a little cooled off."

Spurrier also impressed Reaves with his teaching methods.

"Because of his teaching ability, he makes it so clear," Reaves said. "I had a lot of coaches and it was almost like they wanted to hide the answers from you. The best teachers, the ones that got the most out of you, were the ones who didn't do that. And that's the way Steve was. You knew the answers. He wanted you to know exactly what was going on. Be completely clear about the situation. Have no indecision, and then, like he said so many times, 'Hey, I can't call them perfect every time. If I call a bad play, I want you to check out of it.'"

Bassett died following the 1985 season.

"The new [Bandits] owner, Lee Scarfone, had come in and there was a lawsuit with the National Football League," McVay said. "There was a chance that some teams might [gain entry into the NFL]. You know, John Bassett wanted to stay in the spring. Donald Trump wanted to move to the fall. So that last year when we were going through all the lawsuits and stuff, they let go everyone in the office except for me, Steve and Tim Ruskell. Tim is director of personnel for the Bucs now."

With little else to do but wait, McVay and Spurrier became closer through various activities.

"We played a lot of tennis, and we jogged," McVay said. "Spurrier talked me into running in that Gasparilla race [15K race in Tampa]. We were in good shape. [The Bandits] kept us because the fact things might swing back around."

McVay chuckled when asked if he got in touch with Spurrier's competitive side during this period.

"I played basketball with him, tennis, golf, he really is a great athlete," McVay said. "He could play tennis, he could shoot hoops. I remember playing basketball over at [Hillsborough Community College]. This is a guy who just had some really, really, really strong athletic skills. I mean, he wasn't a blazer, a 4.2 40 guy. In basketball he could shoot; good jump shot. He played tennis, he'd position the ball. The guy really is a good athlete. He's not just some thinker."

A month before the USFL was to begin its first fall season in 1986, the USFL won its lawsuit against the NFL. Unfortunately for the USFL, it was awarded just $1 in damages, which were trebled to $3. Weighted down by $160 million of debt, the league folded before ever attempting to go directly against the NFL.

"I was actually on the [Bandits'] payroll for four years even though the league only played three," McVay said. "But I think we were all greatly disappointed. I think we all had to get up and going. We all loved being in Tampa. This was a very successful operation, but the league collapsed around us. And there were some very talented people. Steve was one of those guys. So it was time, when the league went down, that we all had to go to work. Steve ends up at Duke."

13

BACK TO DURHAM

I ronically, when the USFL folded no NFL teams courted Spurrier to become
their head coach, not even the Bucs once they had a vacancy.

"As long as [Hugh] Culverhouse was the owner, the Bucs weren't going to
show interest [in Spurrier]," Nick Pugliese said. "It was a pride thing, because
the Bandits used to tweak them so bad that they weren't going to stoop that low
to get the Bandits' coach, which was a big mistake on their part. Obviously
[John] McKay didn't like him. Most times, [Spurrier] liked to tweak the Bucs,
that they weren't that good."

During Spurrier's period of unemployment, friends like Graham McKeel
grew concerned about his future.

"The one time I really got concerned was when Steve was finished with the
Bandits and the Bucs needed a coach," McKeel said. "Steve was here in Tampa.
And he didn't get the job. That's when I got concerned about Steve. I was say-
ing, 'This is not good.'"

Tommy Shannon painted a less-than-glowing portrait of his friend during
this period.

"Here's a guy who wasn't making a whole lot of money," Shannon said. "He
was sitting down here with the Bandits. The Bandits were floundering. The
USFL was in a lawsuit. He wasn't even out getting a job when they were in the
lawsuit because he was getting paid by [the Bandits]. So here's a guy who,
frankly, was playing gin five mornings a week over at our country club, Avila. Not
the most conscientious of go-out-and-attack-the-world people in the world.

"I remember John McKay telling [Spurrier] one time, 'Don't stay out of
coaching too long. They might forget who you are.' Jokingly, he said it, you

know. Then the Duke job came along. And the Duke job came along because of [Duke athletic director] Tom Butters, who is a very close friend of Jerri's and Steve's."

Spurrier interviewed with LSU to fill the position vacated by Bill Arnsparger, who left to take the University of Florida athletic director job, but the job didn't become his. Then Steve Sloan left his post as the Duke coach to become the athletic director at his alma mater, Alabama, leaving Butters and Duke looking for a replacement. Butters knew who he wanted to fill the spot.

"I received several calls from football coaches asking who I would hire," Butters said. "I remember I told Andy Geiger, who at that time was [athletic director] at Stanford, and who is presently [athletic director] at Ohio State, I said, 'There is only one guy and that's Steve Spurrier.'"

Butters had strong logic for wanting Spurrier.

"I felt he could move the football as well as anybody I had ever seen," Butters said. "Duke, certainly in the last four decades, we've had our difficulties [being competitive in football] and for us to match up man for man, 70 deep with other schools simply wasn't possible. One of the reasons Steve was hired was I thought he had that edge. With a limited number of football players, and if he could keep them healthy, he could simply outscore them.

"Keep in mind I'm a great believer in defense. When I hired Mike Krzyzewski [as the Duke basketball coach], I thought at 34 years of age he was the best defensive coach in America and I thought he was going to work out. We simply didn't have the luxury of being able to build a program based on defense at Duke University in football."

Butters recalled Spurrier being interviewed by the search committee.

"We sat in a meeting with [Spurrier] and every person on that search committee asked every imaginable question and I didn't say anything," Butters said. "And finally at the end of the interview I said, 'Steve, what's the most exciting thing about football to you?' And he looked up and said, 'Coach, there isn't any question about that. It's when the other team punts. When they punt, all we've got to do is catch it. And then we've got that ball for four downs.' Now that in itself tells you everything you need to know about the way Steve Spurrier thinks. It is so indicative of his personality as a football coach."

Duke hired Spurrier for the job in January 1987. Even today Butters marvels at Spurrier being available.

"I was amazed at the time that [other teams] didn't recognize that this was one of the more gifted offensive minds in modern-day football," Butters said. "It was clear to me, and I would have assumed it would have been far more clear to those in the game who are far more astute than I."

Spurrier, who had coached with NFL legend Norm Van Brocklin on Rodgers' staff at Georgia Tech, reported that Van Brocklin advised him not to take the Duke job, but Spurrier told him, "That's a great idea. But nobody else is askin' me. This is my only chance."

Spurrier had his own beliefs for why suitors weren't knocking down the door to have him coach their teams.

"My reputation of playin' golf and not workin' hard, I guess, was not what they were lookin' for," he told *The Sporting News*.

Butters wasn't worried about Spurrier's work ethic.

"Some football coaches believe you win by outworking everyone else," Butters said. "Steve was never that way. Isn't now and won't be at Washington. He's got a feel for the game, a knack for the game that doesn't require of him or his assistants the 15-hour day that so many of them tend to do. He could simply move the football. He just had that ability to move it."

Duke never has been an easy school to produce a football winner. When Spurrier took the job, the average SAT score for Duke freshmen was 1,320. Understanding the reality of the school, Spurrier wouldn't even consider a proposition 48 athlete for his program.

"Those kids wouldn't be interested in Duke anyway," Spurrier said.

Typical of the Head Ball Coach, he put a positive spin on his situation.

"We're a different school, but we have our advantages," Spurrier told the *Tampa Tribune*. "Duke is ranked third in the country academically, behind only Stanford and Cal-Berkeley. A scholarship here is worth $17,500 a year. And I can show a kid where the average Duke grad has an income of $76,000 a year.

"We have a chance to get the top student athletes in the country. We have a lot to offer them. But it's reasonable for a kid to say he wants to play on a winner and go to a bowl game. We haven't been able to show them that in the past."

Spurrier was realistic about the situation as well.

"The way I look at it, we can find our place somewhere in the middle of the conference, and some years we can do a lot better than that," he said. "We're never going to have the players in the numbers that Clemson has, but we can recruit the top players in the country that have the academic background—and there are a lot more players like that than some people would have you believe. We've got to get faster and bigger and quicker."

Spurrier sounded excited as the 1987 season approached.

"It's a great challenge to come to Duke, basically because they haven't had a lot of success here in football," Spurrier told *USA Today*. "Anything over six wins would be the first time in 25 years. . . . The administration here wants an exciting, competitive program. We're not content to just be average or mediocre and wait for the basketball season to begin.

"I'm looking forward to coaching a game again. I haven't coached a game in two years now, since June 30, 1985, so I'm certainly not suffering from burnout."

Spurrier's enthusiasm could be heard from his players as well. Quarterback Steve Slayden addressed what differences Duke fans would see in the 1987 team that they had not seen under previous coach Steve Sloan.

"Going deep, that's the most significant thing about what we're doing different with the offense this year," Slayden told the *Charlotte Observer.* "I don't want to say anything about how things were [under Sloan], but we never really threw deep in the past.

"We've got more options and more different types of plays, and I've got more freedom, but more responsibility to choose a better play from our audible options. We'll do a lot of things. We're having a lot of fun. Coach Spurrier loves it. He'd be out there playing if he could."

Added receiver Doug Green: "Our offense didn't do much in some games last year. I think a lot of it was because defenses knew we were going to run almost all our routes the same way and to the middle of the field. And we hardly ever adjusted at halftime. . . .

"Now, Coach has got everybody involved, which should free up more receivers. We've got more corner and sideline routes, we have the freedom of getting into them whichever way that's the best at the time, and we're throwing more down the field. It's going to be exciting, but it might take some time to get it all down."

Duke alumni were excited about the prospect of what Spurrier might do with their program, but they were skeptical, seeing the inevitable before it happened: Spurrier's success would lead him elsewhere.

Spurrier shrugged off the hypothetical scenario.

"I hope to stay here a long time," he said. "To my knowledge there's never been a football coach leave Duke for another coaching job. They've either gotten fired or retired. So it's silly to worry about something that hasn't happened in the whole history of the school."

The 1987 Duke slogan was "Air Ball '87" and Spurrier did nothing to disappoint.

Shortly after getting hired, Spurrier began to solicit Duke alumni for an innovative first play of the season and he drew a nice response.

"We got some good ideas to draw from," Spurrier said. "I guarantee you it'll be a wild opening play. I've got it in mind. I've already seen it work in a game, just not with these players. We've got to do it. We've promised all our people. I just hope we're not on our own 2-yard line."

The first play of the season turned out to be as promised: an end sweep, re-verse to the flanker and a pitch back to the quarterback, who ended the play with a pass to the halfback who had started the sweep.

David Alfonso attended the game as a sports reporter for the *Tampa Tribune*.

That first play "was something bizarre, something different," Alfonso said. "I can't recall whether it was successful or not, but they scored on that first drive and beat them handily."

Air Ball '87 was underway with Duke's 41-6 defeat of Colgate on September 5, 1987. Alfonso said the writing already was on the wall about Spurrier's future.

"As an alumni [of the University of Florida] and somebody in the business, [Spurrier's coming back to Florida] seemed like the obvious thing to happen at some point," Alfonso said. "Galen Hall was the interim coach [at Florida] no matter what. Everybody knew that wasn't going to be long-term, especially with Spurrier available. He was the most obvious choice and the perfect choice for the job. Maybe some people saw it coming before others. Once he started coaching at college and had success at Duke, I think everybody realized what the inevitable was."

Duke followed the Colgate victory with wins over Northwestern, 31-16, and Vanderbilt, 35-31, before losing 42-17 to Virginia on the road. Spurrier's first year ended with a disappointing 5-6 mark, but the Blue Devils had lost close ones to Clemson (17-10), Maryland (23-22), Wake Forrest (30-27) and North Carolina State (47-45). Football in the Atlantic Coast Conference had just begun to get interesting. Duke led the ACC in total offense and scoring; 54 percent of the team's offensive plays were passes.

Tom McEwen laughed recalling what Spurrier had told him about his defensive philosophy at Duke.

"He told me 'I told our defensive coordinator to blitz every down, that's the only way we can do it, blitz,'" McEwen said. "Apparently it worked. What he managed to do at Duke was one of the great achievements of all time."

Despite having most of his starters back and quarterback Anthony Dilweg and receiver Clarkston Hines, the Blue Devils were penciled in by football forecasters to finish last in the ACC in 1988. The Blue Devils then proceeded to beat Northwestern and The Citadel to get off to a 2-0 start heading into the big game on their schedule, Tennessee at Knoxville.

Tennessee had been installed as 13-point favorites in the game that would be played in front of 90,000 hostile fans at Neyland Stadium.

"I remember seeing [Spurrier] around the hotel before the game," Alfonso said. "What I recall was how surprised I was that he was as loose and entertaining as he seemed to be with people who were guests and not part of the inner circle. [Spurrier] still had time for friends. He wasn't ruffled, or anxious, or whatever. He was how he always is, confident and under control. I don't think there are many head coaches who do stuff like that. It's hard to tell when he's nervous."

Spurrier told friends from Tampa, "This game is a big, big step for us. We've got a good chance to win it."

Which is exactly what Duke did, taking a 31-7 lead in the third quarter en route to a 31-26 victory.

"That was an amazing thing to see Duke pound Tennessee like that in Neyland Stadium," Alfonso said. "That was a funny thing. Obviously the crowd couldn't believe it. It was a real quiet, big place.

"It was like smoke and mirrors. The passing game, if you're good with it you can be competitive against a physically superior team. As far as Spurrier was concerned, passing was the only way to win that game. He wasn't interested in making it close, he wanted to win the game. And that's the kind of game where Duke could have just as easily gotten beat 50-20 as winning."

The difference in athleticism between the two schools was obvious.

"Tennessee had a wideout who was an Olympic sprinter," Butters said. "There was a marked difference in the quality of the players. [Duke winning] was a remarkable demonstration of good, sound, offensive football."

The '88 team finished 7-3-1 and did not go to a bowl, but Spurrier was voted the ACC's Coach of the Year. Butters recalled an incident from the '88 season, which was one of the few times he had a disciplinary problem with Spurrier.

The ACC had instituted a gag rule in regard to coaches making negative comments about the officiating.

"We go to North Carolina State and we're winning the ballgame by three points," Butters said. "Nine seconds left, fourth down, State's got the ball deep in our territory. They throw a pass incomplete. Our ball. Our game. Three or four seconds go by. Late flag comes. I turn to my wife and tell her I'd meet her at the car. I tell her, 'I've got to get to the room before [Spurrier] talks to the press.' While I'm going down, they've got one more play. They kick a field goal, tie the game and we go from there. I get to the clubhouse, I have to run down four flights of stairs, and I get there too late. He's already lambasted [the officials].

"Next day I get a call from Gene Corrigan, who was then the ACC commissioner. He says, 'Tom, I heard about what Steve said about the officials.' I said, 'You don't have to worry [about investigating it], it's true, I heard it.'"

Corrigan told Butters he would not allow Spurrier to coach in the next week's game against North Carolina.

"I said, 'That's fine, you come down and tell him, I want to be present,'" Butters said. "So he does and Spurrier goes off. And all he can say is, 'I have a right. Coach, I've got a right to say what I said.' I said, 'I think you have a right, the Constitution of the United States thinks you have a right, the world thinks you have a right. But it isn't what you have a right to do, it's what you have a responsibility not to do.' And he looked at me and he nodded his head and he said, 'You know, Coach, you're right.' He never complained. It was an amazing turnaround for him."

Butter's called the athletic director and football coach relationship between Spurrier and him "very smooth sailing."

"I respected him not only as a coach, but as a man," Butters said. "Steve's different than most, he's a very, very complicated individual. I'd rather play golf with him than anyone I can think of simply because he takes that four-hour period of time to grind it out more seriously than anybody I know. So consequently, it's more fun to beat him than anybody I know. He was a pleasure to work with and I can say nothing but good things about him."

Having added close to 10-years of coaching experience to his resume, Spurrier seemed to understand he owned a talent as an offensive mind and he knew how to harness that talent. Particularly when it came to working with the quarterbacks, such as John Brantley at Florida, Mike Kelly at Georgia Tech, Ben Bennett during Spurrier's first stint at Duke, John Reaves and Jimmy Jordan with the Bandits, and Steve Slayden and Anthony Dilweg during his second stint at Duke.

"What I've tried to do is research how I can really help that quarterback when he drops back to pass," Spurrier said. "Tell him what I wasn't told as a pro to help him be successful. Most of the things I've learned have been since I've been coaching."

While Spurrier had created a method of teaching that could be applied to all of his quarterbacks, he was smart enough to leave room for treating each as an individual.

"I coached each of [the quarterbacks] about alike," Spurrier said. "But each was a different personality."

Spurrier had grown comfortable enough with his coaching to confront his detractors, whom did not believe he had the right work ethic to be a head coach.

"I think all of the people here know what's expected of them and I just don't think you have to be real formal and serious all the time," Spurrier said in the 1989 *ACC Football Yearbook* published by Four Corners Press. "There's plenty of time to be real serious and there are other times when you don't have to be all that serious. I really believe you can be successful without trying to take yourself so serious.

"We're not a coaching staff that goes around bragging that we're going to out-work everybody else. I'm sure you've seen coaches who tell the alumni and newspaper people and everybody else how hard they're going to work, and no-body is going to outwork them. It's funny, I've seen so many coaches not win who say that. I don't know what that means. Everybody works hard here, but the main thing is the quality of hours you put in, not the total hours."

Duke assistant Barry Wilson, who had been with Spurrier at Georgia Tech and with the Bandits, said Spurrier "keeps all the elements of our football team, his personal life and us as a staff in some reasonable perspective."

"Even during times you might consider a very busy season for football, we somehow manage to encompass a loose atmosphere and yet work hard enough to be successful," Wilson said.

In line with his ability to keep those around him loose, Spurrier's practices often had an element of fun. During a spring practice in which heavy rains forced a move inside, Spurrier staged a dunking contest inside the Card Gymnasium. Dunking basketballs gave way to field-goal kicking contests during the regular season.

Spurrier sounded at the time like he might stay at Duke for a long time, even though rumors of him going to Stanford, California and LSU began to circulate.

"When I got into coaching, I felt like this was something I enjoy and I felt I had a chance to be pretty good at it," Spurrier said. "Our coaches don't feel this is a job. We don't say we're going to work in the morning; we say we're going to Duke. You hear people say, 'This beats working for a living.' That's my attitude. This coaching beats working for a living. This is fun. We can't wait to get to the office, can't wait to coach the players, can't wait to go to the meetings, can't wait to get in the games."

No doubt, much of Spurrier's enthusiasm stemmed from being at Duke and dealing with the intelligent kids he dealt with on a daily basis.

"The way Duke runs its athletic program is as close to perfect as you can be in college athletics," Spurrier said. "There is a nice balance here between being a student and an athlete. We don't have athletic dorms. The players eat in cafe-terias on campus. They live with other students and go to class with other stu-dents. They enjoy college life as well as big-time college athletics.

"We don't worry about players going to class or flunking out—we graduate 90 percent of our players. We seldom have to worry about players getting into trouble. The reasons the players are here are to earn a degree and be the best football players they can along the way."

Even Jerri Spurrier gave off signals the couple was happy where they were and might remain in Durham.

"We used to say one good thing about coaching is you never have to clean your house, you just move," Jerri said. "Well, I'm not going to say we'll never move again. But for the first time in our life we feel very comfortable."

While Duke and Spurrier were upsetting the order of the ACC, Florida was struggling.

Florida had found success under Coach Charlie Pell in the early 1980s, but in October 1984, an NCAA investigation uncovered 59 violations by the Florida football program and the Gators received three years probation. Pell was fired three games into the 1984 season and Galen Hall took over, leading the Gators to their first-ever SEC championship. But the conference denied the Gators their title as well as a trip to the Sugar Bowl. After Hall's Gators won nine games in 1985, they didn't win more than seven in the following four seasons.

Thanks to Spurrier's 1988 success, the rumors began to circulate that Hall would be fired to make way for Spurrier's glorious return to Florida. According to McEwen, only Arnsparger, the Florida athletic director, stood in the way of such a return.

"By [1988] we all knew that it was just a matter of time until Spurrier returned [to Florida]," McEwen said, noting Arnsparger stood in the way of the move.

A meeting of University of Florida alumni was held at the Tampa Hyatt following the 1988 season.

"There were about 50 people there," McEwen said. "Everybody was saying, 'fire Galen Hall and hire Steve.'"

McKeel remembered the meeting as well.

"I was there, Tom was there, and a lot of other Florida people," McKeel said. "We were trying to get Arnsparger to make a move. We said, 'There needs to be a change. This is going nowhere.' Arnsparger said, basically, 'Bullshit, I'm in charge, [Hall] is staying.' And we were at an all-time low as far as football goes at Florida. [Spurrier's coming to Florida] should have happened a year before it did."

McEwen tried to rationalize with Arnsparger.

"I don't know what was the matter with Arnsparger," McEwen said. "I asked him, 'Bill, they've got Jimmy Johnson at Miami and Bobby Bowden's at Florida State, when they go see a recruit, would you rather have Galen Hall or Steve Spurrier talk to someone? Pretty good question, wasn't it?'"

Shannon, who is one of the more successful Florida alumni in the state, said he never attended such a meeting.

"I would never have tried to get Galen Hall fired," Shannon said. "I liked Galen. I thought he was a helluva coach. He was an asset to the university. He came through for us when we needed some help. I thought Steve was the right progression following him up. But I never would try to make a power play. Most guys are full of baloney if they think they can influence those programs. We had a very strong president back in those days, Marshall Criser. I don't think Graham McKeel or Tom McEwen or anybody was going to influence him."

John Reaves later coached with Arnsparger at Cornell and did not detect any animosity toward Spurrier.

"Arnsparger didn't have anything but great things to say about Spurrier," Reaves said. "I'd heard some people say [Arnsparger didn't like Spurrier]. As far as my being around Bill, he never had anything but great admiration for Steve."

Hall guided the Gators for part of the 1989 season before resigning after the NCAA uncovered more violations. Adding steam to the problem was the fact the Gators were still on probation at the time of the infractions, creating an "overlap" situation. The Gators had a 5-1 record when Gary Darnell took over on an interim basis, finishing the season with a 7-5 record. Rumors about Spurrier returning to Florida intensified.

"I'm not looking to leave," Spurrier said during the 1989 season. "I had a couple of chances to interview for jobs last year and told those athletic directors to find somebody else."

However, when the idea of being able to compete at a higher level was mentioned, Spurrier didn't give Duke a resounding vote of confidence about his future.

"Coaching at a program like Duke is a challenge, but then again I don't have to worry about it until it comes up," Spurrier said. "If somebody wants to offer me a deal you can't refuse, then I'll have to worry about all those things then."

Butters knew Spurrier would have to go if offered the job.

"Steve had an itch that needed to be scratched," Butters said. "And going back to his alma mater, who should have hired him long before they hired him, was simply that itch. He had to get back to it."

With his alma mater in disarray, Spurrier accomplished what might be his finest coaching feat to date by leading the Blue Devils to an 8-3 record and the school's first ACC football title in 24 years, which earned Duke a bid to the All-American Bowl.

Typical of Spurrier, he managed to ruffle a few feathers along the way.

Duke finished off the 1989 regular season with a 41-0 shellacking of rival North Carolina on November 18 at Chapel Hill. Spurrier led the team back onto the field afterward to pose for a photograph underneath the scoreboard to commemorate the event. North Carolina coach Mack Brown was not happy when told of the scene that had taken place on his field. Brown's ire was relayed to

Spurrier, who constantly referred to Brown as "Mr. Football." Spurrier addressed Brown's anger in the fashion that has cast him as cocky and arrogant: "I don't see why [he's mad]. I've won more games on that field than he has."

"That was a helluva party," said Dan Clark, a red-shirt freshman on the '89 Blue Devils. "We locked in our ACC championship [with the win]. Had we lost, we would have finished second. So it was a big game. Everybody was ecstatic. It was like, we're going to go out on the field, we're making a point. We beat UNC at home, full stadium and it doesn't happen that often."

Butters laughed about the aftermath of the North Carolina rout.

"I'll never forgive Steve for that," Butters said. "Let me tell you, I love him like a brother. But he didn't have to face [North Carolina] again. We have not beaten them since then."

Arnsparger called Butters the day after the North Carolina game to ask for permission to talk to Spurrier about the Gators' coaching job. Arnsparger then called Spurrier.

"I don't have any idea when we'll get together," Arnsparger told the *Tampa Tribune*. "I talked to him and he probably needs to study his schedule and anticipate when we can get together. . . . The timetable [for finding a coach] depends upon finding the person we'd like to have, then finding out when that person is available."

Spurrier went to Gainesville the following Saturday and met with interim Florida president Robert Bryan and Arnsparger.

"We had a nice conversation for an hour or two," Spurrier said. "That was about it. It went fine. We're planning to meet again in a week to two weeks."

Rumors about Spurrier heading to other destinations also began to circulate. Included in the rumors were NFL jobs with the Atlanta Falcons, New York Jets and Phoenix Cardinals.

"I'm still the Duke coach and I'm still free to talk to other schools and other teams," Spurrier said. "Nothing has changed. [The Falcons rumor came up] two or three weeks ago. I didn't know that one was back up again. I think it was Phoenix last week and the Jets the week before."

Duke wouldn't stand in Spurrier's way to go elsewhere, but they were prepared to offer him a package said to be competitive with any coach in the country to have him stay.

"Steve has to speak for himself, but I think he's happy at Duke," Butters said. "It's an unusual school for a lot of us and a great spot to work at."

Others at Duke didn't feel Spurrier would return to his alma mater.

"Steve is the kind of guy who wouldn't like to answer to 15 or 20 Bull Gators [the school's top supporters] every week," said Bob Harris, the radio voice of

Duke football and basketball in an article appearing in the *Atlanta Journal-Constitution*. "He has told me several times that he could stay here without the pressure and coach ball the way he likes to coach it."

Rumors of other teams' interest gained momentum when team officials from Atlanta and Phoenix visited Durham to speak with Spurrier in early December. Spurrier seemed most interested in the Phoenix post.

Because "it's in the NFL, in a warm-weather city and they play in a good stadium to throw the football," Spurrier said. "Those are things that would interest anybody. I'm listening. I'm listening to any team that wants to talk to me."

Florida offered Spurrier the job and he accepted. Spurrier told his players he would be taking the job prior to the Blue Devils' 49-21 loss to Texas Tech in the All-American Bowl. Later he regretted telling them.

"I told the team the day before [the bowl game] that I wasn't going to be their coach anymore," Spurrier said. "I love you guys and all that stuff. So we get to the game and one guy was loafing down the field on the kickoff cover and I yelled at him, 'Get on down there!' And he looked at me sort of funny. Like, 'You're not my coach any more, don't yell at me, you're not even my coach.'"

Butters didn't stand in Spurrier's way, but he did offer a word of caution to Spurrier about the arena into which he was about to set foot.

Butters "told me, 'Steve, if you take that Florida job, they're going to write things about you that you didn't do,'" Spurrier said. "'They're going to quote you about things you didn't say.' And I said, 'Wait a minute, that's never happened to me. I've coached with the Bandits. I've coached at Duke.' He said, 'You haven't ever coached at Florida. That's a different job.'"

Butters further told Spurrier, "If you go 8-3 here, you'll be an icon. If you go 8-3 at Florida, you'll be looking for a job in four years." But even Butters wanted him to take the job.

"As much as I wanted him to stay at Duke, he needed to fulfill that itch," Butters said. "He needed to scratch it.

"I'm pleased with the way things turned out for the University of Florida and Steve Spurrier. It could have turned out better for Duke, but I certainly had no regrets that he was here and we had him for that short amount of time. And I have no regrets about him leaving. I think it was the right decision."

Butters contrasted Spurrier's decision with that of Krzyzewski, who turned down an offer by the Boston Celtics to coach in the NBA.

"So here were two separate coaches who made decisions that were 180 degrees different, and I think they both made the right decisions," Butters said.

Spurrier called Arnsparger the day after Duke lost its bowl game, December 30, 1989, at 6:05 P.M. to officially accept the position as head coach of the Gators.

Spurrier's contract was for five years and worth in excess of $500,000 annually. The contract included clauses allowing him to renegotiate after two years and one allowing for extensions if Florida was placed on probation.

"After talking with [Arnsparger], I realized this is the place I wanted to be ... the place I should be," Spurrier told the Associated Press. "Our family loves Gainesville, the atmosphere here. This is where I belong."

14

GOING HOME

Tom McEwen summed up the feelings of Spurrier's friends when he said of Spurrier gaining the Florida job, "We were all so happy. Everybody wanted Steve Spurrier to succeed. Except those he rubs the wrong way. And he rubs people the wrong way only because he's honest, I think. He's an honest guy. Totally honest and I don't think he'll ever change."

John Reaves had an idea of what kind of whipping Spurrier was about to hand out to SEC teams.

"When he got the job, I was quoted as saying, 'This was just what the doctor ordered,'" Reaves said. "SEC teams were all running the ball and playing cover three all day. You knew he was going to take the thing by storm. And he did."

Spurrier arrived to the campus of his alma mater understanding he needed to get the program back on track after it had suffered through the embarrassment of two separate scandals.

"I told the guys first of all that this is a very good team," Spurrier said. "Of course, I'm telling the Redskins the same thing right now. We've got a good team, now we've just got to go out and improve it and play like a good team.

"First thing we needed to do at Florida was eliminate all excuses for why we couldn't be successful. Florida had for some reason built up a lot of bad excuses for why Florida could not win the SEC. We should not be playing Auburn and Georgia back-to-back. They're too good, we can't beat both of them back-to-back. Can't beat Georgia in Jacksonville. Florida's got too many opponents, everybody hates Florida. FSU, all the schools up there, hate Florida, because we're the biggest school in the SEC and blah, blah, blah. So we need to eliminate all of that. And we did."

Spurrier came up with his "four-point plan," which called for the following measures to be taken to return the program to greatness:

- Find and sign players who would excel on the field as well as the classroom.
- Return Miami to Florida's annual schedule.
- Change the playing surface of Florida Field from artificial turf to natural grass.
- Build strong relationships with high school coaches and administrators.

"My commitment is to try to make Florida football the best in the state," Spurrier said. "Right now we are No. 3. There is no doubt about it."

Gator players bought into Spurrier immediately.

Kirk Kirkpatrick chose to attend Florida after being nationally recruited by the likes of Notre Dame, Florida State, Clemson, Georgia and UCLA as a senior out of Brandon High School, just east of Tampa city limits.

"I really wanted to be a Gator," Kirkpatrick said. "Thinking back on it, I probably made a poor decision going there, individually, specifically football related because Florida didn't pass to the tight end. I don't know what made me think they would all of a sudden start going to the tight end by me going there, but I just wanted to be a Gator and that was a big thing."

Evaluating his abilities, Kirkpatrick called himself "an undersized 220-pound tight end."

"Which is not the best scenario in a Galen Hall–style offense," Kirkpatrick said. "You know, he came from Oklahoma from the wishbone days more or less. He coached Billy Sims and all of those guys. Galen, from what I know, is a very nice guy. I played for him for three and a half years. But I don't think I had a close relationship with him at all. Not that I don't like Galen. He just wasn't very close to me. He never got close with any of the players, I didn't think.

"I can honestly say I had a much closer relationship with Coach Spurrier. I don't really know why. But I think Coach Spurrier was much more of a player's coach at the beginning. I think he probably had a lot more fun during the first few years than he did at the end."

Kirkpatrick's mentality prior to Spurrier's arrival was to simply get his final year out of the way.

"Yeah, you know, I blocked for Emmitt [Smith], I think I was second on the team in catches my junior year," Kirkpatrick said. "But it wasn't anything. I think it was 18 catches. So it was pretty much block for Emmitt, catch two or three passes a game and be happy."

Offense as Kirkpatrick and his teammates knew it was about to change. So was the team mindset.

"I remember, [Spurrier] got the job on New Year's Eve," Kirkpatrick said. "I was excited about it because I knew [in Spurrier's offense] they threw to the tight end a bunch. That was right up my alley. I think the quarterbacks were pretty excited, too. The only one who wasn't excited was Emmitt Smith. I don't think he wanted to be in a passing-type offense where he wasn't featured, and rightly so."

Kirkpatrick's first impression of Spurrier was of a coach who was organized but laid back.

"He met with us the first week of January of 1990," Kirkpatrick said. "He came in really fired up. I had never met him before.

"He came in there with a swagger and the attitude that, 'Hey, we're the University of Florida, we have the best athletes, the best facilities, there's nothing we don't have. Why can't we beat Auburn? Why can't we beat Alabama? Why can't we beat Georgia? What do they have on us? I mean, you guys are better athletes, why can't we beat them?' That's what we really needed."

Kirkpatrick said the speech appealed to the team's sense of logic.

"Because before it was always like, 'Oh my gosh, we're at Florida and we've got to play Auburn and Georgia.' And when you look back on it, why were we sweating out people from Birmingham, or Augusta, Georgia, who played high school up there?" Kirkpatrick said. "For some reason we would get all worked up and lose to Auburn or Georgia, and I mean, it was a joke. We had the best high school athletes in the nation at our school. [Spurrier] just gave us confidence. Why not us? Why not now? 'You guys are great athletes, we're going to bring a system in here. There's no reason we can't beat those teams.'"

Smith had just finished his junior season and was named a consensus first-team All-America selection and the SEC Player of the Year by league coaches. At that time he had rushed for 3,928 yards during his college career, the top total in school history and fifth all-time in the SEC; he held 58 school records.

"I wasn't worried about [Smith going to the pros]," Kirkpatrick said. "I was just happy we were going to be throwing the ball. Emmitt was fantastic. I don't mean to say anything negative about Emmitt, because he was the total team player. But he was so good that you almost have to focus your offense around him for the fact it's different than basketball. You know, Michael Jordan can dish the ball around and stuff like that. But in football, he was the offense. And why would you not have the offense built around him? It's not a knock on Emmitt. Emmitt's a great guy, a great player and a great teammate. But it almost made us one dimensional."

Spurrier responded with indifference to the question of whether Smith should turn pro.

"He didn't care," Kirkpatrick said. "Steve Spurrier is Steve Spurrier. You know, he didn't get that impressed with anybody. I don't think that's a bad thing. He was like, 'Well, if Emmitt wants to go, we're just going to roll along.' He's not going to let one person stand in his way, good or bad. He wanted to have Emmitt and he wanted to coach Emmitt, and he said that, but when Emmitt said he was going pro, [Spurrier] didn't try to stop him. He said, 'Hey, that's his prerogative, that's his life. If he wants to do that, good for him. He's been a good Gator. Go and get it, Emmitt. And that's the way he was, which was the right way to handle it."

Smith opted to skip his senior season and enter the NFL draft where the Dallas Cowboys selected him in the first round and he has gone on to have a tremendous career.

"Probably worked out best for everyone," Spurrier said. "Emmitt was ready to go pro. He'd had a wonderful career. And it gave Errict Rhett a chance. We really didn't have any real big stars going into that season. . . . I'm sure Emmitt would have been fine. We still would have won a championship with him. But sometimes it's the time to go pro and sometimes to stay. Probably for Emmitt, right then it was best to go pro."

And the way things turned out, it appeared Smith's decision to move on was best for the Gators as well.

Kirkpatrick noticed a lot of changes heading into the first spring practice under Spurrier.

"I remember, I was doing a little more running, because before, Galen always had a big weight-lifting regimen," Kirkpatrick said. "I remember there were things in the dining hall, where before, we had fairly fattening foods, Spurrier was into lean foods.

"Galen's pregame meals were usually steak and eggs." Kirkpatrick laughed. "That was 1989. Spurrier came back and we started eating pasta and chicken breasts, something light. I remember the meals [when Hall was coach] on the night before games. We would have these huge meals. Prime rib, very, very heavy. Then make the biggest ice cream sundae you can possibly make. [Spurrier] got rid of all that. He had fresh fruit, chicken and pasta. And that was pretty much it. When you think about it, it's like, wow, how could the previous coaching staff not have seen that. You know, I probably shouldn't say that, I just don't think the previous coaching staff had the vision Spurrier had. When you look back on it, they were fairly clueless."

While many felt the talent level was down at Florida when Spurrier arrived, David Alfonso remembered what Spurrier thought after viewing his new players during the early part of spring practice.

"He said, 'Shoot, there's some pretty good talent around here,'" Alfonso said. "We didn't have anything like this at Duke and managed to win a few games.' He was pretty happy about his talent upgrade, even though it wasn't anywhere near what it needed to be to achieve what he wanted to achieve."

Spurrier told a story about having a lunch with Alfred A. McKethan, a big Florida booster, whom the school's baseball field is named after, and discussing the talent level prior to his first season as the Gators' head coach.

McKethan "was in town and we had lunch one day with the president of Gator boosters, John James, at a downtown restaurant," Spurrier said. "And Mr. McKethan said, 'We're not expecting too much out of you these first couple of years, but after that we think we're supposed to be good at football here at Florida.'

"I said, 'Mr. McKethan, we're going to be good the first two years. Now that third year, I don't know who is going to play.' Because recruiting was really down. I said, 'We've got a heckuva team this year and next year. We've got juniors and seniors. We've got plenty of ballplayers. We're going to be good this year.' He looked at me sort of funny, you know how most coaches say, 'Give me three or four years.' I said, 'We've got a team that last year was third in the nation in total defense and we've got eight starters coming back. And we've got guys who can run and catch. Ernie Mills, Terence Barber, Kirk Kirkpatrick, Tre Everett. We've got to find us a quarterback, but we're going to find somebody who can throw it.' We found Shane Matthews. I inherited about as good a team as really any we had at Florida."

Spurrier's playbook was different than what Kirkpatrick expected.

"I'd seen so many playbooks during my time at Florida," Kirkpatrick said. "We had four different offensive coordinators in my first four years. And they all had much more complex playbooks than Spurrier's. And that's what's surprising is that people always think Spurrier's offense is so complex. Spurrier's got all the plays, but they're all based on his master plan. I had an easier time assimilating Spurrier's offense than anyone else's."

Kirkpatrick believes part of Spurrier's success is his ability to simplify.

"It's an easy offense to learn," Kirkpatrick said. "He requires a more cerebral type athlete than other people for the fact that the plays are simpler, but on the other hand, there are so many different branches to them. If you can assimilate that, it makes it much easier."

Kirkpatrick elaborated by saying the receivers are reading coverages when they are running their routes.

"It's basically cover two or cover three," Kirkpatrick said. "Cover two, you're running a different route and cover three you're running another route. You're moving on the go a little bit, but he blows the doors off of any offensive coordinator I've ever been around."

In contrast to the image Spurrier portrays from the sideline in which he looks tighter than a balled fist, Kirkpatrick said Spurrier knows how to make a team relax. The atmosphere at the team's first spring practice under Spurrier was totally different than what the Gators were used to experiencing.

"I just remember it being a lot more fun," Kirkpatrick said. "It was a much more relaxing atmosphere."

This atmosphere carried through right through the regular season.

"I remember our first game," Kirkpatrick said. "We played Oklahoma State, it was Spurrier's first game. Before [when Hall was the coach] you have to understand, the way the Gators were before, you talk about just nerve-racking, gut wrenching. The coaches were so uptight between Galen and the training staff and the equipment staff; they were always just so nervous about the game. You'd have butterflies and you'd be just sick to your stomach about this. They were so strict that if you were laughing on the team bus on game day, didn't have your game face on, they'd get after you. I mean they really would. I remember thinking when I was a freshman or sophomore if you got caught smiling you might get benched. I mean it was that bad. They were that uptight. And that's why the Gators sucked. We were so uptight about everything.

"And I remember the first game [with Spurrier as coach] against Oklahoma State and I don't know if this is a fact, I swear I remember [Spurrier] doing this. He was definitely swimming in the pool. [Quarterback] Shane Matthews and I were walking to our pregame meal. I think our game was around 3:30 and it was about noon or 11:30, and we're walking to the pregame meal at the hotel, the Holiday Inn West in Gainesville, and Shane and I are walking. And I swear Spurrier's in the pool with a couple of other coaches hanging out. . . . He was that relaxed is what I'm saying. I remember him looking over at us and saying, 'Shane, Kirk, you ready for a big game?' And we're like, 'Yeah, Coach.' Then he's like, 'All right, we're going to have some fun today. We're going to toss it around.' And I remember that atmosphere. And it made you so loose and confident because you were prepared. You knew your assignments. You were in good shape. But you were also having fun."

Reaves joined Spurrier's staff prior to the 1990 season as the tight ends' coach; he also assisted with the coaching of the quarterbacks.

Spurrier "actually talked to me about joining him up there at Duke," Reaves said. "But the position only paid $20,000. I'm like, 'Dang Coach, I've got a mortgage, kids, I don't know if I can afford that. Thanks anyway.' So I was in real estate [in Tampa] and it was going real well. Then in '86, they did the tax reform, real estate went way down, got to be hard to make a living in real estate. Plus, my first passion was always coaching. So I wrote him a letter in '89 and told him if he got the Florida job or a pro job, whatever, I'd appreciate it if he kept me in mind. And sure enough, he got the Florida job. He called and hired me to be a coach."

Reaves remembered the pool scene Kirkpatrick recounted.

Spurrier "used to like to run on Saturday morning before the game," Reaves said. "We'd take a run down and around about a three-mile loop, thirty-minute run then hop in the pool. But it wasn't like we were lounging out there getting rays. It was take a run and get in the pool."

Reaves had no recollection of Spurrier drinking a beer, but he does remember the relaxed atmosphere.

"Steve was the same way with the Bandits," Reaves said. "There's enough pressure already. You know, give me a break and let me play. The way he is, I think he understands that."

Spurrier's black and white approach is the same on and off the field. Reaves said Spurrier will let you know what he's thinking. When combined with Spurrier's competitive nature, this can lead to some interesting situations.

Reaves has played golf with Spurrier in the past, but laughs and says, "He won't play with me too much because I'm not any good. You can't play with him too long if you can't shoot close to par."

Reaves remembered a golf outing Spurrier arranged for the coaching staff.

"He'd do those from time to time," Reaves said. "We'd all put $20 in the pot and he had this points thing based on handicap. So whoever won at the end of the day got the pot. There was a low net and a low gross winner."

Reaves stressed the outings took place in the off-season, noting Spurrier put away his clubs on August 1 and didn't pull them out again until football and recruiting seasons were finished.

"So we're out playing Golden Ocala, which is a nice course," Reaves said. "He'd get us out on some nice courses. [Golden Ocala] had holes there that are replicas of famous golf holes around the country. Including one that's like the par three at the Masters that goes over the little lake with the bridge. We come up to that one and he pulls out a 7-iron or whatever, and pops it right up there on the green. So I pull out whatever I'm hitting and hit it in the pond right before the green. Steve's kind of impatient as we all know, so he takes his cart back there on the other side. I drop and hit my second shot over the green and it lands in a sand trap up on top of the green that's kind of angled down. The whole green angles down to that pond and I'm like, 'Oh lord.' So I drive up there and he's still tapping his foot because he can't putt yet. I got to whack out of that trap and I go down to the other side of the green, you know, off the green. I three putt or four putt then I pull the pin and he two-putts for par. So when we're going to the next tee box he goes, 'Whadya have Johnny?' And I go, 'Seven, Coach.' And he says, 'It was an eight, wasn't it?'" Reaves laughed. "He counted every stroke. I thought I could cheat him out of one, he counted every one."

Critical to any football team is the quarterback, and Spurrier's teams have not been an exception. However, while Spurrier always seems to find the right guy to run his offense, the quarterback he chooses to be his starter is not always the guy everybody expects.

"He wants the guys who make the decisions," said Chris Harry, who covered the Gators from 1990 to 1999 for the *Tampa Tribune* and *Orlando Sentinel*.

When Spurrier arrived, Shane Matthews was fifth on the Gators' depth chart. Kyle Morris and Donald Douglas were among those ahead of Matthews entering the first spring game under Spurrier.

Spurrier's "first spring game they were re-doing Florida Field, so they were playing [the game] in Jacksonville," Harry said. "I think there were like 40,000 people there and he had this little quarterback derby going on. Kyle Morris was his first-string quarterback, he threw four interceptions. Shane Matthews threw three touchdowns and no interceptions. All of a sudden, boom, he's the starting quarterback."

Spurrier historically has looked for one qualifier that separates his quarterback candidates.

"[Spurrier] wants someone who can make the right decisions [at quarterback]," Kirkpatrick said. "And that's the key thing. I can't imagine how good Spurrier's offense would be if he got a quarterback who had an absolutely rocket arm, somebody like [Drew] Bledsoe."

Kirkpatrick thought about his statement a moment and seemed to realize that even Bledsoe might not be the right guy for Spurrier's offense.

"But he needs somebody cerebral, who can make the right decisions," Kirkpatrick said. "All of the quarterbacks who have done really well for him have been smart people."

Matthews thrived under Spurrier, winning back-to-back SEC Player of the Year honors and finishing fifth in the 1992 Heisman voting.

Spurrier instilled confidence in his players.

"At first look at the team, I was probably one of the players you'd figure who had some confidence," Kirkpatrick said. "But in reality I really didn't because I didn't have any success at the collegiate level, really. I mean, I was a starter and caught a few passes, but it was nothing great. But he instilled a great deal of confidence. And he said right during spring practice, 'Kirk, you're as good a receiving tight end as I've ever coached,' something like that. That really got me excited, gave me confidence."

Reaves spent five years on Spurrier's staff and still marvels at how he ran his practices and guided his staff.

"Most coaches script on a sheet of paper every play that's going to be run at practice," Reaves said. "During this drill we're going to do this, blah, blah, blah, all the way through practice a script sheet. [Steve] doesn't script practice. He's got his list of ball plays and goes out there and wings it."

Execution is Spurrier's pet peeve, which paints the portrait of a perfectionist. Yet Spurrier continued to coach without working his staff ragged.

"He didn't want you to be in there watching film to all hours of the night," Reaves said. "He respected your time with your family. Thursday night you had to be out of there right after practice. He didn't want you in there; he wanted you home with your family. And Friday wasn't so grueling. He didn't want us to sit up there and pontificate like a lot of coaches who like to get up there and give their oratory."

Lee McGriff said that while some consider Spurrier lazy for the hours he keeps, the normal rules of judgment should not be applied to him.

"What you've got to know about Steve is he coaches with creativity," McGriff said. "Most coaches coach with discipline and work. Like a general, calculation, motivation, organization. Steve's like an artist. And I don't know anybody like him. He may be playing golf, but I promise you while he's playing golf, those wheels are turning. He's freeing his spirit."

Spurrier's first game as head coach came against Oklahoma State on September 8, 1990, and his "Fun and Gun" offense made an immediate impact.

"When they opened up with Oklahoma State, the first game, and there he was, spreading the field, and they went up the field in about four or five plays into the end zone, there it began," McGriff said. "That was just such a telling time. He came out firing with no hesitation. No respect. No concern. Just, here we go. This is what we do."

Spurrier's friends were emotional when Florida destroyed Oklahoma State 50-7.

"It was extremely special," Tommy Shannon said. "We have one of those outdoor boxes [at Ben Hill Griffin Stadium], they call them vomitories, where people walk underneath you. Coincidentally, Jerri Spurrier picked her seats to be exactly on that row, even with us, about 10 seats down. And Jerri gets there early every game and she's got her daughters with her and her son-in-laws. What I do remember is Jerri came down and was standing with us when they said, 'Here come the Gators!' And my wife and I were standing side-by-side and Jerri was standing right in front of me, and we watched Steve run onto that field for the first time and every one of us were crying like babies."

The Associated Press ranked Florida No. 24 after the rout of Oklahoma State; they would never miss another AP poll for the remainder of Spurrier's tenure as the Gators' coach. The next week the Gators went to Tuscaloosa and beat Alabama 17-13 and moved to No. 19 in the AP poll.

The Alabama win "was a big deal," Harry said. "They had this momentum and everything. Spurrier will tell you that was one of the biggest wins of his career because it was his first SEC win."

Then the penalties for the NCAA infractions came down days later and the ruling made Florida ineligible to compete for the SEC title.

Harry said Spurrier was crestfallen and recalled how he asked the media to follow him to an area in the bleachers where he addressed them.

"He had that look," Harry said. "He told us how it was unfair. Went on this rant about playing Clemson every year at Duke and he never complained. 'But I'm complaining about this. This isn't fair for these seniors.' He had no problems with scholarships or anything like that. He had a problem with the fact they would not be recognized as champions if they won the SEC. That was an injustice to the seniors. Nobody on the team had anything to do [with the infractions]."

Today Spurrier continues to call the news of the penalty "disappointing."

"We'd just beaten Alabama in a big, huge game, which, when I look back, might have been the biggest game early to help us go on to win all those championships, to beat Alabama in 1990," Spurrier said. "But after that I told the guys, 'If we win the SEC, I'll guarantee you I'll always include you in all those other SEC championships we're going to win in the future.' And they looked at me and said, 'We know Coach Spurrier and these guys are going to keep winning 'em, so we may as well get one, too, let's go get it.' That's what I told them, I said, 'I'll always include you.' And I always have."

Florida went to 3-0 after dumping Furman 27-3 then defeated Mississippi State in Gainesville and progressed to the No. 10 spot in the AP poll heading into their game with LSU on October 6 in Gainesville. After beating LSU 34-8, the Gators were off to a 5-0 start for only the third time since 1976, and they went to No. 9 in the polls.

Kirkpatrick credited Spurrier for a proactive coaching approach in which Spurrier worked more on what his team was doing than spending time worrying about what the other team would be doing.

"I remember there would be practices where we'd throw against air a lot of times," Kirkpatrick said. "We'd just run our plays against no scout team defense, nobody. Just to get our timing down and routes right. You know, he gets pissed off if you run a yard too far before you make your break, or a half yard short. Little things like that. He wants you to know exactly where 10 yards or 12 yards, exactly where your break is. And if you go a half a yard too far he gets pissed off."

Despite the attention to details, Spurrier's practices were not marathons.

"I heard rumors Charley Pell's practices would be three and a half, four hours," Kirkpatrick said. "And tons of contact. Galen wasn't much better. Galen did pretty much the same thing, long practices, lots of hitting. [Spurrier's] practices were an hour and 45 minutes. We didn't do that much hitting. But we were probably just as hard hitting as any of the other teams. He just has a unique approach that works for him. I don't know if it works for everybody, but it works for him. We hit just as well. We tackled just as well. We were as hard-nosed as everybody else. It's just a different type of style. And now that I've gotten older, I've realized, I really don't want to criticize the old coaching staff, but there were a lot of just boneheaded old-time ideas that needed refreshing."

Spurrier himself concedes his ideas on coaching are different.

"I read something once that I think is so true: If you want to be successful, you have to do it the way everybody does it and do it a lot better—or you have to do it differently," Spurrier said in a 1997 *Sports Illustrated* article. "I can't out-work anybody, and I can't coach the off-tackle play better than anybody else. So I figured I'd try to coach some different ball plays, and instead of poor-mouthing my team, I'd try to build it up to the point where the players think, Coach believes we're pretty good; by golly, let's go prove it."

Such a philosophy dawned on Spurrier while at Duke.

"Obviously, coaching at Duke University, for us to win games and continue being a coach, I had to do it differently," Spurrier said. "And we had to do it differently than, say, the coaches at Clemson and North Carolina and Maryland. So we had to have a little different offense and a different way of doing things. And hopefully that would give us a chance to be successful because our talent level certainly wasn't quite at the level of those other teams."

Long hours are not a prerequisite for Spurrier.

"I don't work as long hours, but I do believe the hours I'm working at football I get as much done as those guys that take twice as many hours," Spurrier said. "I think they waste a lot of time sitting around, shooting the bull, maybe watching the same tape over and over again. They want to watch it eight or 10 times. So I'm not hung up on how many hours you work. My thing is what you do when you're with your players and coaching them.

"John Wooden [famed UCLA basketball coach] said your most important time is when you're with your players. I think, if you look back in college, at Florida, I was probably with our players more than any head coach was with his players in the country. I don't know how any coach could have been with them any more."

Thoughts of an undefeated season in Spurrier's first year back ended in Knoxville on October 13 when Tennessee whipped the Gators 45-3.

Kirkpatrick remembers the game as one of the few times Spurrier got on him for his performance.

"Well, I'm not trying to brag on myself, but I did drop only one pass during my career at Florida, a touchdown against Tennessee [in the 1990 game] that I just flat out dropped," Kirkpatrick said. "It was a corner route and it would have been like a 30-yard touchdown and the score at the time was like 7-0 Tennessee. It would have tied the score. . . . I should have definitely caught the pass.

"[Spurrier] didn't jump on me. He just wanted to make sure I wasn't giving him an excuse. He said, 'What happened here? What did you do wrong? Was the light in your eyes?' And I was like, 'No Coach, I just dropped it. I didn't concentrate on looking the ball in. Maybe I was too concerned with getting my feet in, but I just flat out dropped it.' And he was like, 'Are you sure the lights weren't in your eyes?' I said, 'No, I just flat out dropped it.' I think I gained a little bit of respect from him. I sort of knew what he was doing. He was fishing around for an excuse and I didn't want to give him an excuse just for the fact he doesn't like excuses."

Spurrier had often said about the outcomes of games, "I've found once they're over, they've over. The most important game in your whole life is the game that's coming up next."

Despite the disappointment of the Tennessee loss, Spurrier moved on to the next opponent.

"We were favored, I think, in that Tennessee game," Kirkpatrick said. "But [despite the outcome] I don't remember [Spurrier] being too pissed off about it. His thing was just to regroup."

Florida followed the Tennessee loss with a 59-0 win over Akron and a 48-7 defeat of No. 4 Auburn.

In addition to beating Auburn, Spurrier further irritated Tigers fans in 1990 with his mouth. When Spurrier learned about a campus fire in an Auburn dorm, where some books were burned, he chirped: "The real tragedy was that 15 hadn't been colored yet."

Georgia was Florida's next opponent.

"I remember before the season we wanted to win the SEC and we wanted to beat Auburn and Georgia, which had been our nemesis for so long," Kirkpatrick said before remembering Spurrier's words before taking the field against Georgia. "He said, 'We should beat them. We should beat them by a bunch. Let's take care of business.' We believed him and had a pretty good result."

The Gators embarrassed Georgia 38-7 giving them an 8-1 record and moving them to No. 6 in the AP poll.

Florida then beat Kentucky, coached by Bill Curry, 47-15.

Spurrier would have his way with Curry-coached teams in future years, often running up the score. To Curry's credit he managed to look at Spurrier and the beatings objectively when asked if coaches hated Spurrier for said antics.

"I don't know if he's unpopular among coaches," Curry told *The Sporting News*. "If he is, it's probably because coaches don't like getting beat."

Spurrier's sideline antics already were drawing notice. Spurrier would throw his visor or look as though he were going ballistic on a player. Kirkpatrick said pictures don't always tell an accurate story.

"I don't know of too many people who are the offensive coach, the offensive coordinator and the play caller," Kirkpatrick said. "He calls everything. He calls every offensive play that goes in there. I mean, he wears his emotions on his sleeve. He's trying to make the call and reading the defense from the sideline, which is a terribly hard thing to do. It's hard to see the coverage and the formation and things like that. He's seeing it all. I guess from years of practice. He's that involved in the game. And he gets disgusted when the quarterback checks off to a play that he shouldn't check off to. That's when you see him going nuts is when the quarterback is checking off to something or he's not checking off to something. That drives him nuts, and that's usually when he's going bananas."

Norm Carlson also believes the depiction of Spurrier gathered from his sideline antics is inaccurate.

"A national image has been created that's not really him," Carlson said. "He's involved in everything, so he is demonstrative and he is into the game. Plus, being the offensive coordinator, he's handling personnel there. So he's not going to be like the stoic coach at most colleges who stands on the sidelines with his arms folded. Then he wore a visor. And the first year or two, he threw it a lot."

Carlson said this prompted the networks to station a camera across from him trained to capture his image the entire game.

"And *Sports Illustrated* in particular, because I've had one of their pho-tographers tell me this, they would take one of their photographers with a big lens, stand on the east sidelines and all he did was snap pictures of Steve Spurrier," Carlson said. "That's three hours of pictures of him. If you're any-body that's working at their job, if you sat there and took pictures of him all day long you would catch some shots that aren't necessarily typical, but things happen when you're under pressure and into the game. So what they would run would be the angry, demonstrating something, doing something, which helped create this image that he's a madman, out of control or some-thing."

Florida's final game of the '90 season was a 45-30 loss to Florida State in Tal-lahassee.

Despite having a record that would have won the SEC title and earned the Gators a berth in the Sugar Bowl, Florida was not eligible.

Being champions on the field and not being recognized stayed under Spurrier's skin.

"I've never seen Steve so mad as when they didn't let us have that SEC cham-pionship," Reaves said. "And he's still mad. He's still mad about it to this day when they took that SEC championship away from us based on an alleged, they never proved it, an alleged child support payment."

During Spurrier's farewell press conference after his resignation as Gators coach, Spurrier spoke about his first Gators team.

"I always go back to that 1990 team, our first team here," Spurrier said. "Galen Hall left a very talented team, a very talented team in '90. That team still has not gotten the recognition that they deserved."

Spurrier added he hoped the Gators would one day recognize that the '90 team was an SEC Champion, even if the SEC did not allow it to happen.

"They won it just as much as any of the others," Spurrier said. "And to tell me a child support payment four years prior is the reason they were not called champions is wrong. And I'll always think it's wrong. Not a lot of people around here agree with me, but we're all entitled to our opinion and that '90 team will be recognized here, hopefully, some day."

According to NCAA findings in 1987–88, Coach Galen Hall gave a player, Jarvis Williams, $360.40 to pay for overdue child support.

Despite not officially winning the SEC in 1990, the 1990 Gators brought a new standard to the school. Matthews led the SEC in passing, completing 229 passes in 378 attempts for 23 touchdowns and 2,952 yards. Kirkpatrick led the SEC in receiving with 55 catches and seven touchdowns. Both were All-SEC selections.

"That year [1990] changed the mindset of the Florida fans because we spanked Auburn and Georgia pretty good back-to-back," Carlson said. "That's one reason why Steve holds the '90 team in such high esteem because they set the tone."

While the 1990 team set the tone, Spurrier's 1991 team tore down long-standing walls for the Gators.

The Gators took a No. 6 AP ranking into the 1991 season and looked worthy from the outset, thumping San Jose State 59-21. Spurrier offered up some lip service prior to the Gators' next game against Alabama when he said the Gators would beat the Crimson Tide by at least 30 points. Matthews threw three touchdowns and Alabama's offense never got the ball inside the Florida 25 as the Gators took a 35-0 victory for their first-ever victory against Alabama in seven tries at Gainesville.

"The '91 team was our first conference champion," Spurrier said. "The first conference game was Alabama [at Florida]. We got ahead of them a bunch, beat 'em 35-0. But anyway, I got a letter from a Gator fan after the game that said, 'Coach, you need to calm down on the sideline. You're too stressful. You're too emotional. You need to calm down a bit. Head coaches don't act like you do. I'm afraid you're going to burn out too fast if you keep sort of ranting and raving and so forth on the sideline.' So I read the letter and said, 'Maybe this guy has a point here. Maybe I can be successful and act like all those other coaches do. Be under control let the assistants do the yelling and so forth.' So the next week I tried to do that. I was very calm through practice, very calm on the road trip, very calm on the sideline. And we went up to Syracuse and played like a bunch of zombies. Got our butts kicked 38-21 I think. So I came back home and apologized to the players. I said, 'Fellas, that style might work for some people, but it doesn't work for us. It doesn't work for me.' That's the only way that I think I have a chance to be effective is to coach like my personality. Coaching is a very individual profession in that you've got to do it your way. And there's all kinds of ways to do it just like anything. It's the only way it works for me. So I think my players understand that when I'm yelling at 'em. I'm yelling at everbody and I'm also trying to praise them every opportunity I get. And that's my style of coaching."

After the Syracuse loss, the Gators ran the table.

First they took care of Mississippi State in a road game in Orlando. The Bulldogs had figured they would make more money playing in Orlando than Starkville, Miss., so they sold the game. Florida won 29-7 and Mississippi State did indeed make more money thanks to the pro-Gators crowd at the Citrus Bowl.

The Gators beat LSU 16-0 at Baton Rouge then avenged the previous year's loss to Tennessee by defeating the Vols 35-18 in Gainesville. Wins over Northern Illinois (41-10), Auburn (31-10) and Georgia (45-13) followed.

After defeating Georgia, Spurrier lobbed a shot over the bow of Bulldogs coach Ray Goff. *The Sporting News* quoted Spurrier as saying:

"Why is it that during recruiting season [the Bulldogs] sign all the great players, but when it comes time to play the game, we have all the great players? I don't understand that. What happens to them?"

Said Auburn coach Terry Bowden: "Poor Ray Goff. Steve'd beat Ray real bad, and then he'd talk about all the great players Ray had, which, of course, made Ray's job even tougher."

The No. 5 Gators welcomed Kentucky to Ben Hill Griffin Stadium on November 16, 1991, and hoped to finish off a quest Gators fans had longed for for 60 years: the school's first SEC title. All Florida needed was a victory over the underdog Wildcats, and a crowd of 84,109 couldn't wait to begin the celebration.

Matthews led the Gators to a 28-6 halftime lead with three touchdown passes and even caught a touchdown from Alonzo Sullivan. Kentucky held off the celebration with three unanswered touchdowns to cut the lead to 28-26 with less than eight minutes remaining. However, the Gators would not be denied on this historic day, and when Rhett ran for a two-yard touchdown with 2:22 left in the game, Florida had a 35-26 victory and a 7-0 record in the SEC.

Spurrier gathered his team afterward to join Gator fans in celebrating the school's first official SEC championship.

Florida finished the regular season with a 14-9 victory over FSU in Gainesville giving the school its first 10-win season. They completed the season with a disappointing 39-28 loss to Notre Dame in the Sugar Bowl.

Spurrier nicknamed Ben Hill Griffin Stadium "The Swamp" following the '91 season, explaining, "The swamp is where Gators live. We feel comfortable there. And we hope our opponents feel tentative. A swamp is hot and sticky and can be dangerous."

Nicknames aside, Spurrier had his work cut out for him in 1992, a season that saw the SEC expand, adding Arkansas and South Carolina. The expansion made the SEC a 12-team conference with East and West divisions, with the winners of each division slated to meet in a championship game played at Birmingham's Legion Field. The Gators were put in the East with Tennessee, Georgia, South Carolina, Vanderbilt and Kentucky.

A 35-19 win over Kentucky opened the season, but losses to Tennessee (31-14) and Mississippi State (30-6) followed, putting the Gators below the .500 mark for the first and only time during Spurrier's tenure at Florida.

The Gators responded by running off seven consecutive wins over LSU, Auburn, Louisville, Georgia, Southern Miss, South Carolina and Vanderbilt.

The Gators finished their SEC schedule with a 6-2 mark, which tied them with Georgia. Fortunately for the Gators, their two-point victory over Georgia was the tiebreaker, earning them a trip to the inaugural SEC Championship Game.

Florida finished the regular season in Tallahassee, where the Seminoles took a 45-24 win. On December 5, 1992, the Gators played Alabama for the SEC Championship and trailed 21-7 late in the fourth quarter before tying the score at 21. But Alabama defensive back Antonio Langham's interception return for a touchdown earned the Crimson Tide a 28-21 victory and a trip to the Sugar Bowl. The Gators finished the season with a 27-10 victory over North Carolina State in the Gator Bowl for a 9-4 overall record.

"The '92 season was one of the most fun [seasons] I've had [as the Gators coach]," Spurrier said. "It was one of the most fun because that was the least talented team by far of any team we've had. I remember we were at the [1992] Sugar Bowl and Shane Matthews said, 'Coach, who's going to play offensive tackle next year?' We didn't have anybody. And I said, 'Somebody will show up, we can't worry about that now.' Well, who showed up were two true freshmen, Reggie Green and Jason Odom. We played the '92 season with two high school fifth year guys, Reggie Green and Jason Odom. They played well.

"I think it's the only year we've ever been underdogs to Georgia. And somehow or another, we won that one 26-24. Even the Alabama [SEC] championship game of '92 was a favorite game because we were the underdogs. We weren't supposed to have a chance against the No. 1 team in the nation. I think they were No. 1 in every defensive category. And even though we didn't get it done, it was a fun game. Our team really competed hard. I'm proud of that '92 team. Just like all the championship teams. Even though they didn't win one, they probably maxed out their potential pretty good in '92."

15

SEC BULLIES

The Gators had evolved into the team to beat in the Southeastern Conference after the '92 season.

"The next four years were our hey days, '93 through '96," Spurrier said. "Danny Wuerffel, Terry Dean played a bunch during that time, too. Chris Doerring, Jack Jackson, Willie Jackson, Ellis Johnson, Kevin Carter, can't really mention all the really good players we had during that time. And that was an era that I don't know if the SEC was quite as good.

"Seemed like every time we played Tennessee, good things always happened. We were able to really maximize those four years with four SEC [titles] and a national there."

A critical event for what was to come for the Gators occurred during the 1992 season on the recruiting trail, the area where Spurrier received the most criticism.

Spurrier already had tabbed a gem of a quarterback when Eric Kresser made an early commitment to the Gators. Some might have been satisfied with Kresser alone. Spurrier was not, resulting in the recruitment and signing of Wuerffel from Fort Walton Beach, Florida. Alabama and Florida State each wanted Wuerffel, but Wuerffel liked the idea of being coached by a former Heisman Trophy winner with a wide-open offense.

With Shane Matthews graduated, the Gators opened the 1993 season with Terry Dean at quarterback. Despite having an unestablished quarterback, the Gators were ranked No. 8 before their first game against Arkansas State on September 4.

The Gators did what they were supposed to in a 44-6 win, leading to the first of six consecutive SEC contests when the Gators traveled to Lexington to play Kentucky.

The Wildcats appeared to have the game until Spurrier went to his bench to replace the ineffective Dean with Wuerffel. Even after the move, the Gators trailed 20-17 with eight seconds remaining and the ball on the Kentucky 28; Spurrier figured he had enough time to throw one more pass before attempting a game-tying field gold. That's when Wuerffel noticed Doering had nobody covering him in the slot position. What would be the first of many touchdown passes between the two gave the Gators a 24-20 win.

The Gators went on to win seven of their next eight games; a 38-35 loss at Auburn was the team's only blemish, but not enough to keep them from returning to the SEC Championship Game for a rematch with Alabama.

FSU snapped the win streak by beating the Gators 33-21, which was the Gators' first loss in The Swamp under Spurrier. Florida recovered to win its second SEC title with a 28-13 win over Alabama then took their first-ever Sugar Bowl victory by beating West Virginia 41-7. The Gators finished the season with a school-record 11 wins and a No. 5 ranking.

FSU won the National Championship in 1993 but was embarrassed following the season during the so-called Foot Locker scandal where FSU players received, among other things, free shoes from a local Foot Locker retail store. Spurrier couldn't resist tagging Florida's rival "Free Shoes U." And he connected the dots from there, alleging free merchandise was only the tip of the iceberg.

"We didn't get as many blue-chip players as FSU got, but I'm starting to understand," Spurrier was quoted as saying in *The Sporting News*. "When [the blue chippers] would get called and asked why didn't they go to Florida, why did they go up there, they said they were more comfortable [at Florida State]. I always suspected what that 'comfortable' meant. And now I think everybody is realizing what that 'comfortable' means."

Spurrier never took back his comments, nor did he issue an apology, even after Florida President John Lombardi addressed Spurrier's remarks by saying, "The University of Florida has no standing to criticize any other university. The good thing about Coach Spurrier's insights is nothing is ever a mystery."

Lee McGriff remembered the '93 season for another reason. His son, Travis, was a senior at P.K. Young High School in Gainesville and had caught Spurrier's eye enough to be recruited by him. When asked if it was a thrill for Travis to be recruited by Spurrier, McGriff answered, "It was. There are multiple answers."

"Travis went to the [Gators] football camps, at one point I thought he had a chance to be a college quarterback, then my midget genes caught up with him,"

Lee McGriff said assuming Spurrier's high-pitched voice when describing a conversation with Spurrier after Spurrier had seen Travis at camp. "Steve tells me, 'Hey, Trav's pretty good. He runs around like you.' And of course, he tells Travis that. And it was all Travis' coaches could do to get him to play quarterback his senior year. And I said, 'Great Travis, what are you going to do, throw it to yourself?'

"Then [Florida] recruited him, but as Steve does in his loose fashion, he'd given me every signal that they had intended to sign Travis, and Trav was being recruited by other schools. But Steve took his time, [assuming the Spurrier voice] 'Well, you know, we'd like him to come over here. We'll give him a scholarship.' That's about as formal as he gets. And of course he did come to visit Trav at our house just to do it. But of course, he was just like an old shoe coming in there, being relaxed, Margie [McGriff's wife] and Steve's wife, Jerri, are real good friends. That was all real neat. I mean it really was. It got a little scary there. But that's the way it is when you're dealing with Steve and he's in charge. He never really lets you know where he stands. And it started making us uneasy. But then they stepped forward and offered Trav a scholarship. Of course we were very excited, him going to Florida. The prospect of playing for Steve was really exciting."

McGriff and Spurrier were friends, but the friendship didn't rule the way Spurrier handled Travis McGriff.

"It was an exhausting process, I can tell you that," Lee McGriff said. "Steve's not very communicative on a personal level. And he did some things with Travis that made no sense at the time. And not that coaching and playing football is a sensitive environment. But, you know, the path along the way was rugged [for Travis]. Travis came in with an extraordinary group of players. Ike Hilliard, Reidel Anthony, Jacquez Green, Nafis Karim, and a guy named Jamie Richardson. And that's a pretty phenomenal group of people. That group was unbelievable, four or five guys making all conference and All-America."

McGriff figured his son would be redshirted as a freshman.

But Spurrier said "he was not going to redshirt three of them, Trav included," Lee McGriff said. "Which told me Trav [was considered to be] in the top three. Then it got weird from there. They ended up redshirting [Travis]. And that was sudden. There was no communication with Travis. I mean literally. He found out about it in the dining hall standing in the line, kind of matter of fact. Steve just kind of passed by, 'Hey, we're going to redshirt you.' Which is fine, ultimately I always thought that was the best thing to do anyway. But there was no communication. So I guess what I'm describing, there was no personal touch. Steve is a unique bird, it's not that I expected him to do anything special for Trav, but at the same time, when I say no special touch, there was no communication to Trav about how things were, where things were headed or how he was doing."

Lee McGriff said his son spent the next "two or three years fighting like a dog to find his spot" around "a very distant Steve."

Ultimately, Travis McGriff's story had a happy ending as he went on to star for Spurrier and currently plays in the NFL.

"Trav worked through it all and rose to the top eventually," Lee McGriff said. "He reaped the benefits of being in Steve Spurrier's offense."

The 1994 season began how the '93 season ended, with Wuerffel and Dean splitting time at quarterback and the Gators went into their first game holding the No. 1 spot in the Associated Press poll.

On September 3, New Mexico State came to The Swamp, and Dean treated them rudely by throwing seven touchdowns in a 70-21 Gators win. The polls then treated the Gators rudely on the following Monday by dropping them from No. 1 to No. 2—a spot they regained the next Monday after a 73-7 win over Kentucky.

Running up the score would be a charge leveled at Spurrier throughout his coaching career, but he justifies the charge by saying: "I hope I'm accused of running it up as long as I'm a coach, because I really believe that teams that can score a lot of points will score a lot, and teams that can't score a lot will whine and moan about those who can."

Tennessee became the next victim, losing to the Gators 31-0 in Gainesville.

Wins over Ole Miss (38-14) and LSU (42-18) followed as the Gators rode their No. 1 ranking into a meeting with Auburn on October 15 at The Swamp.

Not only were the Gators 5-0 and ranked at the top of the polls, but this was a revenge game for the Gators after the previous year's loss. In Auburn's first year under Terry Bowden, the Tigers had gone 11-0 but were not bowl eligible because they were on NCAA probation.

In the end, Florida lost 36-33 when Auburn threw a touchdown with 30 seconds remaining. But the Gators had been sloppy throughout, committing six turnovers, while Auburn had none. The game also brought about one of the bigger controversies in Spurrier's 12 years at Florida.

Dean had been having a marvelous season in '94, throwing touchdowns in great enough numbers to be considered a Heisman candidate. That was before the Auburn game.

Dean threw four interceptions against Auburn, prompting Spurrier to jerk him from the game. Wuerffel finished the season at quarterback with Dean seeing little action.

"Terry was a tremendous physical talent," John Reaves said. "He could run and throw. Probably could run a 4.6 40 or close to it, threw a beautiful ball, had

SEC BULLIES

a nice release and everything. He was an excellent player. A very good player. He, unfortunately, had a couple of bad games and didn't understand that Steve demands that upper echelon performance continually.

"Terry started out, I think in '94, as a Heisman candidate and we won a bunch of games, won fairly handily, including beating Tennessee. And then we played LSU and beat them, but he had kind of an off day. Steve got frustrated with him, 'Listen, we expect you to make these throws' and 'you've got to get better.' Then we played Auburn and Terry fumbled a snap and threw four interceptions that day. And he put Danny in there. Danny made some plays, actually got us ahead then threw an interception late and we lost. [Auburn] marched down and scored. And so [Spurrier] decided to go with Danny."

Reaves said comments in the paper didn't help the situation.

"There were some things said in the paper, unfortunately," Reaves said. "I think mainly by Terry. He didn't think it was right that he'd been benched. And I can't remember, but I think Steve took offense to that. Then Danny went on a roll, he was playing brilliantly. Terry didn't get much of a chance to play again, although I think Steve wanted to give him that opportunity to play again. But it was like they were butting heads."

Chris Harry spoke about the comments Dean made to the media.

"I guess [Dean] hadn't played well the week before, or the week before that, and Spurrier told him if he didn't play better he'd put Wuerffel into the game," Harry said. "[Dean] made a reference to how 'Coach put a lot of pressure on him to perform.' He probably got baited into saying he put too much pressure on him. Spurrier said a couple of days later, 'I'm putting too much pressure on a quarterback. I don't want to do that.'"

Reaves liked Dean and remembered not wanting to see him finish his career on the bench.

"I'd been benched by Steve before [with the Bandits] and had an opportunity to play again," Reaves said. "So I went to Terry, I said, 'Terry, I don't know if this will happen or not, but if I were you I would go in and apologize to Coach Spurrier. I'd go in and tell him you are sorry for what happened in the media. You didn't mean it. He was right. And if you do that, I bet he'll give you a chance to play.' But he wouldn't do it. And so he never got a chance to play again. And really, Steve wanted to give him another chance, because I remember hearing Steve kind of lamenting about what happened there. It bothered Steve, too. It was a little bit of a power struggle."

The Gators followed the Auburn loss with lopsided victories over Georgia (52-14), Southern Miss (55-17) and South Carolina (48-17) before Vanderbilt put up a good fight in a 24-7 loss at Nashville, setting the stage for a meeting with

THE STEVE SPURRIER STORY

FSU in Tallahassee in what had to be one of Spurrier's most disappointing games at Florida.

With Wuerffel playing quarterback, the Gators built a 31-3 lead going into the fourth quarter. But the Seminoles quickly cut the lead to 31-17 with 10:04 remaining, and it appeared the only thing that could stop FSU was the clock. FSU quarterback Danny Kanell led the 'Noles on touchdown drives of 73 and 60 yards, leaving FSU one point short after their final touchdown. Should they kick the extra point and take the tie, or go for two points and risk losing? That was the question facing FSU coach Bobby Bowden, who elected to kick the point and take the tie, rationalizing his team had come from so far back that a tie would feel like a win. Whether FSU felt like it had won or not is a point for debate, but from the Gators' viewpoint, a 31-31 tie after leading 31-3 felt more like a loss.

The Gators had to put the FSU tie behind them with Alabama waiting to play the Gators in a rematch in the SEC Championship Game. The game proved to be one of the most exciting contests in the young history of the conference's title game.

Alabama entered the game undefeated and ranked No. 3 in the country and took a 23-17 lead in the fourth quarter. To some the situation might have looked dire for the Gators. To Spurrier, the situation offered the chance to serve up a history lesson.

First he used an old favorite from the 1953 Notre Dame playbook. Protecting an undefeated season and trailing Iowa 7-0 in the first half, Irish coach Frank Leahy, who was coaching his final season for Notre Dame, called upon tackle Frank Varrichione to fake an injury in order to stop the clock. Notre Dame had the ball on the Iowa 12 with no timeouts when Varrichione dropped to the grass clutching his back. Notre Dame scored on a touchdown pass on the next play en route to a 14-14 tie; they finished the season 9-0-1.

Wuerffel limped off the field to make way for a play especially designed for his backup, Eric Kresser, who possessed a powerful arm.

The logic was flawless. Most teams will blitz the backup quarterback, who normally has seen little playing time and is suddenly thrust into the game, which makes for a combination of nervousness, confusion and botched performance. In Kresser's case, the Gators had practiced the play all week and he was primed to enter the game and complete a 25-yard pass. The play was critical as it moved Florida into Alabama's side of the field.

In addition, Spurrier went to a wild formation during the drive that saw multiple receivers lined up wide on each side, leaving the defense in total chaos.

Wuerffel capped the 80-yard drive with a two-yard touchdown pass to Chris Doering. When the extra point was good, the Gators had a 24-23 win and another SEC title.

Joe Biddle remembers being in the press conference after the game when somebody asked Spurrier about the spread formation he'd used.

"Somebody asked, 'Steve, we've never seen you run that, what is that?'" Biddle said. "And he said, 'that's Emory and Henry.' Of course, I'm the only one in the audience who probably knew what Emory and Henry was, I think."

Biddle explained the story that dated to their youth in Johnson City.

"They used to have a small college bowl game in Johnson City," Biddle said. "I think they called it the Burley Bowl. It was a tobacco industry sponsored bowl game. And Emory and Henry played in it one year. And we'd go to that game occasionally if the weather was halfway decent. There wasn't a whole lot to do in Johnson City, except maybe kick the tires. And we'd go watch it. That's where Steve first saw that formation and evidently remembered that thing and put it out there against Alabama."

Giving names to plays or formations was nothing new to Spurrier.

"He always did that with his plays," Biddle said. "He had one in his playbook named after Lonnie Lowe, a classmate of ours who just died recently of cancer. He has one named after me. I said, 'How'd you come up with that?' And he said, 'Well, Tampa Bay Bandits, Bandit back, b-back, and the pass route he ran on this particular play was right across the middle, so I just took the b-back and the middle and made it Biddle.' So blame me if it doesn't work. You'll probably see a variation with the Redskins."

Reaves recalled other plays Spurrier has named after people.

"That middle screen is named 'Margie' after his mother," Reaves said. "His option play to the right is 'Ralph' after Ralph Campbell, former general manager of the Bandits. Option play to the left is 'Loni' after Loni Anderson. He has a play called the 'Mills Route' after Ernie Mills who made a great play against Alabama in 1990."

Florida played a rematch with FSU in the Sugar Bowl and lost 23-17 to end what in many respects was a disappointing season. Nevertheless, the Gators had a 10-2-1 record. Clearly Spurrier had raised the bar for expectations in Gainesville and the program's fortunes continued to climb higher.

Wuerffel returned to lead a talented Gators team in 1995 that was ranked No. 5 in the preseason polls prior to their 45-21 opening game against Houston in Gainesville. What followed was the magical immaculate season Gator fans had never before experienced, nor have they experienced it since.

After four consecutive lopsided wins over Kentucky (42-7), Tennessee (62-37), Ole Miss (28-10) and LSU (28-10), Florida experienced one of their closer victories of the season with a 49-38 win over Auburn. Despite the margin, Spurrier managed to slap down the Tigers by sloughing off his team's effort by commenting, "We didn't necessarily do all that well today."

Said Auburn coach Terry Bowden of Spurrier in an article appearing in *Esquire*: "There are some people that it's fun to compete against. Steve's not one of them."

If anybody thought the Gators were letting up, that line of thinking was quickly dismissed in their next game against Georgia.

Because Jacksonville's Gator Bowl was still being modified, Florida had to travel to Athens to play the Bulldogs for the first time in 63 years; the previous year the game had been played in Gainesville.

At The Swamp the Gators took a 52-14 win in 1994, so the Bulldogs were talking revenge at historic Sanford Stadium. Instead, the Gators humiliated the home team.

Not only did the Gators defense hold the Bulldogs to 281 yards, they were riddled by Wuerffel and Kresser, who accounted for seven touchdown passes, a record number for an SEC conference game.

The Gators' final touchdown was the first caught by Travis McGriff as a Gator and was the last straw for Bulldog fans, who accused Spurrier of poor sportsmanship for throwing the late touchdown in a 52-17 win.

Spurrier never believed in making any players have to lay down on the ball in the name of sportsmanship. So when he was asked about throwing the late touchdown, his answer hardly could have been considered a surprise.

"Because no visiting team has ever scored 50 points in this stadium and we wanted to be the first," Spurrier said.

The Gators continued to pummel their opponents in the next three games, beating Northern Illinois (58-20), South Carolina (63-7) and Vanderbilt (38-7) before their final game of the regular season against FSU in Gainesville.

The 'Noles entered the game ranked No. 6 in the country and were riding a four-game streak in which they had not lost to Florida. FSU gave Florida their closest game of the season but came up short 35-24, and Florida had an 11-0 record, the first-ever perfect season in Gator football history. The victory moved Florida to No. 2 in the national rankings behind Nebraska, whom Florida earned the right to play in the Fiesta Bowl following a 34-3 shellacking of Arkansas in the SEC Championship Game.

Unfortunately for the Gators, the Arkansas win marked the end of the fun.

Playing in one game for a national championship was what every Gator fan wanted. Spurrier's offense could not be stopped by any team according to conventional wisdom. And true to form, the Gators took a 10-6 first quarter lead before the game turned into a Cornhuskers rout.

Led by Nebraska quarterback Tommie Frazier and running back Lawrence Phillips, the 'Huskers ran for 524 yards on a night when their offense accumulated 629 yards. The Big Red defense hurried Wuerffel all night, resulting in a safety and an interception return for a touchdown. When the final gun sounded, there were no doubts about Nebraska being No. 1 by virtue of their 63-24 win.

Spurrier didn't look his best for a national television audience, particularly when he went off on Wuerffel following a safety.

Nebraska obviously had a superior defense on the field, yet when the Gators were backed into their own end zone, Spurrier elected to go with a set employing five wideouts. Wuerffel dodged the rush on the first play but was slammed for a safety on the second. Spurrier greeted Wuerffel with a thrown visor and a face of anger. The Gators' fortunes continued to deteriorate after the episode.

Tom Shannon spent time with Spurrier before and after the Nebraska game.

"Our room happened to be a few rooms down from [Spurrier's] in Scottsdale," Shannon said. "And we spent a lot of time watching ballgames that day, our families kind of hanging around together. But he didn't face it any different than any other ballgame. He relaxes. He likes to talk about other things. Then, obviously, about two or three hours before he's getting ready to leave the hotel, we just excused ourselves because a guy's got to concentrate on 'where I'm coming out and what I'm going to do.' But he was very relaxed to be with.

"[After the game] I think he was like everybody else. The game was just a gigantic disappointment, tough crowd, first time to the big dance. Nebraska probably travels better than any team in the country and [the stadium] seemed like it was a sea of red. And actually, the first quarter was pretty neat. After that it was Katie bar the door."

Even though the Gators had come up empty in their attempt to claim their first national title, Spurrier was hot coaching property. Returning to Tampa was a tempting scenario that presented itself in January 1996.

The Bucs offered Spurrier $2 million a year to take charge of the beleaguered franchise.

Spurrier "obviously didn't know if the franchise was going to end up in Cleveland, Baltimore, or Los Angeles," Nick Pugliese said. "I think he and Jerri talked that night and he was thinking about taking that job, but the thing that made him say no was he could take that job tomorrow and the next week they could be moving to L.A. They didn't want to move to L.A. They loved Tampa and they would have wanted to stay here."

Spurrier turned down the Bucs to stay put in Gainesville.

16

THAT
CHAMPIONSHIP
SEASON

Danny Wuerffel started his senior season of 1996 as a Heisman candidate based on his being the perfect mechanic for Spurrier's offense. Having a quarterback like Wuerffel was like having a coach on the field and the Gators had a talented tandem of receivers in Anthony Reidel and Ike Hilliard; Spurrier's offense had all the necessary weapons. Bob Stoops, an emerging coaching talent, held the job of defensive coordinator and the Gators had plenty of defensive talent, highlighted by defensive backs Anthony Lott and Lawrence Wright and linebacker James Bates.

They opened the season with wins against Southwestern Louisiana (55-21) and Georgia Southern (62-14) to set the table for their first legitimate opponent, Tennessee.

An NCAA-record crowd of 107,608 showed up at Tennessee's Neyland Stadium to watch the 1996 Florida–Tennessee game. Revenge and redemption were on the minds of Vols fans. Revenge for the 62-37 drubbing the previous year in The Swamp; redemption for much-heralded quarterback Peyton Manning, who seemed to play well against every team he faced, other than Florida.

Manning entered the 1996 season as the preseason favorite to win the Heisman. No doubt Manning's name was erased from more than one ballot after his four first-half interceptions against the Gators.

By five minutes into the second quarter Wuerffel had thrown four touchdown passes and Florida held a 35-0 lead. Tennessee cut the lead to two touchdowns with just over eight minutes remaining, but the Gators' offense did what it had to by staging a 13-play drive that killed six minutes before stalling out. The final score of 35-29 was not indicative of what transpired that day in Knoxville.

Spurrier didn't endear himself to Tennessee fans later when he examined Tennessee's list of goals for the 1996 season and crossed out national championship and SEC champions. Tennessee had lost to Memphis so Spurrier crossed out "State Championship." But, according to Spurrier, Tennessee was Knox County Champion.

Florida moved to No. 1 in the polls by virtue of the Tennessee win and they took their new ranking out for a spin the next week by trouncing Kentucky 65-0. Six consecutive wins followed over Arkansas (42-7), LSU (56-13), Auburn (51-10), Georgia (47-7), Vanderbilt (28-21) and South Carolina (52-25), giving the Gators a 10-0 mark to go along with their No. 1 ranking as they went to Tallahassee on November 30, 1996, for the season finale against No. 2 ranked FSU.

Eight years had passed since the top two ranked teams in the country had met so late in the season making for an off-the-charts pregame buildup.

FSU defensive coordinator Mickey Andrews had studied the previous season's Fiesta Bowl when Nebraska maintained constant pressure on Wuerffel and noted: "We learned a lot from Nebraska."

FSU coach Bobby Bowden could see some cracks in the Florida offensive line as indicated by his comments leading up to the game.

"I wish I had an extra week to get ready," Bowden said. "Because there are some flaws in Steve's blocking system, but I just don't know if we can get everything in and get it all down."

Florida planned to double-team Florida State's imposing defensive ends, Peter Boulware and Reinard Wilson. Boulware had plans of his own.

"The only way to stop Wuerffel is to make sure he's on his back with the ball," Boulware said.

Florida's extra attention paid to Boulware and Wilson opened things up for FSU's inside linemen, Andre Wadsworth and Connell Spain, in addition to creating lanes for blitzing linebackers and defensive backs to charge in and tee off on Wuerffel.

"If we had more time [to throw] we would have killed them," Anthony said. "There were times when we'd get 10 yards deep, turn around, and Danny was already on the ground."

Said Wuerffel: "They just kept coming and coming. They kept bringing the heat. All you can do is hang in there and hope for the best."

"Pooh Bear" Williams, FSU's 300-pound fullback, powered over for a touchdown following Boulware's blocked punt that gave the 'Noles the ball at the Gators' 3. The score gave FSU a 10-0 lead with 3:07 remaining in the first quarter. Thad Busby's one-yard touchdown toss to Melvin Pearsall made it 17-0 FSU early in the second quarter.

Wuerffel whittled away at the FSU lead by throwing two touchdown passes to Jacquez Green to cut the lead to 17-14 at halftime.

The contest evolved into a defensive struggle with neither team being able to sustain a drive in the third quarter. Williams finally ended the drought when he scored from the one to give FSU a 24-14 lead with 7:15 left in the game.

Wuerffel led the Gators to a late score, but the ensuing onside kick failed and FSU had a 24-21 upset victory, which saw FSU get whistled for three roughing-the-passer violations against Wuerffel.

Florida dropped to No. 4 in the polls and their chances for a national championship appeared dashed. Meantime, Wuerffel was named the Heisman Trophy winner, making Spurrier and him the only coach and quarterback to own Heisman Trophies. Wuerffel had endured the demanding coach and was rewarded accordingly.

"More than anything, [Spurrier] wants you to achieve your potential," Wuerffel said. "Sometimes you have to get through the bark to get to the bite."

Florida played Alabama in the SEC Championship Game in Atlanta.

Alabama had the sixth-rated defense in the country and took a 7-0 lead in the first quarter, but Wuerffel proved too much for the Crimson Tide, throwing for six touchdowns for 401 yards in a 45-30 Gators win.

The win earned the Gators their fifth SEC title as well as earning them a bid to the Sugar Bowl for a rematch with No. 1 FSU.

Spurrier immediately took the offensive toward the FSU defense, accusing them of late hits to Wuerffel and generally playing dirty during the course of the FSU game. Wuerffel had been tackled 26 times, and one of the FSU players said after the game that the Seminoles' defense tried to knock Wuerffel out of the game.

"The day after they beat Alabama, it was inevitable they were going to be matched against FSU [in the Sugar Bowl] and he called us up to this little room and told us all about the late-hit shit," Chris Harry said. "Danny Wuerffel and FSU, our mouths dropped, all the shit he was saying. Coaches just don't say that kind of stuff. . . . A couple of weeks later he asked a few of us to come up into his office and showed us a tape. He'd point stuff out with his little laser. And he showed this one, and this guy does come in and puts his helmet in his back. And I laughed. He looked at me and he says, 'Nothing funny about that Chris Harry.'"

Spurrier continued his crusade to have the officials take extra care to look out for his quarterback during the coming Sugar Bowl. He addressed the situation by playing on the fact Wuerffel was a devout Christian.

"Danny's a New Testament kind of guy," Spurrier said. "He turns the other cheek. Now, I'm more of an Old Testament guy. You know, an eye for an eye."

Bowden told his players in a December 21 meeting, "If I wasn't a good Christian man, I'd tell every one of you to go out and kick Steve Spurrier's ass."

Bowden made light of Spurrier's remark outwardly, but he told *Sports Illustrated*, "Don't know why he had to do that. I wish he hadn't. I guess I should be used to that with him by now."

John Reaves called Spurrier's action "one of the most brilliant coaching jobs [Spurrier] did."

"Talking about the late hits took so much pressure off the team," Reaves said. "Took the focus off the team and put it on him. And it frustrated Bobby Bowden so much in defending himself that I think it distracted them from game planning and playing. And I think the players rallied around Steve to support him and the position he took because people were just blasting him [for the things he said]. And I think that was brilliant."

Harry added: "He had his players believing there was an injustice, his offensive linemen believed it, there was a lot of shouting going on at the Sugar Bowl."

The chances for a national championship were out of the Gators' control, but they improved the week after their loss to FSU when Texas upset Nebraska in the Big 12 Championship Game, moving the Gators to No. 3 in the polls and knocking No. 2 Nebraska out of a Sugar Bowl bid. Further good fortune smiled on the Gators on New Year's Day in the Rose Bowl.

The Rose Bowl still staked claim to the Big 10 and Pac 10 champions in 1996, keeping No. 2 Arizona State from playing FSU, which provided two breaks for the Gators. First, it allowed the rematch with FSU to happen. In addition, the situation made possible No. 4 Ohio State's upset of Arizona State in Pasadena.

The stakes for the 1997 Sugar Bowl, which had been tabbed "ReDeaux on the Bayou," had been raised. The winner of the contest between the in-state rivals would gain more than bragging rights; they would win a national championship as well.

Shortly after the conclusion of the Rose Bowl in which Ohio State scored the winning touchdown with 19 seconds remaining, Spurrier held a team meeting at the team hotel, a Holiday Inn in Gonzalez, Louisiana, and addressed his players about the Mulligan they had just received.

"Gentlemen, they say God helps those who help themselves," Spurrier said. "We've got a chance. It's in our hands."

Nick Pugliese, who is a Florida alumnus, decided to go to New Orleans as a fan rather than report on the game. Walking around the French Quarter the night before the game, he ran into Jerri Spurrier, whom he knew from his days covering the Bandits.

"I had gone to the Gator hotel to meet some people and was walking back to my hotel and here comes Jerri Spurrier all by herself, walking with a bag," Pugliese said. "She gave me a big hug. We talked about 20 minutes and she said how nervous she was and she told me, 'We've got to win. We've just got to win tomorrow night. This means so much to everyone. Steve's nervous. I'm nervous.' She was like a nervous wreck. I gave her a hug and said, 'I hope Florida wins tomorrow night.' I guess she was just trying to get away from it all."

Looking for some positive karma in the game, Florida wore blue pants. And after winning the toss, Spurrier deferred to the second half—the first time he had elected to do so during his tenure at Florida. But the biggest change came in Spurrier's decision to keep tight ends and running backs in on any given play to help combat FSU's tenacious rush and buy extra time for Wuerffel. Further help came in continued use of the shotgun formation, which Florida had used effectively against Alabama in the SEC Championship Game. Wuerffel lined up in the shotgun 21 times in the first quarter.

"I was hoping they'd blitz more, but once they saw the shotgun, they chickened out," Spurrier said.

Wuerffel connected with Ike Hilliard to give the Gators an early 7-0 lead and pushed the lead to 10-3 on Bart Edmiston's field goal. Wuerffel's 31-yard touchdown pass to Hilliard gave Florida a 24-17 halftime lead.

FSU cut the lead to 24-20 with a field goal early in the second half before the Sugar Bowl became a Gators love fest when Spurrier's troops put 28 unanswered points on the scoreboard. Hilliard scored three touchdowns, Willie Jackson scored twice while Wuerffel completed 18 of 34 passes for 306 yards and three touchdowns; he also scored one himself.

The Gators had a 52-20 victory and their first football national championship.

"God has smiled on the Gators," Spurrier said.

Afterward, Spurrier spoke of Wuerffel.

"I like Danny for every reason you can think of," he said. "Accurate passer, makes plays, leads the team—he's got it all. Florida State tried and they still couldn't knock him out of the game. Anybody who didn't put him on their Heisman ballot is listening to that NFL draft bull crap and couldn't have seen him play."

Tom Shannon remembers being with Spurrier immediately following the game.

"Tom McEwen was with me," Shannon said. "Tom had flown up to the game with my wife and me. When the game was over I dragged Tom with me over to where the team was partying. And boy, it was just a great celebration with a lot of kissing and hugging and loving. And everybody was just as happy as they could be. And I told Tom, you better call Linda [McEwen's wife] and tell her we're not getting home until about four in the morning. He goes, 'Oh shit, man, I knew I bummed the wrong ride.' I said, 'Screw you, it's my plane, you're with me. I ain't missing this celebration.' He loved every minute of it."

17

HIGH EXPECTATIONS

Steadily progressing each year, while simultaneously setting a high standard, Steve Spurrier had achieved what he aimed for when he took the Florida job. Winning Florida's first national championship put the program and Spurrier on top of the college football world.

Though Spurrier had his critics, he didn't forget those who had helped him, like Ray Graves.

Out of the blue, Spurrier called his old coach and invited him to lunch.

"Something was going on, an alumni thing or something, and he wanted me to meet him for lunch," Graves said.

While spending time with his old coach, Spurrier said, "Here," and Graves felt him slip something into his pocket that felt like a box.

"That's when he said, 'I didn't win a championship when I was playing for you, but you've got a ring now,'" Graves said.

Spurrier had given Graves a national championship ring.

"That was a nice thing to do," Graves said. "A touching moment. We have a close relationship we'll always share."

Others didn't share the same warm fuzzy when it came to Spurrier. More and more his image to schools outside of Gainesville was of an intolerable crybaby, cocky and arrogant. In short, Spurrier was not a well-loved man around the South.

In Knoxville, 100 miles from his hometown, Vols fans considered Spurrier public enemy No. 1. Why? Because Spurrier beat the big Orange and the victory usually came with the Head Ball Coach's own unique touchdown dance.

Because Tennessee did not win the SEC many of the years when Florida did, the Vols went to the Citrus Bowl, which earned the following from Spurrier:

"I heard they just hung a new sign outside the Citrus Bowl in Orlando: WINTER HOME OF THE TENNESSEE VOLUNTEERS."

Or: "You know you can't spell Citrus without U-T."

And, finally: "I know why Peyton [Manning] came back for his senior year. He wanted to be a three-time star of the Citrus Bowl."

Still, Spurrier's friends say his image is unwarranted.

"He's really a family man," Graves said pointing out Spurrier is an excellent father to his four children and grandfather to his seven grandchildren. "He's an interesting person. I guess I know him about as well as anybody. You can't, in a few words, say what kind of man he is.

"Of course, after the season he likes to get away. I've always said he's a lot like Bobby Dodd where he plays golf and gets away from everything. Comes back with a clear mind."

Graves said he's never spoken to Spurrier about the agonizing facial language he employs on the sideline, but Graves has attempted to get Spurrier to tone down some of his remarks.

"Norm Carlson and I have tried to tell him not to say everything he says," Graves said. "Like [Bobby] Bowden said a couple of years ago, 'You know, Steve says what he thinks.' But he's going to say it. I don't care he's going to say it. He's going to criticize himself, or his players. He's always going to be that way. I think the players who play for him, they know his personality and I think they respect him for that."

Graham McKeel smiled when asked about the prevailing perception of Spurrier.

"Nobody likes the guy," McKeel said. "I've never heard so many people hate a guy in my life. I just can't understand how people can hate somebody like that, but I guess it's the image he portrays. But he doesn't care. He does what he wants to do and he says this is the way I'm going to do it, and, I mean, he can just piss more people off than anybody I've seen in my life.

"That guy at Georgia, [Ray] Goff, he just ran him out of there. [Spurrier] was on his ass from day one. He says this guy is worthless and no good. I couldn't believe it. And sure enough, poor Goff, he ran him off."

McKeel sees a different Spurrier on the field than the one he saw as a player.

"I don't remember him as a friend and a teammate as a whiner, so the personality that came out as a successful coach, I didn't really remember that as Steve's personality," McKeel said. "Just the perfectionist and all that kind of stuff, you can see that's what he expects and that's what he did himself. And that's what he expects of his quarterbacks today."

Graham Spurrier acknowledged the fact people truly seem to hate his brother.

"Especially up here [in Tennessee]," Graham Spurrier said. "But the people who say bad things, they don't know him. You take fans, a lot of big university fans. They just don't like to lose. They can't stand to lose. It was especially goading up here, because he's from here. He's a Tennessee boy. A lot of people think he's a traitor and all that, because he beat them eight out of 12 years. You know, that's a pretty good whippin' there. Eight out of 12. But that was his job, he was at Florida now. A lot of people don't understand that. Of course, they're blinded by their loyalty to UT. And you know, that's fine. That's part of it. But the people that really knew him, they were behind him. Except when they played UT and they still say bad things about him. They really do. Now I'm used to it. I just take it with a grain of salt and go on."

Graham Spurrier's Johnson City hangout is an establishment called "The Cottage," where visitors can grab a cold beer and some good food, particularly the burgers and pizza.

"Just a neat little ole place," Graham Spurrier said. "It's been there for years. I went there in college. And it hasn't hardly changed. You can go in there and know there's not going to be any problems. There's no riffraff, they don't allow it. Just a very well-run place. Steve usually comes and stops in when he's in town. And they've got a big picture of him hanging there. Of course, most of the people who go there are rabid UT fans, though I've converted a few to Gator fans who come down with me every now and then.

"A couple of years ago Steve was in town one Saturday, and I'll never forget this. There were about five or six guys sitting at a big round table on the first floor as you come in the door. They're big UT fans and they rag me a little bit about the Gators and Steve. And I'd say, 'Well, one of these days he'll come in and you can see for yourself. So he stopped by there and they were all there. He sat there with them for a couple of hours and they asked him everything under the sun. When he left they said, 'I can't really believe what a nice guy he is.' I said, 'I've been trying to tell you guys that.' After that they didn't really condemn him any more. Of course, they weren't happy when he beat them, but no more saying the bad things about him and stuff, because they finally got to know him."

Tom McEwen said he's never asked Spurrier about his sideline demeanor.

"They use the word 'whine,' like he's a whiner, a complainer," McEwen said. "Fact is he speaks his mind.

"When he complained about Florida State hitting Wuerffel late, he asked if any of the coaches in the Atlantic Coast Conference [the conference to which FSU belongs] thought he was wrong. He welcomed their comments, nobody said a word. Steve is so loyal to his friends. He's extremely loyal to us. He'll fly down here to our party. He always returns my calls. To this day, what I admire more than anything else is his innovativeness, his honesty and his loyalty. He's black and white, absolutely black and white."

McEwen was being honored at a banquet at Tampa's exclusive Old Memorial Golf Club, and the people conducting the ceremony asked him who he would like to come down and take part in the ceremony's question and answer portion of the program. McEwen wanted Spurrier, who gladly made the two-hour drive from Gainesville to be with McEwen.

"He stayed there over an hour and a half answering questions," McEwen said. "Now these are guys from all over the country. A lot of them are from Kentucky and [Spurrier's Gators] beat the shit out of them.

"Everybody's drinking, which is fine, and one of the guys asked Steve, 'Coach, I had a lot of money on that [Florida–Kentucky] game and I lost it because you threw a 70-yard touchdown pass on the last play of the game. Why did you do that? How do you think I feel about that?' And Steve said, 'Why don't you ask [Kentucky coach] Hal Mumme how he feels about it? On the previous series he had the ball and he threw three times. If he doesn't pass, he can run the clock out. If he's going to pass, I'm going to pass.'"

Larry Smith said, "I kind of get ticked off at all these people saying he's a whiner."

"Maybe he takes things too far some times, but he's brutally honest," Smith said. "He says exactly what he believes. And it seems people aren't used to that. Most people are more reserved."

Smith has his own theory for Spurrier's sideline antics.

"I guess it appears he gets frustrated on the sidelines, because he doesn't have [the same kind of control he had as a player]. In other words, he can't throw the ball for the kids. But he knows where he wants him to throw it. It seems to me it's a natural frustration when you're as involved in the coaching as he is. Most head coaches, they delegate that to their assistants. Probably if you watched their assistants, the guys in charge of the offense and defense, they'd be doing the same thing. So he's a head coach who actually coaches, which is a bit unusual in this day and age."

Pepper Rodgers had a story when asked about Spurrier's "evil genius" label.

"One time my wife told me, 'Pepper, I hate to tell you this, everybody doesn't think you're cute,'" Rodgers said. "And that's like Steve. Steve, everybody doesn't think you're right on. Now, having said that, those people who didn't think I was cute, my reply was, 'Well, they don't know me.' I think that Steve says what he thinks. And I think anybody who says what they think, well, they're going to make some people mad. Honesty won't make people like you as much, sometimes, as not saying what you think. You've heard the saying, 'If you can't say something nice, don't say anything.' Well, Steve's honest. He just goes right on ahead and says it. . . . But again, everybody doesn't like everybody. That's just the way it is. But I promise you this, if Steve was losing to all these people, they'd like him a lot better. Just remember that one."

Shannon believes Spurrier's competitiveness drives his label.

"He's a grinder," Shannon said. "We've probably played 1,000 games of golf together. With me he's fun. I have a lot of fun. I've been in matches with him where other people are there and he's a grinder. He doesn't like to lose, but I know him well enough to tell you, he doesn't like to lose any more than you don't like to lose. Or than I don't like to lose. Sometimes he shows it a little more. To me, I don't know how you would consider that. I've seen him smile and joke about missing a putt. I've seen him walk off the golf course. Have you ever walked off the golf course?"

A visitor replied, "No."

"Well, I haven't either," Shannon laughed. "The idea is going out and having a good time. You lose a few bucks, you win a few bucks. Everybody likes their money. Nobody likes to lose. I'm not into analyzing Steve Spurrier, other than I know him as a friend. And if he called me and he had a problem, I'd go help him. Steve's a regular guy. He's a very compassionate father; he's a spectacular family man. He's been very lucky himself. He's been very fortunate."

Shannon added he believes partial credit for "evil genius" must be given to the fact Spurrier coaches football like a basketball coach.

"I've always compared Steve to Rick Pitino," Shannon said. "If you watch Rick Pitino on the sidelines, ranting and raving, going up and down, and the vein popping out of his neck, that's the same heat Spurrier's under when he's calling play, to play, to play. He's not just the head coach, he's the offensive co-ordinator. So he's checking off in the heat of battle with the quarterback. Coor-dinators are throwing their headsets up in the box. You just don't see it."

Spurrier concedes he is more like a basketball coach than a football coach.

"At coaches' meetings I probably try to spend more time with the basketball coaches than the football coaches," Spurrier said. "People expect a head coach in basketball to really coach his team. He's in the forefront. That's kind of the way I was as an assistant coach, coaching the offense at Georgia Tech and at Duke, and that's the way I always figured I wanted to do it if I ever became a head coach."

Spurrier admires John Wooden. When Rodgers coached at UCLA, he knew and observed the legendary basketball coach. And while Rodgers believes Spurrier and Wooden are different, he believes they are alike as well.

"They're two very different people," Rodgers said. "But the one thing John Wooden had, John Wooden was more concerned about what he did and what his players did than what the other team was doing. And I think Steve is like that. Too many of these guys in the profession spend all their time running around looking at scouting reports on what the other team is going to be doing, and too little time on making their players better."

Rodgers added: "Steve's the kind of guy people will play for because of his reputation; that's what John Wooden got."

Spurrier tells a story about *Orlando Sentinel* columnist Mike Bianchi telling Spurrier about covering the 2002 Final Four and observing fiery Gary Williams. The Maryland coach was yelling at his players and totally involved, which is the way basketball coaches coach.

"And [Bianchi] said, 'I thought that's the way Steve coaches football. Gary Williams at Maryland, you guys coach alike,'" Spurrier said. "I said, I've always said I coach like a basketball coach, but very few football coaches coach like that. And that makes me different. If you're not a Gator, you're saying, 'He's loud, he's yelling at everybody.' But really, the only guy I'm usually yelling at is the quarterback, to get his attention, to shake him up a little bit."

Spurrier's success whet the appetites of Florida faithful. No longer was an SEC Championship good enough, it was expected; anything less than a national championship became a disappointment.

Using the above-mentioned criteria, Spurrier's final five seasons at Florida were a disappointment: Just one SEC title and no national championships. No doubt the pressure cooker Spurrier had created worked on him. At his farewell press conference after announcing his departure from Florida, Spurrier addressed the lofty expectations by noting how much he missed being classified the underdog.

"Being the underdog is a little more fun at times," Spurrier said. "It was more fun the first few years here when Florida had lost to Auburn and Georgia so many times. And listening to them say, 'We've beaten them so many times before, blah, blah, blah.' It sort of added a little more pizzazz to us. Now we're just carrying on. Now it's almost a disgrace every time we lose. It's a relief when we win. Hey, we got 'em when we weren't supposed to. It's always a little more fun that way."

The Gators opened the 1997 season at No. 2 in the polls, this despite the graduation of the ultimate Spurrier disciple, Wuerffel.

In hindsight "certainly the success we had with [Wuerffel] there will probably never be equaled," Spurrier said. "I don't see how any other quarterback will win four SECs and a national [championship] during his four years at Florida.

Danny had a good team around him. But he was special. His passes seemed to just get there. They'd be inches away from a defender, but they just seemed to almost always get there. And his leadership qualities; everybody loved the guy and he was so smart with the ball.

"He was a good listener, too. We could yell in audibles occasionally, he knew what to look for and he has a wonderful understanding of the game. He works at it. He's mentally prepared to play very well. Some of our other quarterbacks later just weren't mentally as quick as Danny was."

Doug Johnson became Spurrier's new signal caller. Johnson was a headstrong, dual-sport athlete, who would clash with Spurrier during his tenure with the Gators. But the Gators appeared as though they would not skip a beat with Johnson as they ran off five wins to start the season. But a visit to Baton Rouge to play LSU resulted in a 28-21 loss. A win against Auburn followed before a 37-17 loss to Georgia, the Gators' only loss to the Bulldogs in Spurrier's 12-year tenure as coach of the Gators.

Twice-beaten heading into the season finale against FSU, Florida remained a dangerous team for the Seminoles to beat and retain their No. 1 and No. 2 rankings in the polls.

Neither of the Gators' quarterbacks, Johnson nor Noah Brindise, had distinquished themselves, and word was out FSU knew how to read the Florida hand signals for calling in plays. Addressing both problems, Spurrier decided to alternate his quarterbacks on every play.

Throughout the game, Brindise or Johnson stood next to Spurrier and listened to their coach's call for the next play. Somehow it worked. The quarterback tandem completed 19 of 36 passes for 336 yards and no interceptions, including the 67-yard Johnson to Jacquez Green pass that set up the Gators' winning touchdown for a 32-29 upset victory.

The Gators finished the season with a 21-6 victory over Penn State in the Citrus Bowl, giving them a 10-2 mark.

In 1998 Spurrier's Gators entered the season with their usual high expectations, which they basically lived up to other than the fact the '98 team earned the distinction as the lowest-scoring team of the Spurrier era.

Florida lost to Tennessee 20-17, which paved the road for a Tennessee national championship; FSU handed the Gators their second and final loss of the season before the Gators handled Syracuse 31-10 in the Orange Bowl, giving the Gators their sixth-consecutive 10-win season.

The streak of 10 wins a season ended in 1999, a season highlighted by the Gators' September 18 defeat of defending national champion Tennessee 23-21 at The Swamp. Disappointments were delivered by Alabama, which handed out the Gators's first loss with a 40-39 overtime victory and later administered a 34-7 clubbing in the SEC Championship Game; Florida State, which won 30-23 in the final game of the regular season; and Michigan State, which defeated the Gators 37-34 in the Citrus Bowl.

Despite all the success the Gators' program had enjoyed under Spurrier, the nine-win season brought grumblings about whether Spurrier had lost his magic. Unfair, yes, but Spurrier had created the lofty expectations through the many successes his teams had enjoyed during his tenure.

Today Spurrier maintains he has no frustrations about raising the expectations and hopes of Gator fans.

"That's sort of the way you want it," he said. "There's a saying, 'It's better to be disappointed occasionally than to not have high expectations.' If your expectations aren't too high, you're not going to achieve too much, usually. So it's okay to be disappointed when you don't quite hit your expectations. That's part of it. You just have to handle that."

Spurrier's father, the Rev. J. Graham Spurrier, died in April 2000 at his home in Green Cove Springs, just south of Jacksonville, Florida. The Reverend had become a familiar fixture around Gainesville during Spurrier's reign, attending all of the Florida home games.

"He had not only an influence on [Steve Spurrier], but on everyone he encountered," said John Hoke, Florida's defensive coordinator at the time. "He was just that kind of guy. He always had a smile on his face. He always had a good word for everybody."

John Reaves called Spurrier's father a devout Christian man.

"He walked the walk his entire life," Reaves said. "I mean that guy never skipped a beat. . . . He'd come to every home game and some away games. And then at the Gator room at home games, three hours before the game, we'd host recruits that were up there. He'd shake their hands and welcome them and Coach Spurrier would give [the recruits] a little speech and he'd introduce his father and his brother, Graham. His dad, every time I'd see him [Reaves held out his hand like he was shaking hands and went to a deep voice], 'John, how is your relationship with Jesus Christ?' Steve had a wonderful relationship with his father."

Graham Spurrier said his father was very proud of Steve.

"We hardly missed a [Florida] game," Graham said. "Watching with my dad was great. Of course Dad was still in his critiquing mode, even then. We'd come home and Steve would call and he'd say, 'Steve, why'd you do this?' But he'd do it in a positive way. Steve understood.

"Dad, toward his latter years here, bless his heart, really started tickling me. We'd pull up in the parking lot. And we had a good spot, right next to the gate [at Ben Hill Griffin Stadium], we'd get out and he'd start saying, 'You know who I am?' And of course he never used to do that, but he was proud in his latter years and he'd tell everybody. Of course everybody would take pictures with him. He'd eat all that up. It was good."

In the background during this trying period, Spurrier took the time to watch some game films brought to him by a set of parents who traveled from Bloomington, Indiana, to Gainesville with their son, who hoped to convince the Gators to recruit him to play quarterback. Spurrier took a look at the boy's highlight film and saw something. Spurrier then cued the Danny Wuerffel highlight reel, circa 1996, when Wuerffel threw 39 touchdown passes.

"All of the receivers were just wide open and I was thinking, 'This is the place I want to play,'" the youngster would later say.

Spurrier decided to offer the youngster a scholarship, and that youngster's name was Rex Grossman. Grossman was redshirted during the 1999 season and hardly considered the favorite to win the quarterback job during the 2000 season.

Spurrier had incumbent Jessie Palmer in addition to Brock Berlin from Shreveport, Louisiana, who was named the nation's top quarterback recruit the previous year.

The Gators breezed in wins over Ball State (40-19) and Middle Tennessee (55-0) to start the 2000 season before traveling to Knoxville to play Tennessee. Palmer played the entire game and rewarded Spurrier's faith in him by leading a 91-yard touchdown drive that culminated with a three-yard touchdown pass with 14 seconds remaining to beat Tennessee 27-20. The win moved the Gators to No. 3 in the rankings, but after defeating Kentucky 59-31 in their next game, the Gators suffered their only loss to an unranked team during Spurrier's tenure when Mississippi State rolled to a 47-35 win at Starkville.

Grossman became the quarterback almost exclusively from that point on, passing for 3,896 yards and 34 touchdowns in 2000, leading the Gators to their first SEC championship since 1996 with a 28-6 win over Auburn. The season ended on a low note when Miami crushed the Gators 37-20 in the Sugar Bowl, but the future looked bright.

Florida had designs on a national championship in 2001, which would be a magical sort of event since it would be played at the Rose Bowl, a site closed to conferences outside the Pac 10 and Big 10 for years. But with the revolving site for the championship game in place thanks to the Bowl Championship Series, the 2002 Rose Bowl truly would be the "Granddaddy of them all."

Florida's fortunes took a sad turn on July 19, 2001, when Eraste Autin, an incoming freshman, collapsed near Ben Hill Griffin Stadium after a voluntary workout. The 18-year-old from Lafayette, Louisiana, died a week later in Shands Hospital. Nobody has been able to explain why the tragedy occurred. Autin did not collapse until at least 20 minutes after his workout before staff members rushed him to Shands.

Spurrier was devastated.

"It's hard to figure out what we did wrong," Spurrier said. "Did we push him too hard? He finished the drill, drank some water, and joked around with the girls who are our student managers. Everything seemed fine. And then he was gone."

Outside linebackers coach Jim Collins told the *Atlanta Journal-Constitution* Autin's death "really affected" Spurrier, who said player safety "is the biggest responsibility I have as coach."

"We don't even hit that hard in practice," Spurrier said. "We try to make the game as safe as possible. It was just frustrating and difficult to understand why it would happen."

Florida started the 2001 season by reeling off lopsided victories over Marshall (49-14), Louisiana-Monroe (55-6), Kentucky (44-10), Mississippi State (52-0) and LSU (44-15). Missing from the folds of victory was the early-season mega-matchup against Tennessee that was put off until December 1 due to the September 11 terrorist attacks. The postponement made the October 13 contest against 5-1 Auburn the Gators' first true test of the season. And the game turned out to be one of those games in which the Gators seemed destined to lose, and did 23-20 on a last-minute field goal.

The chances of grabbing a spot in the Rose Bowl looked remote after the Gators' loss, but the Gators followed their lone loss with victories over Georgia, Vanderbilt and South Carolina to give them an 8-1 mark heading into the FSU game.

FSU came to The Swamp a flawed but improving team. The Gators showed no mercy, accruing 453 yards of total offense en route to a 37-13 victory. But the story of the game became the sideshow of Spurrier accusing FSU's Darnell Dockett of intentionally twisting the knee of running back Earnest Graham after Graham was tackled and trapped in the resulting pileup. Replays from earlier in the game showed Dockett when he tried to stomp on Grossman's hand when he was out of bounds on his back following a play.

Spurrier addressed the incident at his Sunday press conference the day after the game.

"Earnest came off the field and said the guy twisted his leg after he was down," Spurrier told the *St. Petersburg Times*. "We'll look into it. I'm not accusing anybody of anything, but if that did occur, something certainly needs to be done. We can't watch guys twist guys' legs after they are on the ground and so forth. But we'll let the proper people take review of how he got hurt."

Spurrier said he watched the tape and "it didn't clearly show the guy, but the guy was sort of doing something down there."

"I hate to bring it up, but still, I've got to say something on behalf of Earnest Graham," Spurrier said. "If this happened, we'll let the proper people . . . look at the thing because I know Bobby Bowden would never have a player intentionally try to twist a guy's leg in the bottom of a pileup."

Further fodder came in a *St. Petersburg Times* report that said Dockett was overheard after the game asking his teammates: "Did you all see what I did to Earnest Graham?"

FSU's Bowden downplayed the idea of Dockett intentionally hurting Graham.

"In the history of college football, I've heard of people twisting ankles, but I don't know how you could twist a knee," Bowden told the *St. Petersburg Times*. "I heard the same thing on [Spurrier's] radio show, and I'm not mad at him saying it, if that's what [Graham] thinks. Whether it happened or not, I don't know, I saw the replay, and I couldn't tell."

Upon further review, the "Battle of Wounded Knee" incident wouldn't die. Spurrier's criticism of FSU intensified the week after the game.

"Would I say it surprises me an FSU player did that?" Spurrier said. "No, it doesn't surprise me. It doesn't surprise me Bowden won't do anything. That's the way they do business at FSU. It's the way they run the show up there. It doesn't surprise me at all."

Dockett denied all charges.

"You can look at the film; it's an aggressive tackle," Dockett said. "I didn't intentionally pull his leg or anything. For Steve Spurrier to just call my name out like that, it seems like he's whining over something that's nothing."

Robert Gillespie, the Gators' tailback who would replace Graham for the upcoming Tennessee game, said the injury was intentional.

"We've got it on film," Gilllespie said. "It's clear cut, no question about it, and it's ridiculous for that to happen. I think if their administrators or whoever don't take care of it, that shows what kind of people they are also."

Graham released the following statement, which Spurrier read at a press conference:

"We will all have our day in court. That's after the season stuff. We have time to settle that, ain't nobody running from it. There is plenty of time for that when the season is over, trust me."

FSU athletic director Dave Hart responded.

"Across the board the consensus opinion is that looking at video clips that were e-mailed to several people from Gainesville that they are truly inconclusive," Hart said. "I've talked to Darnell Dockett one-on-one. I've talked to Bobby a couple different times about this. We've done our due diligence despite the very poor manner in which this was handled by the head football coach in Gainesville."

Hart added: "I think [Spurrier] is a very good football coach, and he has an outstanding football team this year. But it probably would be good if somebody'd just spank him and put him to bed and hope he wakes up all grown up."

Hart contacted the American Football Coaches Association to report what he perceived to be unethical behavior by Spurrier.

Spurrier's response came in typical don't-back-down Spurrier style.

"Sometimes the truth hurts," Spurrier said. "I'm glad they're thinking. What did Sun Tzu say? 'Better your enemies talk evil of you than nothing at all.'"

Amidst the controversy, Florida moved on to their game against Tennessee, but the "Battle of Wounded Knee" incident hardly was finished.

Everything was at stake in the Tennessee game. The SEC East title, a berth in the SEC Championship Game and, most importantly, a win against Tennessee followed by a win in the SEC Championship Game would earn a spot in the Rose Bowl against undefeated Miami.

With 1:10 remaining in the game, Grossman capped a 10-play, 66-yard drive with a 2-yard touchdown pass to Carlos Perez and the Gators trailed 34-32. But Grossman's pass to Jabar Gaffney on the two-point conversion attempt fell incomplete.

"We thought we had a decent play on," Spurrier said. "They covered it, they changed coverages, and we didn't throw to who I thought we maybe should have."

The Gators' ensuing onside kick failed as well, giving the Vols the upset victory and their first win in Gainesville since 1971. No SEC championship, no Rose Bowl, only disappointment in what would be Spurrier's final game at The Swamp.

Spurrier seemed deflated when he spoke the next day of the Gators' 2001 season.

"Our season's over, that's just the way it happened this year," Spurrier said. "It was a year we made some errors in two games. We looked pretty good in those nine wins, but in our two losses, we made enough mistakes to cost us. . . .

"We're very disappointed that we didn't win anything this year. We had a good record, had a lot of good games, but we didn't win anything."

Perhaps it was the fact the Gators were 0-2 without Earnest Graham. The team rushed for minus 36 yards in the Auburn loss and gained just 36 yards rushing against Tennessee; with Graham in the lineup the Gators were 9-0. Maybe it was just a sore that wouldn't heal, but Spurrier continued to rant about the "Battle of Wounded Knee" even as his team prepared for an Orange Bowl date with ACC champion Maryland.

Shortly after Spurrier's Orange Bowl media day press conference ended, Spurrier returned and asked those media members still remaining if they were curious about how Graham got hurt.

"Any of you curious to see that tape?" Spurrier said. "You haven't seen the end zone copy. Come on, I'll show it to you. Since [FSU and certain members of the media] have attacked me and Earnest about lying about it, I think you ought to see it."

Spurrier had the lights dimmed.

"We'll show people what happened so people don't think we're making up what happened," Spurrier said.

Spurrier used a laser pointer's red light to highlight Dockett in the end zone shot he ran several times that showed Dockett on top of Graham after tackling the Gator running back.

"They tried to say Earnest made this up, and that I've made it up, but you see it right there," Spurrier said. "See [number] 45 right there? I've never seen anything like this happen in all my coaching. See that? Now up."

After the Graham incident, he showed a clip of Dockett pushing down his foot in a stomping motion near Grossman's passing hand as Grossman was stretched out on the sideline.

"He barely missed," Spurrier said. "Here it is again. I just want to let you all know I'm not making that up. They're trying to personally attack me about making it up."

Spurrier finished by asking the media members present if any of them would be going to Tallahassee. A cameraman answered yes and Spurrier handed him the tape, instructing him to "take that to them."

Nobody knew Spurrier's last game as coach of the Gators would be the Orange Bowl. Heading into the game, Spurrier did not spare the rod on Grossman, who missed curfew and did not start against Maryland. Instead, Spurrier started Berlin, the touted quarterback whom Spurrier had granted permission to transfer to Miami. Berlin completed 11 of 19 passes for 199 yards and a touchdown before giving way to Grossman, who seemed to have had a fire lit under him. Grossman entered the game with just over six minutes left in the second quarter and the Gators leading 14-10. Calmly, the super sophomore led the Gators on a 10-play, 72-yard drive culminating with a 15-yard touchdown pass to Taylor Jacobs. Before the evening was finished, Grossman had completed 20 of 28 attempts for 249 yards and four touchdowns in a 56-23 rout.

The Gators' 462 passing yards and 659 total yards both set Orange Bowl records and the Gators had yet another 10-win season. Afterward Spurrier sounded content.

"This was one of our best games of the season," Spurrier said. "We didn't win much, but we won the Orange Bowl."

Spurrier waved to the highly partisan Gators crowd when he ran off the field. Nobody knew he was waving good-bye, including those close to him like Pepper Rodgers.

"I go to the Orange Bowl every year," Rodgers said. "I've seen Steve at the Orange Bowl every time he's been down there. I go with FedEx every year since it's been the FedEx Orange Bowl. I go down there with Fred Smith, who is the [Federal Express] Chairman of the Board, and he and I have been friends forever. So I've seen Steve out at several of these bowl games. I went and saw him before this one like I always do. This game, it was ironic that Dan Snyder was there. His team was playing Florida, he went to Maryland. We were sitting in the same box. I called Steve the day after the game. I think he was driving back to Gainesville, or Crescent Beach or something. I asked how are you doing, told him great game, and all that, then I read in the paper the next day that he was going to quit Florida. Then I picked up the phone and told him Dan wanted to talk to him and he did."

When Spurrier addressed the media following his announcement, he spoke of some of the program's accomplishments during his 12 years as head coach.

"Last five years we've not achieved quite as much as [his first seven seasons] . . . only one SEC [championship] in five years and that's the truth," Spurrier said. "But we have gone to three major bowls in the last five years and two Citrus Bowls. Which isn't all that bad. But we still haven't hit the top. . . . I was watching the British Open Saturday. They had an old replay from '62 or '63. Anyway, Gary Player beat Jack Nicklaus in the British Open. It went on to say that Nicklaus had finished runner up in the British Open six times.

"Sometimes you don't always win. You hang around near the top, like our guys have. We've won our share, but sometimes it doesn't work out. And obviously the Tennessee game was a very frustrating time for all of us. One of our most heartbreaking [losses]. But we just didn't really play that well. We just didn't do it that night. And that's what happens sometimes. I'm really proud of the way our guys bounced back in the Orange Bowl, played one of their best games of the year. Which is what we're trying to do, play our best every time out. But sometimes it just doesn't quite work out that way."

Spurrier said the accomplishment of which he was most proud of at Florida was "hanging around at the top."

"Those championships are nice," Spurrier said. "And even the years when they [didn't win championships], still our guys were hanging near the top fighting it out for the SEC championship. I think we figured out that even though we were only on top during seven of the 12 years, the other five, at the end of the regular season, I think we were second place when you did the records before the championship game. So I'm proud that our guys competed every year. Consistency is something I'm really proud of our teams, that they could do that. Every one involved. Obviously our fans here are very responsible for the success we've had here. The Swamp is a very difficult place for the opponent to win and I'm always thanking those people right there."

So why did Spurrier decide to leave? When asked the question, Spurrier brought up a conversation he had with former University of Florida president John Lombardi.

"I said, 'President Lombardi, did they kind of shove you out the door? Did you retire, resign on your own? Did something happen?'" Spurrier said. "And he said, 'Steve, 10 years was enough to be a university president. I was ready to go on and do something else.' And that sort of hit me. At what time is your tenure long enough? At what time have you had your sort of run and when are you smart enough to say, 'hey, this is it. This has been a good run, let's move on'? And somehow late in the year, this year, [he thought] that maybe this was as good a time as any to say good-bye. Although, certainly I was hoping, as we all were, that it would be after the Rose Bowl. But it didn't work out. It didn't work out that that was my last game. So anyway, it sort of starts wearing on you. When do you go? Are you ever going to coach in the NFL? At some point most people thought I'd take a shot at coaching in the NFL. And yes, I'm intrigued to see if our style of offense, my style of coaching, can be successful at the NFL level. So, I need to find that out before I completely hang it up."

Spurrier wants to once again experience the feeling of being an underdog.

"You realize how big a favorite we are all the time," Spurrier said. "And it's nobody's fault. It's just the way it is that we're double-digit favorites over everybody. And I guess we should be because we cover most of them or we get beat. One or the other. But everytime we lose, it's us coaches, we screwed up. Look at what huge favorites the team was and they didn't win. So anyway, that's sort of aggravating. It wears on you a little bit. Maybe, in a way, looking back, it would have been smart not to have scored so many points. If you don't score so many points, then you're not that big of a favorite the next week. But I don't know. I don't know how a basketball coach tells his guys to hold it down. This that and the other. I just always let the guys play. I mean, we put the backups in. Whereas if you look back, well, maybe a 24-10 might have been better than a 52-10. You know, looking back. But I don't know. It would be hard for me to hold the guys back from playing."

Did the Dockett incident have any bearing on his leaving? Florida athletic director Jeremy Foley never offered a rebuttal to the Hart statement that Spurrier needed to be spanked.

"No [the Dockett incident didn't influence his leaving], but since you mentioned that, I sort of think nobody seems to give a damn except for me and Earnest Graham," Spurrier said. "Nobody seems to care. Nobody seems to want to bring up that a guy was intentionally hurt. You know he couldn't play against Tennessee, the biggest game of the year. How important was he? I don't know. You can figure that out. But I wish at some point somebody would make a call, either the NCAA, the football coaches association, the SEC or the University of Florida. Somebody would make a call. Either Earnest and Spurrier are lying or the guy did it and something needs to be done. But right now that fight is in your hands. I've carried it as far as I can carry it. If ya'll want to see something happen, that's up to you."

Three months after Spurrier's resignation, Foley told the Volusia County Gator Club he had received many e-mails from Gators fans asking why he kept his silence when it came to the "Battle of Wounded Knee."

"I've heard people say that is one of the reasons Coach Spurrier is not around," Foley said. "Let me tell you, that is just not true."

Foley said there was not insurmountable evidence Dockett hurt Graham and he felt continued discussion of the matter would be a negative.

"I didn't think the whole situation was healthy," Foley said. "I had doctors tell me you can't hurt that ligament by twisting it. Everyone had an opinion. Trying to change opinions would have been a waste of time, and I don't like to waste time. I like to move on. . . . Steve just handled it his way. I handled it my way."

Spurrier felt from the beginning he would coach at Florida for seven or eight years before trying the NFL.

"I was figuring out, being the head coach at Florida is sort of like being the captain of a big battleship called Gator football," Spurrier said. "And we've had 150 battles and the head coach is sort of like the captain. And I'm sort of like a captain who takes the wheel instead of letting his crew do just about everything. You know, it's just time to move on. A hundred and fifty battles. Won a bunch of them. Now it's time to let somebody else captain this ship for awhile."

Leaving only a Steve Spurrier legacy, which he hopes will include his being "a guy never charged with breaking any rules."

"I don't know why that's so difficult," Spurrier said. "But there's a lot of rule breakers, not so many any more, but there's still a few out there. And hopefully the players, once they leave here, they've learned something about being a good person and they'll be successful once they leave here. That's what I hope happens. That our players say they enjoyed playing for me and the assistant coaches."

Spurrier thanked Florida alumni and fans in his final comments.

"Again, I thank the 'Gator Nation' for the overwhelming support for our teams for 12 years," he said. "The seven SEC championships and the 1996 national championship are memories of a lifetime we will all share together."

18

BRING ON THE NFL

Spurrier arrived in Washington charming and brash for the news conference in which he was introduced to the media. He downplayed his heralded arrival, which local media compared in significance to the arrivals of Vince Lombardi and George Allen, and he went to the heart of the matter.

"We do try to score," Spurrier said. "As much as we can. You play 'til the game ends, then look up and see how you did. We keep trying to score, too. Some people get mad [at that]. But we keep trying. . . . We're very capable of having a big year [in 2002]. How big? We'll find out."

Spurrier joked about how his relationship with high-profile owner Dan Snyder will progress.

"Only time will tell," Spurrier said. "So far we've been fine. I survived Duke twice. . . . I don't think we'll have many problems. If we do, he'll win."

Spurrier cited Snyder's salesmanship as the reason he took the job.

"Dan Synder convinced me this was the best opportunity," Spurrier said. "Basically, he said, 'Steve, you want a challenge? You want to coach at the highest level? You want to coach in a big ballpark? You want to coach where we've got the best fans in the country? I'm giving you that challenge right now."

Whether Spurrier can step up to the NFL is one of the more compelling questions football fans around the country are anxious to see answered. Don't think NFL coaches aren't equally interested to see how he fares.

"I think it's a great endorsement for the NFL that one of the greatest coaches in the college ranks is intrigued enough to come into the league, to wonder if he can do that at this level," Pittsburgh Steelers coach Bill Cowher said in *Football*

Digest. "We're all wondering that. I've never met him, but I have a lot of respect for him and wish him nothing but the best, except when he's playing us."

Spurrier's announcement he would be leaving Florida initially sparked speculation he'd become the new coach of the Tampa Bay Buccaneers, or at the very least coach one of the Florida professional teams. Those scenarios never materialized and Spurrier doesn't regret they did not.

"I've lived in Florida 31 of the last 37 years and I sort of felt like, 'Let's get out of Florida for five or six years and see if we can make it happen on a very big stage,'" Spurrier said. "FedEx Field is the largest stadium in the league. We'll have a go at it and see what happens."

Pepper Rodgers chuckled when asked how Spurrier would do adjusting from college football to professional.

"The only time I ever coached against Steve was during the pro game when he was with the Tampa Bay Bandits and I was with the Memphis Showboats of the United States Football League and he was as good a football coach as that league had, and maybe right at the top of it," Rodgers said. "He certainly was very effective as a professional football coach in the USFL. So to say he doesn't have any pro experience would be wrong. He did a great job down there at Tampa."

Catching up to the speed of the pro game is an element of the pro game any coach has to adjust to when moving from college to pro. Rodgers doesn't see that as a problem for Spurrier.

"It's relative in that [the players] are faster on defense, they've got more time to practice on defense, they've got more players with experience on defense," Rodgers said. "But at the same time you've got the same thing on offense. And it has always come down to who does the best job."

Rodgers pointed out an obvious difference between NFL games and college games by noting, "When you're real good in the NFL, you won't have any easy games."

"There are no Vanderbilts in the NFL," Rodgers said. "But in Steve's last several years at Florida, he went into about 90 percent of his games as the favorite. He won't be favored in 90 percent of the games up here. And I think he likes that. I think he likes that challenge and I think he likes the excitement of proving what he believes in will work at any level. . . .

"All great competitors like challenges and I don't think there's a bigger challenge in the world than the National Football League. You don't get 150, 160 games to prove you can win. You've got 16. Now having said that, 16 is a lot more games than you play in college. But I think Steve has always been one of the great competitors whether it's on the golf course, ping-pong or the game of football. And I think this is a wonderful challenge for him and I think it's invigorating for him."

Bobby Bowden told the *St. Petersburg Times*, "I'll miss [Spurrier], but I'm glad he's gone."

"He needs to tone down the accusations against other coaches," Bowden said. "Up there, reactions to such things will be much tougher. He'll hear it from a far larger audience of critics. . . .

"I've always been a Dallas Cowboys fan, but, no, I won't be rooting against Steve. I will be fascinated to see how it goes. I won't pull against the Redskins unless he has more bad things to say about me. That isn't likely to happen. I'm gone from his life now. He's their problem now, not mine."

Bowden said he wouldn't bet against Spurrier succeeding with the Redskins.

"This is a coach who won in football at Duke in the '80s, a feat that becomes more amazing when you check what [Duke] did before and after he was there," Bowden said.

Rodgers believes Spurrier can bring something new to the NFL.

"There's not a lot that's revolutionary when it comes to the NFL," Rodgers said. "But I do think Steve is a guy who isn't afraid that things won't work. He's so confident in what he believes in, what he's coaching and what he's teaching, that he will try things other people might not try because he's not afraid to do it. And I think Steve will bring a lot of things to the league. He's so dangerous a football coach because a lot of coaches, as they get older, become more conservative, more afraid of what to do, more concerned about errors. Not Steve, man. He comes after it. Steve believes everything is going to work.

"A lot of guys, when they get older, they know it's not going to work, because they found out before it wasn't going to work. I think Steve has changed less in the way he approaches the game than anybody I've ever known. He's totally confident that what he's doing is the right thing. And everybody else has doubts and I don't think he has any. He's going to run his East Coast Offense. He throws the ball down the field. And I think he'll do that better than people have been doing it in the National Football League. I also think one of the things he'll do, he'll do some counter stuff. I never thought the NFL did a real good job with the counter offense. Meaning fake one way and go back the other. I think Steve has always done a good job of that. And I think he will in the NFL."

Spurrier told the *Miami Herald* he has no fear making the jump from college to the NFL.

"I'm not really scared," Spurrier said. "I realize success is not guaranteed, but I think we've got a pretty good team with a chance of being a really, really good team. I'm not scared of the unknown. I've found out that as long as the coaches and the players we have are still on edge, trying to get better, success has a chance. The thing I'm proudest of at Florida is that we won nine games or more every year—no letup, no complacency. We were competitive and persistent every year, and I think we will be here, too."

Contrary to popular opinion, Rodgers said Spurrier doesn't have a head coach's ego when it comes to controlling his team.

"Other than maybe [Jon] Gruden at Tampa Bay, who does a lot of his [offensive] stuff, which he did at Oakland, I don't believe many of the current NFL coaches are hands on like Steve," Rodgers said. "Most of them have an offensive and defensive coordinator and walk up and down the field and play head coach. Steve doesn't play head coach. He plays on the practice field that he's coaching the quarterbacks and the wide receivers and the offense. And he's got a great defensive coach here with the Redskins, but Steve's got so much confidence he doesn't have an ego problem about letting Marvin Lewis take over the defense like a lot of coaches would."

John Reaves called Spurrier a "tremendous technician," which he believes to be Spurrier's edge.

"He knows the passing game and the running game well, but the passing game so well," Reaves said. "And he knows coverages so well. He knows how to beat 'em. So he designs a system that can take advantage of the coverages you're playing. And then he teaches the techniques and mechanics of the individual drills on up.

"So you can beat these coverages, there's holes in all of those coverages. It's just a matter of getting into those holes. But you can't just run some ugly circle route to get into those holes. You've got to do things to set up to get into those holes. Not only is he a great quarterbacks coach, he's a great receivers coach. At teaching route running, catching the ball, etc. It's all set up on timing and steps. You've got to take your steps and throw it. It's one of the things you'll always hear. Like a country western song, you know, take your steps and throw it. It's all set up on timing. If that guy ain't there, he'll get somebody who'll get there."

In looking at the list of successful college coaches who have made a run at coaching in the NFL, many big names have failed, such as Tommy Prothro, Dan Devine, Lou Holtz, John McKay, and Ron Meyer. If this group had a common denominator, it is they tried to take what had been successful for them at the college level and use that method of success in the NFL. Meanwhile, Jimmy Johnson was able to find success in the NFL because he ran a pro-style offense at the University of Miami before making the jump to the NFL. Spurrier must be listed under the same category as Johnson.

"When Steve first got the job a friend of mine said to me, 'He's going to find out this is the NFL, not college anymore,'" Dallas Cowboys coach Dave Campo told the *Bergen County Record.* "I told him wait, that's exactly what they said about us when we came here to Dallas in 1989."

Campo was on Johnson's staff that left Miami for the Cowboys.

In advance of the coming season, Campo had his staff begin breaking down film of Spurrier-coached Florida teams to try and get a feel for what the Cowboys might expect.

"We're looking at everything Steve's done the last seven or eight years," Campo said. "Of course we will have some preseason games and, depending on when we play them, maybe some regular-season games to work with. But we want to get an idea about what he likes to do."

"Steve Spurrier is an outstanding football coach," Jacksonville Jaguars coach Tom Coughlin told the *Bergen County Record.* "His innovations on offense are well established. Now the NFL is different than college football, [as a former Boston College coach] I'm well aware of that, but I think Steve is smart enough to realize that and make the necessary adjustments."

Spurrier is coy about the coming transition from college to pro football. When asked about the biggest challenge from the change, he answered: "I don't know; I haven't played yet."

Spurrier considered the question momentary, then spoke again.

"Obviously, the field's a little different, the hash marks are in a little tighter, the clock starts when the ball goes out of bounds and incomplete passes when the referee winds it," Spurrier said. "It's a little faster game, as far as timewise. But I don't know, the pros play a lot of the same coverages the colleges play. The speed, yeah, the better athletes, so forth.

"But we've got to play before I can say, 'Well, we could do this in college, we can't do this now. I haven't seen anything we've done in the past we can't do now as long as we execute it efficiently."

19

FIRST STEPS

Among Spurrier's first moves as a coach was to procure the services of former Florida stars Danny Wuerffel, Chris Doering, Jacquez Green and Reidel Anthony, all of whom have not reached the same level of performance in the NFL they reached in college. Spurrier's critics point to these acquisitions as a move of vanity, like only Spurrier could coach these players successfully; Spurrier views bringing in the former Gators as a positive.

"Are you telling me that Reidel, Quezzie and Danny can't play?" Spurrier said. "I believe they all can play. Now, we've got to find out. I've seen them play well. We've got all these guys for the minimum, or close to it. They were cheap and available. . . .

"Reidel was a first-round draft pick. Jacquez was a second-round pick. I've seen Danny play in the game, so I don't need some NFL experts to tell me he can't play. I've seen too much. I've seen him against FSU, Tennessee, Auburn, Georgia. All pretty good defenses. Our personnel guys were impressed with Reidel and Quez and Danny Wuerffel. Of course, time will only tell, but obviously I've seen all of these players play very, very well."

Count Wuerffel among the most excited to be playing for his former coach.

"There are probably a whole lot of guys from Florida and other places that would love the opportunity to play for Coach Spurrier," Wuerffel said. "I didn't think I would have the opportunity to play for him. But when it came about I was as excited as could be. . . .

"This is a dream for all of us. Every NFL player could only hope to be in a place where a coach believes in you and the coach knows what you can do. You have to be in the right place at the right time and that's what we can only hope for."

Wuerffel views his opportunity with the Redskins as an opportunity to compete.

"One thing about Coach Spurrier, he's very committed to playing who he thinks is the best person to win," Wuerffel said. "You go to some places and they may bring you in to be the third guy and that's what you'll be regardless of how things may or may not go. That's the way it works. But you could be the sixth guy and start for Coach Spurrier. You can never shut down your effort. You always play and compete. That's all we can ask for."

In Spurrier's mind, each of these players just needed to be playing in the right system—his system. He has since brought in Shane Matthews.

"Nothing is guaranteed, but I've got to believe in the system we've had from Duke to the USFL and back to Duke and back to Florida, if we've got good players like we've had at all those places," Spurrier said. "I don't think the game is a whole lot different. Obviously the talent is much, much better in the NFL, but the defenses these coordinators run are a lot like the colleges. They all interchange. The college coaches all visit the pro camps all the time. So, it's not a whole bunch of different defenses than we saw in college."

Already Spurrier is defending his decision to bring aboard the ex-Gators.

"I knew [the criticism] would happen," Spurrier told the *Miami Herald*. "We have not spent a lot of money on any of these players, you know? When I got here, we had one quarterback under contract and only two or three receivers who played a little last year. We needed receivers and quarterbacks. A lot of our Gator guys were available. That's the way it has worked out so far, but a lot of people don't realize I'm going to have to cut some of these Florida guys because we've got some who are better. The criticism will stop when I release one or two. Marty Schottenheimer had more Kansas City guys here than I had Gators, but that was OK and this isn't?"

Wuerffel defended Spurrier.

"I think it's natural anytime a coach goes to a new place that he brings in some of the guys he's worked with before," Wuerffel said. "Coach Spurrier was so high profile at Florida that it's a little more noticeable."

The former Gators on the Redskins talked about having a comfort level in being back in the Spurrier system.

"It's amazing how much easier it is to play and react when you know what you're doing, and you don't have to think about it," Doering said. "Certainly I have to be refreshed because it's been a while since I've been in this offense. If you spoke English your whole life, then went away for a few years, then came back, you'd still remember English. It's like that."

Matthews called the atmosphere with the Redskins "comfortable."

"It's totally different than what I've been in my other years in the league," Matthews said. "The laid back approach is something I really like. That's how I am, that's my personality—laid back. I'm looking forward to my time here."

Matthews did acknowledge he had some work to do to totally understand the offense.

"It's changed a little bit," Matthews said. "I'd say about 95 percent of it is the same. You have to remember it's been almost 10 years since I've been in the offense. It's going to take some time for me to feel comfortable again. It's not going to happen overnight."

Anthony and Green were both excited about being reunited with Spurrier. Both played for the Bucs, who ran a conservative offense.

"What was my role in Tampa? I didn't have a role," Green told the *Orlando Sentinel*. "I might run a slight adjustment on a safety blitz, but mostly it was clear-outs for Keyshawn Johnson. I might run a 'go' route, but I doubt it."

In addition, Green and Anthony wore the label of the typical "quick, but undersized, Florida receivers." Critics point to their inabilities to get open against a bump-and-run defense.

"No, I can't beat a bump-and-run running [expletive] routes," Green said. "Now [on the Redskins] we see bump-and-run; guess what? We've got routes that get you open. I mean you can't call a 'hook' for me—when I'm 5-feet-9 and 160—and expect me to muscle the man 14 yards downfield, then turn around and catch the ball. No, I'm not going to be able to do that.

"But if you call a hook and tell me I can adjust my route to get open, yeah, I can do that. I can use my quickness for that. Our offense in Tampa was built for big receivers. I don't even know why they drafted me and Reidel. We're with a real coordinator now. Maybe even the best coordinator."

Thus far, Redskins players seem to have bought in to Spurrier's approach.

"I think Coach Spurrier is bringing a player's approach," standout linebacker LaVar Arrington said. "He's probably the closest thing to a player who is a coach. He has the same type of swagger we have. He has the same personality we have. You communicate with him as a coach, but you really see him as a person. And that makes all the difference. He's not so old that we can't relate to him. And he's not so young where we can't respect his wisdom."

In March, Spurrier attended the NFL meetings. When asked if he wanted the Dallas Cowboys to become his Florida State, Spurrier quipped: "Hopefully our Georgia."

Spurrier was 11-1 against the Bulldogs.

He didn't stop there, addressing several topics, like NFL coaches working nights at the office.

"I know there's a perception that since I golf and work out on the treadmill six days a week . . . that I don't work hard," Spurrier said. "Some coaches who spent a lot of hours had a lot of success. Some got fired quickly. Brad Scott had a cot at South Carolina."

Scott's tenure as the Gamecocks' coach was short-lived.

Regarding how involved he will be with the defense, Spurrier said, "I'll pat the guys on their backs when they make a good play, high-five 'em, you know, maybe knock fists like the guys do."

Will his Fun-N-Gun offense work well in the NFL?

"I hope it does well," Spurrier said. "We've got to find a name for it. How about the East Coast Offense? If we don't do very well, we'll hold the name."

Spurrier eagerly awaits the challenge of the 2002 season.

"I like being among those critics up [in Washington, D.C.], guys who've never seen my teams play," Spurrier said. "It doesn't matter what I say right now until we play the game. People can write whatever they want, it's all fair. Until we go play, who knows what's going to happen?"

Spurrier has always maintained the best way to measure a coach is to look at the record of his team before he arrives and after he leaves. Will that be the measuring stick for how Spurrier is remembered at Washington, or will he have to win a Super Bowl to earn a stamp of approval?

"Obviously [winning the Super Bowl] is the goal of every team, 32 teams now," Spurrier said. "Trying for it. It's not going to be easy. Somebody asked me what we were most proud of at Florida, and that was that we were in the hunt every year for the SEC Championship. Twelve teams in that conference and at the end of the regular season we finished first or second every year. We were competitive, we were in the hunt, you have to be competitive, hanging out at the top to get there. I don't think the Buffalo Bills would be considered a failure for going to four Super Bowls in a row. Hopefully it will happen, but we'll see."

Spurrier calls the Redskins' job his "new challenge."

The job is "certainly an opportunity I needed to do before I hang up my coaching career and I'm really looking forward to it," Spurrier said. "Sometimes in life we need something new to stir up our enthusiasm and get us excited to do our thing."

Spurrier has changed teams over the years and found success everywhere he's been, but Wuerffel said no matter what happens to Spurrier, he remains the same.

"He's just a ball coach," Wuerffel said. "That's what he wants to be and it's what he gets a chance to be."